Design for Sport

The Butterworths Design Series for architects and planners

General Editor: Edward D. Mills, CBE, FRIBA, MSIA

Each book in the Butterworths Design Series takes an in-depth look at the design approach to a particular building type or building problem. Basic design philosophies are analysed in the context of the needs of the building user. Truly international in scope and coverage, the series draws on abundant worldwide examples of the best of modern design and planning.

All the books in the series have been specially commissioned from leading architects and specialists of worldwide repute. The Butterworths Design Series complements the publisher's *Planning* Series, and will be an invaluable reference for practising architects, schools of architecture and design, and departments of urban and rural development.

Titles in the **'Design'** series

Design for Fire Safety
Eric W. Marchant

Design for Health Care
Anthony Cox and Philip Groves

Design for Holidays and Tourism
Edward D. Mills

Design for Leisure Entertainment
Anthony Wylson

Design for Shopping Centres
Nadine Beddington

Design for Sport
Gerald A. Perrin

Design for Sport

Gerald A. Perrin

Butterworths

London Boston Sydney Wellington Durban Toronto

First published 1981
© Gerald A. Perrin 1981

British Library Cataloguing in Publication Data

Perrin, Gerald A.
  Design for sport.
  1. Recreation areas – Planning
  I. Title
  725'.8   GV182

  ISBN 0-408-00365-0

Photoset by Butterworths Litho Preparation Department
Printed by Mackays of Chatham

Foreword

The increase in leisure time for large numbers of people due to shorter working hours resulting from the development of new technology and the generally improved standard of living in many parts of the world has made sport, together with tourism and entertainment, a growth area for building investment of considerable significance. This new book by Gerald Perrin in the *Butterworths Design Series* is therefore of special interest and importance. The author has been concerned with the design of sports buildings for nearly twenty years and is internationally recognised as one of the leading experts on the subject. Not only has the value of his research been widely acknowledged but his practical experience has been illustrated in many completed projects with which he has been associated as an architect.

The book is of universal interest, as it covers a wide range of buildings for sport, from small scale examples such as school cricket pavilions to sports centres and the large sports complex capable of accommodating the Olympic games. No less than forty-six schemes from all parts of the world are described and illustrated in detail, varying from the Old Chigwellians Sports Centre in North London to the National Sports Centre, Papendal, Holland, on its 124 ha site on the outskirts of Arnhem. Each case study includes plans and photographs chosen to illustrate the reasons behind the design solutions and underline the importance of good planning, design and management.

In addition to studies of individual buildings, special attention is given to many important matters including flexibility in design, the choice of materials, orientation and floodlighting. Special emphasis is given to facilities for the handicapped who are increasingly enjoying new experiences through parti-cipation in sport, as proved by the 1980 Paraplegic Olympics at Papendal and similar events. Even skiing is enjoyed by amputees and the blind at the Harlow, Essex, Ski Centre. The Therapeutic Centre, Washington, D.C., which is described in this book, was specially designed to provide a wide range of sports related facilities for mentally retarded and physically disabled users in the USA.

Design for Sport will be of great value to any architect, organisation or official authority, in the planning of leisure and sporting facilities, not only because of the detailed information it contains but because of the broadly based approach of the author. In addition to the coverage of specific sports buildings, this book also deals with such subjects as urban rest and leisure parks, the Lee Valley Regional Park to the East of London, and the Gruga Park, Essen, W. Germany. A special chapter is devoted to 'Sports groupings in community facilities' which discusses the integration of sports facilities with other community activities. The Cresset, Peterborough, in the UK, for example is a complex of shops, social and recreational services with many unique features, which the author rightly regards as a possible pattern for the future.

Finally, the Appendix presents in diagramatic form the Olympic regulations governing sports installations. Gerald Perrin contributed the section on Sports Facilities in *Planning Ninth Edition*, where specific sports data is given in considerable detail.

This volume in the *Butterworths Design Series* compliments the other books in the series *Design for Leisure Entertainment* (Anthony Wylson), *Design for Health Care* (Anthony Cox and Philip Groves) and *Design for Holidays & Tourism* (Edward D. Mills).

Edward D. Mills

Preface

'*Sport for all*' has become an evocative slogan in many parts of the developed world, implying universal provision for sport on a scale not seen since it became a substitute for national aggression among the warlike tribes in Greek and Roman times.

The implementation of this policy however, has become the subject of widely differing interpretations. For many, the winning of medals and the boost this gives to national prestige is of greater significance than mass participation by the public at large, or of playing for enjoyment. The dichotomy between both objectives can be clearly seen in the buildings designed to meet these needs – national training centres, superbly equipped, on the one hand, and fun pools on the other. In the latter, a world of make-believe can be enjoyed (at a price), and the often grey surroundings outside forgotten momentarily.

Between these two extremes exist many intermediate facilities which, over the past decade, have come to be regarded by many as among the natural order of things. This alone is quite remarkable compared with attitudes twenty years or so ago, and represents a major breakthrough at all walks of life. The main purpose of this book has therefore been to identify the range of sports buildings which now exist to meet this rapidly expanding market, and to indicate some of the more probable trends which may take place during the 1980s.

It is clear that sport, and its spin-off effect on freetime activities, including entertainment and tourism will shortly become one of the largest growth areas for investment seen this century. This type of relaxation has already crossed many boundaries including those associated with the arts, commerce and science (including medicine).

In this book each section deals with a particular building type by tracing its development over the past ten or fifteen years, and by describing several examples selected for their special contribution to development trends, in the form of case studies. These give considerable insight to the motivating forces and types of sponsorship behind their design solutions, including the increasingly important role now being played by professional recreation management in shaping the design process.

During the selection and analysis of the case studies a common theme emerged almost every time – good design and sensible planning, backed up by intelligent management, are fundamental to successful use. Bearing in mind the large capital sums now involved in this process it goes without saying that a 'best buy' must contain all three ingredients. In an area of architecture not previously noted for its design context, sport is therefore beginning to contribute much to the urban and suburban scene where good design is increasingly essential to the modern quality of life, both in developed and developing societies.

Gerald A. Perrin

Contents

Acknowledgements

The collection of material for this book has taken place over a number of years and involved visits and revisits to many projects built during the past two decades, particularly in Europe. It has also involved meeting and talking with many connected with provision for sport and with players at most skill levels, which was both enjoyable and rewarding.

Thanks are due to these and to all those who helped prepare, collate, and edit the material into its final form, and to those who supplied many of the illustrations including the following organisations:

The Architects' Journal;
Barnsley, Hewitt & Mallinson;
Biwater Shellabear Ltd;
British Steel Corporation;
Building Design Partnership;
Buro Fred Balm BV;
Chapman Taylor & Partners;
The Cresset Ltd, Peterborough;
Cunninghame District Council;
DLW (Britain) Ltd;
Danish Sports Associaton;
Dutch Sports Federation;
Ellis Pearson Ltd;
Faulkner Brown, Hendy, Watkinson, Stonor & Partners;
Gillinson & Barnett;
Irvine Development Corporation;
Jackson & Edmonds;
Kent Cooper Partnership;
Landeshaupstadt Dusseldorf;
Lea Valley Regional Authority;
Mexican Olympic Association;
National Development Commission, Canberra;
Olympiapark, Munich;
Philips International;
Pro Juventute, Zurich;
Reed Harris Ltd;
Resisport Ltd;
Rice Roberts & Partners;
Robert Matthew, Johnson-Marshal & Partners;
Robert Turner Associates;
Seefeld Sport & Congress Centre;
Sport Bader & Freizeit Bauten;
Sporthochschule, Cologne;
Stantonbury Campus, Milton Keynes;
Wimpey News;
W. D. R. and R. T. Taggart & Partners;
David P. Webster;
Working Group for Sport, Recreation & Tourism, International Union of Architects.

Chapter 1

Background to provision

'Play is at the heart of a leisure society. It is an illusory quality rarely seen in Victorian times and is essential to our present way of life'.

Most people feel they understand the meaning of sport, but few can agree a precise definition. Hecksher's description in his book *'The Public Happiness'* comes as close as any to the dictionary definitiion of sport as 'the playing of games, or participation in competitive pastimes involving physical exertion and skill'. Perhaps Shakespeare's view in Henry the Fourth, Part One, is more apposite to contemporary society – 'if all the year were playing holidays, to sport would be as tedious as to work'. Others refer to it as 'recreation', or freetime activities: and for many outside the actual playing arena, sport has become 'entertainment' or sponsored voyeurism to be enjoyed from the confort of one's home.

There is obviously a wide field of interpretation and little would be gained by attempting a more detailed analysis. It is sufficient to say that sport, recreation, or 'freizeit' activities are now widely accepted as a fundamental part of the everyday quality of life, and essential to the mental and physical well-being of any present day society. The reasons generally advanced in support of these views have been fully developed in another volume in this series – *Design for Leisure Entertainment* by Anthony Wylson.

Leisure time is increasing, sometimes as a result of worker negotiations, sometimes through the introduction of automation, and sometimes as we have seen recently, through economic recession. People are accepting earlier retirement, while young people are studying for longer periods, if only as some cynics would hasten to point out, that they may enjoy 12 week summer vacations until their mid 20s. The increasing acceptance by employers of flexitime working enables many people to enjoy a round of golf, or games of squash during the day: while a trend towards homebased jobs has given others the same option.

The rapid growth of games such as squash, badminton, and golf owes much to these particular trends, and many sports have found increased popularity though exposure by the media. Tennis flourishes

during Wimbledon fortnight in the UK while lying almost dormant the rest of the year. Sheepdog trials, and 'Horse-of-the-Year' shows, which were formerly minority sports, now get much support when given in-depth coverage by television. Jogging becomes fashionable when seen being done by heads of state. Celebrity golf, tennis, or cricket matches are watched by audiences of many millions, and in some cases have altered the course of games irrevocably. Generally, all this has been for the best. Lighting standards at stadias have risen immeasurably if only to allow for colour television broadcasts. Buildings are better finished and the facilities less spartan.

Sophistication is looked for at every level of participation, together with many ancillary facilities in the form of hairdressing salons, fashion shows, sauna bathing, under-water jet streams, whirlpool baths, video recordings, and refreshments. Sport is no longer just 'playing games', but is part of the huge leisure market which started to grow in the 1970s and shows

Mirandabad, Amsterdam. View from open poolside refreshment lounge overlooking the wavepool. One of the latest fun pools to appear in north-west Europe. (Photo: Gerald Perrin)

Seefeld Sports & Congress Centre, Tyrol. General view of project which combines facilities for sport, leisure and tourism within a hotel complex

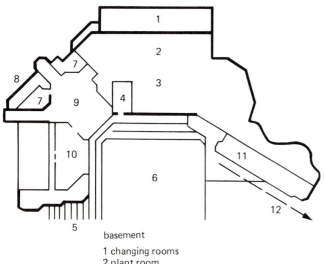

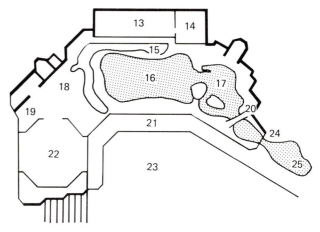

basement

1 changing rooms
2 plant room
3 underside of pool
4 ski depot and store
5 seating
6 ice rink
7 toilets
8 staff
9 foyer
10 meeting rooms
11 changing and toilets
 for ice skating
12 start of ski run

ground floor plan

13 pool cloakroom
14 pre-cleanse/wash area
15 planting
16 pool
17 rock islands
18 to restaurant over
19 information and office
20 bridge
21 glass island terrrace
22 olympic congress hall
23 ice rink
24 moveable window screen
25 heated outdoor pool

Seefeld. Ground and upper level plans showing extent of indoor sports facilities provided in association with hotel and conference provision as part of growing up-market leisure industry now seen in many parts of western Europe. (Architects: Heiss, Drachensky)

Summerland, Tokio. View of free form fun pool (Photo: Hitomi Kawasaki)

no sign of diminishing in the foreseeable future. It is as much part of franchising, and the opening up of sales outlets as any other piece of merchandise found in high street shops or out-of-town hypermarkets.

The effect of the Olympic movement

Some people believe that the modern Olympic movement has had an equally important part to play in shaping design trends, both in the form of training facilities and in provision for the Games themselves – although as others point out – at a cost which cannot be justified morally or financially by the many host nations concerned. It is also said that the Games are out of touch with the mood of present day participants. Coubertin's dream of re-living the spirit of ancient Greece may have been appropriate at the turn of the century, but the range of activities bears little resemblance to those now regularly undertaken by present-day society.

Although still popular, swimming, athletics, the martial arts, equestrian events and water sports, form only a part of activities which attract a far larger audience. Roller skating (and roller dance), ballet (as part of the rhythm and movement group of activities), hang gliding, scuba diving, long distance cycling,

Summerland, Tokio. General view of main hall from one of several open refreshment terraces around the aquatic area. (Photo: Hitomi Kawasaki)

fishing, and similar pastimes all have devotees which globally, amount to many times the number who are bound by conventional sports watched for a fortnight once every four years, albeit by a vast audience.

In many respects, sports architecture reflects this movement. The number of 'one-off' stadia, or swimming pool complexes is still considerable, but the way in which they are now used – as will be described in later case studies – is vastly different, at least in those countries where community involvement of one kind or another is encouraged at the expense of elitism. In such cases the stadium is also a hub for community training and recreation each day of the week. Some stadia include additional facilities other than the running track or central arena. Similarly, swimming pools are now largely places for having fun in (with other pools for serious training and competition). The Summerland project in Tokio has had a profound affect on western thinking in this respect, and in particular, the trend established during the 1970s towards fun pools in the UK, Holland, the USA and West Germany, since echoed in the Middle East, and Indonesia.

Sport at the family level

It is at local level however, that grass root changes give an early warning indication of most future trends in participation. We have already seen for example the way in which many more people are able to play when

Jakarta Leisure Centre, Indonesia. View of aquatic-based fun complex which includes flume-rides, wave pools and roller-coaster slides. (Architects: Biwater Shellabear Ltd)

it is most convenient to their individual lifestyles, and increasingly choose to do so in what used to be regarded as off-peak periods of the day. They still find conventional constraints on complete freedom of choice however by the very nature of their age – constraints such as child-rearing responsibilities, care of others, mobility and income.

The development of professional management 'agents', particularly in the UK, and of private entrepreneurs in the USA, show that commercial enterprise has been quick to see the potential of this market. Creches have been provided to enable mothers or one-parent families to continue playing, and at the same time generate a secondary income to the hire of courts or equipment. At the same time the children concerned have been weaned into the atmosphere of sports buildings at their most impressionable age, and the foundations laid for future generations of user already conditioned into accepting such surroundings as being among the natural order of things. The 'hard sell' by sponsors of a generation ago is over. Emphasis has changed from being one of *need* to one of *demand* as being the determining factor when assessing the provision of facilities at local level.

For much the same reasons, short sharp activities such as squash and five-a-side football have grown in popularity because of their low thresholds of skill, but more significantly because they occupy such a short period of time, and can be arranged during lunch breaks, before breakfast, or on the way home from work. Equally important in the management context is the fact that these sports generate a spectator appeal, and post-play socialising, especially in the bar, if one is provided.

Demand is therefore matched by the general willingness of sponsors to meet it so long as the end product is viable. This, however, only applies to those countries where viability is considered important, in others the state pays as part of the public service accountability to society as a whole. In some countries intermediate policies can be seen working extremely well, for example in Holland and Switzerland where secondary sources of funding have been channelled into sports provision from football pools, state lotteries (TOTO), or the sale of postage stamps (as in the case of the Pro Juventute organisation in Switzerland).

The growth of facilities

It is interesting to see how such contrasts in provision have arisen over the past two decades. The place of sport in the UK – from which many games have grown – has, for example, traditionally occupied a

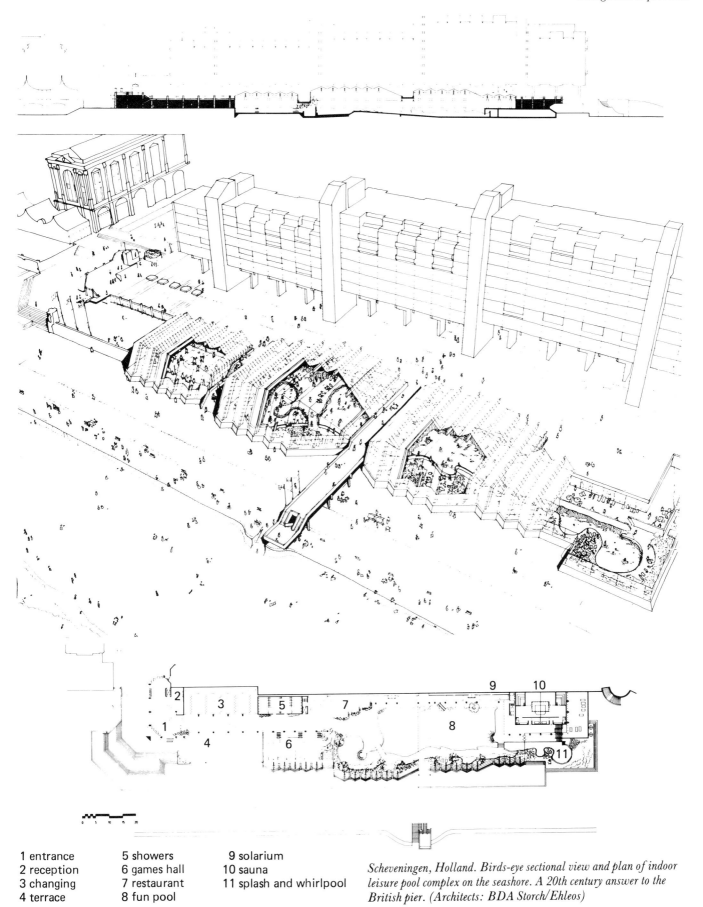

1 entrance
2 reception
3 changing
4 terrace

5 showers
6 games hall
7 restaurant
8 fun pool

9 solarium
10 sauna
11 splash and whirlpool

Scheveningen, Holland. Birds-eye sectional view and plan of indoor leisure pool complex on the seashore. A 20th century answer to the British pier. (Architects: BDA Storch/Ehleos)

surprisingly low priority in central and local government hierarchies of sponsorship and funding. Much of this can be put down to a strong puritanical background still influencing decisions throughout the country – attitudes which continue to regard provision for sport on moral rather than any other grounds where facilities are only 'needed' 'if they are good for one'. Public baths appeared in response to this concept along with many other aspects of Victoriana which remain to this day, a considerable drain on resources and a major deterrent to new capital investment.

Whitley Bay Amenity Centre. Photo of original proposals for a leisure pyramid on the north east coast of England. These were later amended to a more conventional 'fun palace' similar to those at Sunderland, and Bletchley seen in later chapters. (Architects: Gillinson & Barnett)

For much the same reason, policies throughout the country have become known as 'the organisation of shortages', something the British have grown used to living with. One result has been the provision of a thin layer of facilities usually overcrowded from the day they open, built for a fraction of the cost of similar facilities on the European mainland. To paraphrase Johnson, 'it is not done well, but you are surprised to find it done at all'. Ironically, professional management involvement is expensive – amounting in some cases to the equivalent capital cost of facilities within three or four years of operation – although considered necessary in the present context.

By contrast, continental European management is usually centrally located and organised in partnership with local sports clubs, who are often left to run day-to-day programmes themselves. The inclusion of automated devices is a feature of most projects, and to the outsider at least it is a revelation to see the extent to which such devices can be push-button controlled to minimise staff involvement still further.

On the continent provision of facilities has also been on a massive scale compared with that in the UK. The 'mille piscines' programme in France begun during the 1970s is almost completed. By 1970 all first wave projects identified in the 1960 Golden Plan for West German sport has been met, and a secondary programme started which had again been completed a decade later.

Spending throughout Europe has been between twenty and twenty-five times that in the UK, with provision being made even in communities of 4000 or less. The latter often involves the use of community schools especially in country districts otherwise unable to fund large scale facilities themselves. (There are also many examples in the UK and several are described in later sections of the book).

New planning concepts are much in evidence in town and country areas, the former in the form of comprehensive community centres, or new shopping centres where sports provision has maintained public usage until the small hours of each morning. The latter often comprise sports buildings linked to a network of footpaths and trackways used for jogging, cycling, skating, or (depending upon locality) skiing. Olso is a typical example of where an unbroken system of pedestrian and cycle paths link the inner city to the surrounding countryside, and to health spas for winter and summer use. Floodlighting forms part of this system for considerable after-dark use.

Standards of design and finish are generally high, and facilities are regarded in much the same way as hotels may be in the UK. They are places to go to for wining and dining, for wedding receptions, rotary meetings and receptions, and have surroundings equal to, if not superior, to many hotels. Swimming pools in particular are a popular meeting place for eating beside the pool, as in the Mirandabad. In this example, ozone water treatment systems work in parallel with heat recovery methods, and result in odour-free surroundings of a standard thought barely possible in the 'municipal pools' twenty years ago.

The hotel industry in particular has been quick to realise the growing potential of this market. Many hotels now offer sporting facilities as in the case of the Seefeld Sport and Congress Centre, where the facilities include leisure pools, riding, golf, skiing, and ice skating, together with casinos and a nightclub.

The influence of these ideas on other parts of the developed and developing world has been marked by the appearance of many notable sports projects which reflect general trends similar to those in Western Europe. Stadia have appeared in many parts of the Middle East as sport begins to attract popular support. A similar pattern is slowly taking shape in Africa although apart from resource rich countries such as

LOCATION MAPS FOR CASE STUDIES REFERRED TO IN THE TEXT

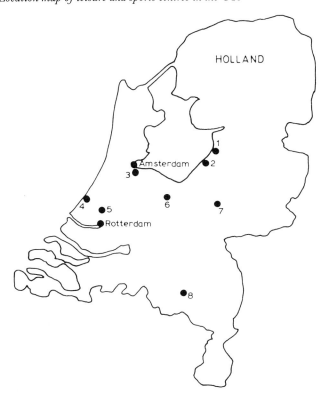

1 Ballymena Town Park
2 Irvine Leisure Centre
3 Royal Commonwealth Pool and
   Meadowbank, Edinburgh
4 Billingham Forum
5 Northgate Arena, Chester
6 The Cresset, Peterborough
7 Stantonbury Campus, Milton
   Keynes

8 Bletchley Leisure Centre
9 Dunstable Recreation Centre
10 Harlow Sportcentre
11 Redbridge Sports Centre
12 Lea Valley Regional Park
13 Eastleigh Sports Centre
14 University of Kent, Canterbury
15 Folkestone Sports Centre

Location map of leisure and sports centres in the UK

1 Gruga Park, Essen
2 Dusseldorf Stadium
3 Munchengladbach

4 Sporthochschule, Cologne
5 Herranalb Thermal Baths
6 Munich Olympic Stadium

Location map of leisure and sports centres in W. Germany

1 Lelystadt Sports Centre
2 De Meerpaal Hall, Dronten
3 De Mirandabad, Amsterdam
4 Scheveningen leisure complex
5 Ahoy Centre, Rotterdam
6 Royal Dutch Football Association
   Training Centre, Zeist
7 Papendal National Training Centre,
   Arnhem
8 Karregat Centre, Eindhoven

Location map of leisure and sports centres in Holland

Nigeria, funding has been more difficult, and heavily dependent upon outright gifts from the outside world. In Nigeria itself, a major programme of sports facilities is under construction which could result in it becoming a major influence in sport within the next decade.

National training centres have taken shape in Hong Kong and Singapore which will almost certainly reshape the future sports involvement on the international scene of both regions; while new development in Australia (part of which is described in chapter 6) has already combined many of the needs for serious training and general recreational sport. Jakarta has also attracted much attention especially from the Middle East, to its huge leisure pool and flume ride complex situated close to high density residential areas whose families can use it as a welcome 'outing' centre away from the hurly burly of urban life a kilometre or so away.

Development in Canada and the USA has also followed the same pattern, except that in the former there is a strong winter sport tradition. In the USA the availability of capital has resulted in ample provision of both competitive and recreational facilities on a scale similar to that seen only in West Germany at the present time. The main difference however is in the way that facilities are provided in the USA with a firm viability objective in mind. This works largely due to the fact that Americans are motivated this way (and often cannot understand why Europeans are so pub-lic-service minded), and also because young people have access to good training facilities throughout their high school and university life. Once they enter outside societies however, continuing participation is usually on the basis of privately run clubs where they expect to pay high (by European standards) membership dues in return for first class facilities provided with every convenience, including in many cases parking space for privately owned aeroplanes.

The case studies in the following chapters will illustrate many of the above points. Perhaps the main theme to emerge concerns the way in which sports architecture is no longer the severely functional expressionism of the 1960s. It is becoming increasingly sophisticated and in most cases is highly organised and well managed. The Olympic movement continues to lead design trends, but the motivation for playing now comes from mass participation at recreational levels. Innovation and relocation of facilities in the form of community centres and urban parks are trends which cannot be ignored.

We are obviously in an age of transition in which ideas are frequently superceded within five to seven years, requiring a building framework which can be altered (without the need for demolition) within the loose-knit framework seen in experimental projects in Europe during the 1970s. Flexibility is necessary to reflect this feeling of impermanence, and the measure of good design will almost certainly become adaptability, not monumentality.

Chapter 2
Small-scale projects

The club has long formed the basis of grass root provision throughout Europe, particularly in the UK where club involvement is a prerequisite for participation outside school or the community sports centre.

Traditional forms of provision normally include the pavilion, clubhouse, and mini sports centre. But with the changing trends referred to in the previous chapter, their organisation and range of accommodation is now very different from what it was ten or fifteen years ago.

A number of factors have influenced this situation. Indoor sports centres (described in chapter 4) have in many cases spawned the remarkable growth of new 'in-house' clubs as the result of management policy. However, not all aims are in this direction and competition for peak user period space is keen. In many cases this has resulted in clubs moving out to other external facilities in youth club premises, or in buildings requiring some renovation. Wider diversification has added to this range of new club provision, and increasing sophistication is another factor.

Perhaps the major influence affecting the decision-making process today is one of inflation, and the need to survive in an age of rapidly rising costs affecting land purchase, capital costs, staffing, and general organisation. These forces are obviously making a significant change to the planning and design of small scale facilities at the present time. The traditional preference for independence is fast disappearing as the economics of coalition become a survival ethic. The introduction of known money-making elements into this situation is now equally important, as is the possible introduction of other forms of commercialism including franchising and advertising to further augment income options. The example at Bishops Stortford (UK) is typical of this trend, as are the descriptions of golf and squash centres selected as case studies later in this chapter.

Optimum use of facilities

It could be said that today we are in a transitional period at this scale of provision. But it is clear that the single activity sports ground and pavilion will continue to fulfill a basic demand for some time to come,

Canons Brook Golf Club, Harlow. Clubhouse forming part of a quadrangle of listed buildings formerly a farmhouse complex (Conversion by Robert Turner Associates). (Photo: Harlow Development Corporation)

9

and recently much thought has been given to possible ways and means of improving even the most traditional of these facilities. Among the suggestions offered are included the possibility of making better use of facilities during weekdays by the letting of rooms to pre-school play groups, the addition of squash courts and bar spaces with the help of subsidies usually offered by local breweries, and committee rooms for mid-week team selection and evening use for chess, cards or darts matches.

The net effect of these suggestions when put into practice has been to increase the overall size of projects and to replace old committee structures with new forms of management control similar to the Sports Trust system seen in the Bishops Stortford example. This type of arrangement also carries distinct advantages in terms of rating and tenure of property if accepted as being of charitable status. A subsidiary effect has also been to up-grade standards of finish to meet this new image and satisfy public demand, as may be judged by the examples included in this section as case studies.

The inherent sophistication called for by these policies has taken many forms. Colour televisions may be frequently seen in committee rooms, and 'snugs' in bar lounges.

Lighting systems often make provision for disco dancing, and dancing zones formed by the inclusion of a suitably inset floor finish. Where squash is included, separate rooms for changing and showering have become almost mandatory in addition to those provided for team games, to economise on space and water heating. Separation is also necessary for security reasons especially where a burglar alarm system has been installed. Digital locks, coin-operated lighting apparatus – fitted with over-ride switching controls – and self-booking arrangements, all form part of these new requirements if running costs are to be kept to a minimum.

The degree to which these buildings can be fenestrated continues to cause many problems, especially in high risk areas associated with isolated locations. The inclusion of vandal-proof glazing although expensive compared with ordinary glass can be very rewarding in such circumstances and has opened up new possibilities in this field. Planning requirements also play a major part in shaping design features such as height, external materials, landscaping and sound emission through glazed areas. The scale relationship of squash courts to clubhouses is frequently a source of some concern in this context, and calls for care in balancing the overall massing of the building by lowering courts into the ground, or by forming earth mounds planted with shrubs or small trees.

Orientation is another factor requiring some attention if optimum viewing conditions for outdoor activities are to be provided. Views to the east are preferred in the majority of cases, as may be seen by reference to the table below; if possible on high ground giving good views over surrounding pitches.

The examples given later in this chapter include many of these points, and should be compared with others illustrated in the United Kingdom Sports Council book *Pavilions*, and the *Handbook of Sports Facilities* published by The Architects' Journal, London. Other examples of small scale facilities may be seen in the section on Urban Parks under the case study of the Lee Valley Regional Park Authority, see page 113.

Orientation

The effect of solar glare on spectators and players can be minimised by the correct orientation of pavilions, stands, pitches and tracks, according to latitude and playing time. For example the table below shows the recommended axis of pitches and tracks, and stand or pavilion orientation for a latitude of 52°N (which is approximately the latitude of London).

Activity	Time of day	Pitch axis	Pavilion orientation
Football	early p.m.	N/S	faces east
Rugby	early p.m.	N/S	faces east
Hockey	early p.m.	N/S	faces east
Cricket	11–12.00	NW/SE	faces south east
Tennis	p.m.	N/S	faces east
Running tracks	p.m.	NNW/SSE	faces east

The sun path diagram is for the same degree of latitude and can be used to obtain the best position for the placing of canopies of louvres in relation to pitch orientation.

In practice however, the increasing use of floodlights and late kick-off times, together with all-weather surfaces, makes such fine adjustments almost unnecessary, although it is always more pleasant to watch play without having to shield eyes from direct glare if these facilities are not available. It is also better to place viewing positions away from prevailing wind directions, which in the UK are generally from the west side of grounds. As west is the main weather side of buildings, windows should be generally smaller than on the east, and detailed to throw off rainwater.

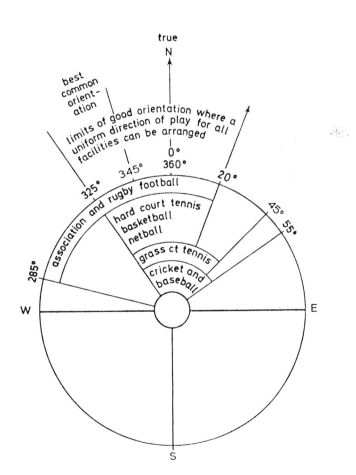

Sun path diagram

DIMENSIONS OF MAIN OUTDOOR PLAYING AREAS

Flat rink bowls – 6 rinks

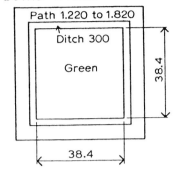

Path 1.220 to 1.820

Ditch 300

Green

38.4

38.4

Crown rink bowls as flat rink but 36.5 x 36.5

Flat rink bowling green

Orientation of sports fields and courts

Tennis

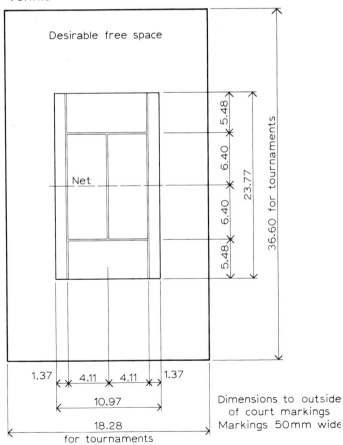

Desirable free space

Net

5.48

6.40

6.40

5.48

23.77

36.60 for tournaments

1.37   4.11   4.11   1.37

10.97

18.28
for tournaments

Dimensions to outside
of court markings
Markings 50mm wide

Tennis courts

Cricket

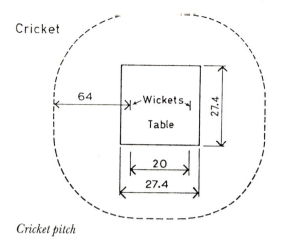

Cricket pitch

Lacrosse (men)

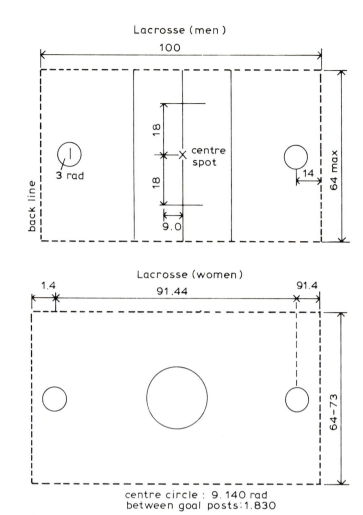

Soccer

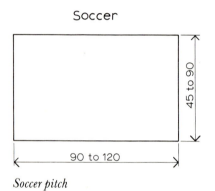

Soccer pitch

Lacrosse (women)

centre circle : 9.140 rad
between goal posts:1.830

Lacrosse

Rugby

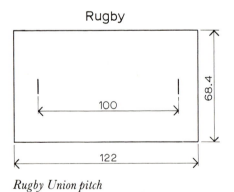

Rugby Union pitch

Hockey

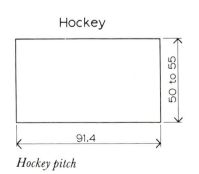

Hockey pitch

Rugby league

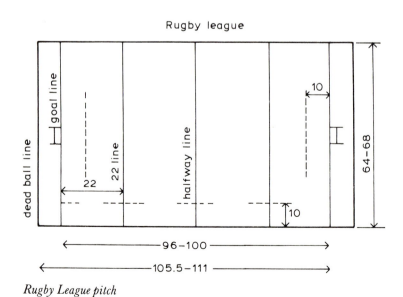

Rugby League pitch

Case studies

Sports Pavilion, University of Essex, Colchester
This project attracted much attention on completion in the late 1960s by the manner in which the traditional close-knit pavilion plan was rearranged to suit site conditions. This created a 'contrapuntal forms' solution much admired at the time, but seldom seen since.

The site in question consisted of an historic glade of trees protected by preservation order on high ground overlooking outdoor pitches on three sides each with access paths leading to the centre of the site. The point at which these paths met became the focal point of the new building – the refreshment wing – and where they came into the project became footpaths leading to the two changing units on either side of the refreshment area, with a common meeting ground between each arranged as an internal patio. This can be seen from the plan.

The final shape of the three units as hexagons reduced the overall massing considerably and achieved an excellent scale relationship with the tall *in situ* trees surrounding the building. This has been further enhanced by chamfering the copings from a point four courses of brickwork below skyline level. Essex red brickwork was used to blend with the green surroundings on each of the windowless changing room units. These are windowless because of high risk from vandalism and also to emphasise the impact of the completely open glass box forming the refreshment wing.

The intellectualism of this concept has been expressed in many small points of detailing. For example, one side of the glass box has been truncated to allow the paving beyond to die away to a point in the direction of the first-eleven pitch. Stepping stones lead to the other pitches. A number of environmental devices have been explored, such as roof-mounted floodlighting to illuminate the glade after dark and produce the impression of a much larger internal space.

Further refinements may be seen in the articulation of each element to reduce the apparent massing, and in the detailing of doors and windows which have been positioned flush with external brick faces and rag-bolted or hinged direct to brickwork without frames in order not to interrupt the general flow of these shapes. Copings are sloped to soften the outline, and paving beyond the social wing is allowed to die away in a point carrying the eye to the playing field beyond.

Circulation in each changing block continues this easy flow pattern, players being able to pass from the central entrance corridors through the changing and toilet areas in a sequence kept to the perimeter of the buildings which avoids any crossing of wet paths. The groundstores are completely separate, and a central heating plant in the female changing block, ducts warm air across to other elements via the central patio. In the refreshment area, tables can be arranged in the traditional long line for after-match teas, or in clusters when the bar opens. Warm air is ducted up the inside glass faces as an invisible curtain preventing condensation. Several of the floor to ceiling height

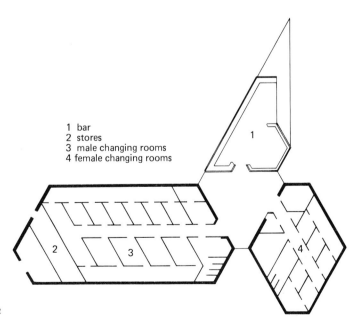

1 bar
2 stores
3 male changing rooms
4 female changing rooms

University of Essex, Sports Pavilion. Plan

University of Essex, Sports Pavilion. A view into the internal patio where access paths converge from surrounding pitches and the main approach road. (Architects: Gasson and Meunier)

University of Essex, Sports Pavilion. An example of the contrast between the windowless changing rooms and the glass-box enclosing the refreshment room

glass panels double up as sliding doors leading to the terrace on the east and south sides of this area, see under 'Orientation' in chapter 1.

Low maintenance cost materials have been used throughout – white painted fletton brickwork intenally, grano topped floors, and patent aluminium section roof members. Colours are limited to the self finish of the materials themselves, plywood, brown quarry tiles (in the social room), galvanised metal and glass. Black neoprene gaskets hold the plate glass sections, and galvanised metal supports at 900 mm centres are braced at the top by transverse and lateral beams, and at the bottom by perimeter seating units with subframes welded to the uprights.

The introduction of intermediate supports (one of which is hollow and acts as a service duct for electrical supplies) has reduced the depth of transverse beams and kept structural cost to the minimum. The project was in fact built well within the clients' cost limits of £50 per square metre (which by 1980 had risen to £300), and well vindicated the university's decision to place this work with one of the smaller practices.

Clubhouse and squash courts, Bishops Stortford, Hertfordshire

This project was completed in 1979 following considerable discussion on ways and means of up-grading existing social and toilet facilities on the site, and improving annual income. The senior cricket club had played on the ground since the days of W. G. Grace (who played there on several occasions in the late 1800s), and had been joined between the two world wars this century by tennis and hockey sections

retaining their individual identity by building separate changing rooms and playing on self-contained areas of the grounds, leased from the local authority.

Like many organisations in the same situation, modern times have begun to erode this structure, with inflation biting deeply into resources, and traditional voluntary effort achieving less each year despite considerable local support for these facilities. In 1978 a special meeting decided the time had come to form a corporate identity in the form of a Sports Trust with charitable status and to include two squash courts and a larger bar and refreshment room with the object of improving annual revenues, increasing membership, and achieving a greater measure of viability.

Planning requirements largely dictated the siting of the new squash courts as an integral part of the existing clubhouse, at right angles to each other and recessed into surrounding made up ground used as tennis courts, in order to reduce their scale and massing in relation to the old building and site as a whole. Planting requirements were another feature of the planning consent resulting from the site position in relation to the urban green belt around the town .

Development took place within the constraints of tight fixture lists and bar bookings throughout the seven month construction period. A day nursery let to an adjacent school used the main clubhouse area. This is a typical feature of such improvements, calling for considerable goodwill on all parts, not least the contractors and their insurers.

The final form of the building achieves a fine balance between day users (squash players and the pre-school play group), and peak evening time use. As

1 old clubhouse
2 new squash courts
3 new changing rooms, showers and toilets
4 new 'snug' and momento display area
5 old cricket pavilion
6 upper and lower tennis courts
7 car park
8 banking between tennis courts, used to reduce scale of squash courts

Bishops Stortford Sports Trust Pavilion and Squash Courts. Plan (Architects: Perrin Associates)

15

there is no full time management, squash members control their own booking arrangements, the entry system (by means of a digital locking device with a numbering code changed every month), and lighting controls to the courts (by means of coin-operated light meters or using an over-ride switch for competitions). Entry to the clubhouse is prohibited during mornings while the pre-school play group is in residence, and unauthorised entry at other times can be controlled by an elaborate burglar alarm system.

The 'snug' extension to the clubhouse gives a good view over the main cricket square, while providing a display area for old prints, photographs and club momentos which give so much 'atmosphere' in this type of building, and provide a sense of belonging for so many generations of users. It also serves as a television room for the nursery group. Financial and material help to enlarge the bar was provided by a local brewery as is often the case at the present time. Maintenance costs have been minimised by the use of good quality straw-coloured facing brickwork internally, timber-lined ceilings, and stained timber linings to frames and partitions. Ventilation is provided to the internal changing room by means of a fan mounted in the rooflight above, operated by the light switches. Hot water supplies are controlled by two immersion heaters, one at the top of the main storage cylinder for use in the kitchen and bar areas, and one at the bottom for shower water. Both are controlled by time switches to economise on costs.

The overall result has achieved the immediate objectives set in 1978 to increase income and membership, with the minimum amount of upkeep or management control. The plan form will allow future growth should further squash courts be considered necessary (over thirty courts are in use within a seven mile radius of the project, although demand shows no sign of being met at present). The final appearance of the extension has done much to improve the image of the ground as a whole, and to attract membership from a much larger catchment area in the face of strong competition from other local clubs and organisations.

Old Chigwellians Sports Centre, North London

Chigwell School is a well-known public school with a soccer/cricket playing tradition going back many years, and a strong old boys' society to carry on this tradition in adult life.

In 1978 the opportunity arose to lease a playing field site adjacent the school sports pitches, and to build a permanent home for the old boys which would serve as a focal point for future school leavers until well into the next century. A fund-raising campaign

was launched, discussions were started with local planners (as the site was in the Green Belt), and plans drawn up which were eventually approved on the basis of the strong relationship between the old boys and the school.

Construction work commenced in 1979 and the building was completed in the summer of 1980. Features of the resulting complex reflect many of the points made in the introduction. The client wanted an 'up-market' atmosphere in keeping with the age range of the users and their expressed preference for good standards of finish and materials, a welcoming atmosphere for their guests, and an economic planning solution which would minimise day to day running costs.

The resulting plan form sets out to reflect most of these objectives. The two squash courts have been placed at right angles to each other, as at Bishops Stortford, to reduce their apparent mass when viewed

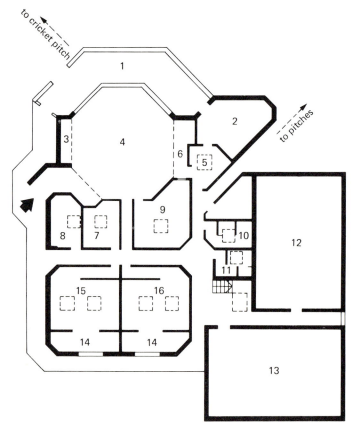

1 terrace	9 committee
2 store	10 men's squash changing room
3 snug	11 women's squash changing
4 club room	12 squash court 1
5 kitchen	13 squash court 2
6 bar	14 showers
7 men s'toilets	15 changing 1 (home)
8 women s'toilets	16 changing 2 (visitors)

Old Chigwellians Association, Pavilion and Squash Courts. Plan (Architects: Perrin Associates)

from the outside, and are further reduced in scale by one story high changing rooms between them and the approach road and car park.

The hexagonal shape of the clubhouse has been used as a further means of breaking up the rectangularity of these courts, and at the same providing an interesting internal shape reflected externally by the sloping roof and use of asbestos slates as a contrast with the red brickwork of the squash courts at the rear. The clock housing completes this contrast in shapes, while being very much in keeping with surrounding property known locally as 'millionaires row'.

The two main functions of the building – social and play – are separated by a central corridor between the clubhouse and the changing room wing. Squash players arriving by day use a digital lock at the side entrance to gain access to their own changing rooms and the courts. Weekend users use the same entrance to enter larger changing rooms adjacent, to which they can return after play without entering any social areas. A bar steward is available at mid-day to open the bar and clubhouse during weekdays, and again in the evenings when social areas become fully operational. A committee room has been placed between the clubhouse and one side of the bar in which members can select teams, or watch television. A hatchway can be used for refreshments without the need to go into the main clubhouse.

Finishes in the clubhouse consist of straw-coloured facing bricks, timber-lined sloping ceilings, and a carpeted floor coloured dark brown as a foil to the brickwork. The bar counter has been finished in orange-coloured mosaic tiles with brass edging strips, as the main source of strong colour in the room. Mirrors behind the bar optics increase the feeling of space within this area, and reflect the outside trees and grass pitches seen through the full height windows overlooking the main cricket square. A small terrace defined by traditional white boarded fencing has also been provided for this purpose.

Finishes in the changing areas are sparse by contrast in an effort to keep capital costs to a minimum, and to provide only better finishes where they were in the public eye. Ceilings are therefore of exposed woodwool slabs spray painted, and blockwork has been used in preference to brick. Full height tiling has however been provided in all shower areas as experience has shown that paint finishes in these locations deteriorate rapidly with use. Pipework is concealed throughout to avoid replacement costs through horseplay, as is all electrical conduit which has been built into the structure at no extra cost. Painted finishes have been limited to doors and changing area blockwork.

Light fittings in the clubhouse have been arranged to emphasise activity areas – downlighters over the bar concealed in a timber housing containing glass shelves: downlighters in the centre of the room for possible disco dances: orange lights in the 'snug': spotlights to pick out various plaques, photographs and paintings on enclosing wall surfaces. Strip lighting has been concealed above each of the windows behind curtaining to emphasise the latter and give a further sense of atmosphere after dark.

The single storey structure has been designed to accommodate a first floor if required at a future date. The squash courts can also be added to without disruption should the existing provision prove inadequate.

Multi-purpose hall, North Romford Community Association, North London

This project is typical of many urban 'local sports centres' which now form a major part of UK Sports Council strategy. They fulfill a very real need for indoor sports facilities where they can be reached on foot in 'round the corner' situations existing as in this case in a thriving community association used for many other functions not necessarily connected with sport.

The history of this project is common to many in and around large conurbations. The demand for indoor space in the existing accommodation had reached such proportions by the mid-1970s that many well-supported groups such as local badminton and volleyball clubs were forced to look elsewhere for space in which to train and play. Even today much of the area is still classified as being in a considerable state of deprivation for such facilities. Discussions concerning the possibility of extending facilities to include a hall large enough for such games have continued over many years, and the final decision to proceed was made in 1979.

The brief called for two badminton courts, one volleyball court, four-a-side football, table tennis and judo facilities, with provision to be made for occasional lettings to wedding parties, dances, and social functions. The client in this case was the community association, and contributors to the construction cost included the local authority, the education authority and the regional sports council.

The dimensions of the hall conform to present recommendations made by the national UK Sports Council, although it is accepted that these are to a recreational standard and may be extremely restricting in terms of height for badminton, or length for volleyball. Nevertheless they fulfill the main objective of meeting basic needs in the area, and are more than

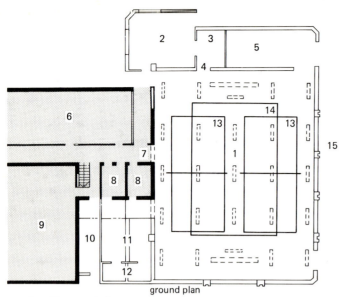

1 multi purpose hall
   (6.700 m high overall)
2 meeting room
3 kitchen
4 service to hall
5 equipment store
6 existing community association facilities
7 access from existing facilities
8 existing toilets
9 existing hall
10 plant room
11 changing rooms
12 showers
13 babminton courts
14 volleyball court
15 car park

ground plan

*North Romford Community Association, Multi-purpose Hall. Plan
(Architects: Perrin Associates)*

adequate for other groups requesting space in the hall, including yoga classes, keep fit groups, and ballet classes.

In addition to the hall the brief called for a meeting room, equipment store, and changing rooms to service the hall itself, as indicated on the plan. Local planners called for an extension to the existing car park, and a certain degree of rehabilitation work to outside fencing and landscaping.

Constraints were imposed by the local authority landlord on any structural alterations to the existing building, and particular attention was paid to alternative means of escape in case of fire. The final form of the building therefore resulted from these requirements, and the structural solution avoids any need to alter existing walls or foundations, by building over these where the new meets the old.

The final decision to opt for a 'black box' solution in the main hall was taken after comparative cost exercises had been undertaken with alternative roof light systems, although it was accepted that the latter were probably the cheaper in terms of annual running costs. The final timber finishes to the structural roof and ceiling add considerably to the warm inviting

atmosphere in the hall, as do the cinnamon coloured brick walls, and beech floor (which surprisingly was obtained for half the cost of synthetic finishes).

The fluorescent lighting arrangement makes allowance for the fact that no lights should be positioned directly over badminton courts, and can be switched to suit either the needs of this activity or volleyball. Subsidiary lighting of a 'softer' nature is also provided for wedding receptions and dances.

The project is one of a number now used as models for future similar projects by the UK Sports Council, and was constructed well within cost yardsticks set at the time for this type of building.

Squash centres

The growth in squash raquets has been remarkable over the past decade in the UK, Australia, the USA and is beginning to appear in significant strength in Japan and continental Europe. Some of the reasons for this have already been referred to in chapter 1, especially the revenue-earning characteristics of the game. Other reasons include the shortness of the

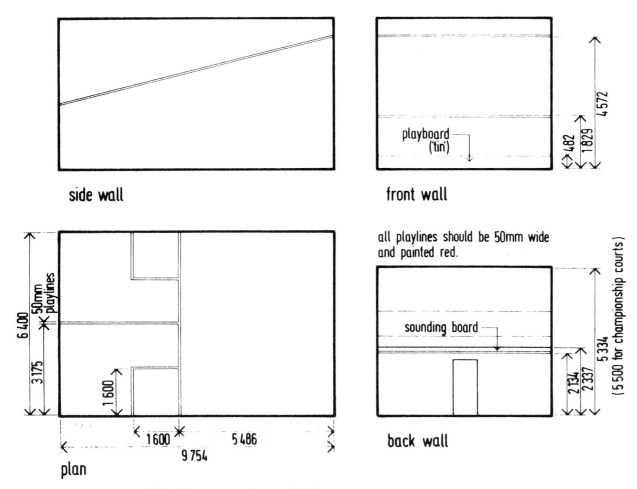

side wall

front wall

playboard
('tin')

482

1 829

4 572

all playlines should be 50mm wide
and painted red.

plan

6 400

50mm
playlines

3 175

1 600

1 600

5 486

9 754

back wall

sounding board

2 134

2 337

5 334

(5 500 for championship courts)

Squash court data diagram. Main dimensions are between finishes

*Wembley Squash Centre, Championship Court. Viewing at rear of
court only. More recent projects employ three sided glass walled courts
or plastic lined courts with open-top viewed from high level seating.
(Photo: Ellis Pearson Ltd)*

game, its attraction for men and women, its low threshold of skill level before enjoyment can be had from playing, and its low degree of organisation required from those who wish to play. From the sponsorship point of view courts are relatively cheap to maintain and staff, and with good management can be made to pay their way within a short time of opening. The original capital cost can be regained within four to five years.

For these reasons many indoor public sports centres now include some squash court provision, and in some cases have developed a separate squash membership playing section as at the Harlow Sportcentre (see page 77). The growth of commercially-run squash centres has been particularly noticeable in the USA and the UK during the past decade, and later case studies in this chapter give several examples of the design approach in the UK which are typical of this movement.

Other examples of provision have been illustrated in the case studies of the Old Chigwellians Sports Centre, and the Bishops Stortford Sports Trust complex. The Kingswood Squash Centre in Basildon, Essex, has grown from eight courts in 1970 to nineteen by 1980, while in an eight-mile radius there are many more courts all fully booked at peak user periods. Similarly, there are over forty courts within seven miles of the Harlow Sportcentre which is less than twenty miles away, with demand showing no signs of drying up in the foreseeable future.

One reason for this is the nature of the players who have attained some proficiency at the game and find themselves playing three or four times a week in order to keep match fit. Experience shows that, at this stage, many either take up membership of several centres just to ensure a booking, or belong to several others where social conditions may be better after play. As a rule of thumb therefore it has been found that 100 members per court give very comfortable playing conditions, 125 reasonable conditions, 175 produce a sound economic return on investment (but borderline comfort conditions), and 190 members or over give rise to conditions likely to lead to many players going elsewhere. Many courts operate best at around 80% to 90% utilisation fourteen hours a day, seven days a week.

Design trends are changing in much the same way as in other indoor sports facilities – increasingly reflecting the greater sophistication looked for today by players and spectators alike. Whereas ten years ago most courts were arranged in rows for cheapness by repetition, they are now often broken up into smaller units, often at right angles to each other, for instance the at the Bishops Stortford Pavilion on page 17. The courts are frequently without first floor viewing galleries, and play is often watched through glass rear walls as at Penkridge, Staffordshire shown below.

Players are lightly clad and susceptible to temperature changes and now look increasingly for sophisticated air-conditioning systems to achieve better comfort conditions. Some form of air movement and background heating outside the courts is in any case essential to avoid the traditional complaint of condensation on walls and floors (where slipperiness can result in injury). Lighting systems are also becoming increasingly sophisticated to allow for several levels of

Viewing area between rows of glass backed squash courts at the 4C's Squash Club, Penkridge, Staffordshire.
(Photo: Ellis Pearson Ltd)

competition should this be a management objective. The lighting arrangement at the City Squash Centre for example can be adjusted for recreational level play, training, and high level competition including colour television coverage.

There is a strong trend towards glass-sided walls with one-way vision glass to increase spectating options again where these form a firm management commitment. Although relatively expensive at present, saving is made on maintenance and replacement costs common to all existing plaster finishes. Where glass walls have been installed it has often been found necessary to provide a microphone point and loudspeaker arrangement at high level to enable players to hear decisions being called by umpires during major competitions.

In all cases white backgrounds are essential to all walls and ceilings: as are sprung timber floors using either beech or prime grade maple selected for their evenness of colour. The use of green squash balls is now obligatory at most centres to reduce wall markings and subsequent maintenance costs.

Back-up facilities outside courts usually include a carpeted viewing area (e.g. the Penkridge Squash Club), good changing rooms – separate to normal changing areas if part of a larger sports complex – an easily-run bookings system for messages and announcements, comfortable seating arrangements, and most important of all, a good bar lounge, run on club membership lines. There is also some indication that sauna suites, hairdressing facilities and a trimnasium (keep-fit or leisure conditioning room) can be an added attraction and revenue-producing source given the right management input, and design expertise.

City Squash Club, London

The redevelopment of old commercial premises in and around the City of London has led to the inclusion of sports facilities in some of the most unlikely locations in recent years. The City Squash Centre has replaced a group of Victorian shops and offices opposite Aldgate East underground station in a part of London which only the inexperienced would attempt to reach by car.

From this point of view the risk factor must have appeared high by any standards, but has been offset in practice by the nearness of the location to the famous 'Square Mile' comprising banking and financial institutions in the City of London. Many thousands of young business people working here are eager to play 'breakfast' squash before starting work or during their lunch break. An increasing number also appear keen to stay on in the evenings until after the rush hour has ended.

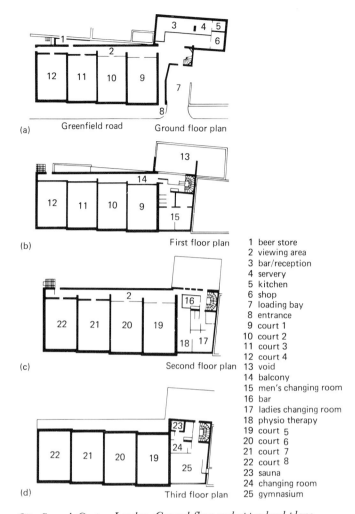

1	beer store
2	viewing area
3	bar/reception
4	servery
5	kitchen
6	shop
7	loading bay
8	entrance
9	court 1
10	court 2
11	court 3
12	court 4
13	void
14	balcony
15	men's changing room
16	bar
17	ladies changing room
18	physio therapy
19	court 5
20	court 6
21	court 7
22	court 8
23	sauna
24	changing room
25	gymnasium

City Squash Centre, London. Ground floor and upper level plans (Architects: Barnsley, Hewett & Mallinson)

City Squash Centre. Entrance and reception leading to the social and refreshment area. (Architects: Barnsley, Hewett & Mallinson)

As may be expected, the external appearance of the Club presents a blank anonymous aspect, four-stories high, to the street. The building is further emphasised by what might be called a 'hole in the wall' entrance consisting of a single door leading to a narrow corridor beyond, which opens into a double height reception area, carpeted and well lit by concealed fittings. This also serves as a health food lounge and social space.

Good quality, straw-coloured facing brickwork provides a warm inviting background to these facilities, which are much used by non-playing social members. Changing rooms are at upper levels approached by a circular staircase from this area, and the eight courts are arranged in groups of four placed over each other; two serving as competition courts, two as coaching courts, and the remainder as general match play facilities.

Individual coaching forms part of a highly personalised service to members for which fees are set proportionately high; for example, VIP membership in 1980 was £500 a year at the top end of the scale (for which a valet service is included) and social non-playing membership, £25 per annum, both exlusive of Value Added Tax. Personal lockers, a laundry service, hairdriers, cosmetic appliances, and a hairdressing salon are also included in this service.

All courts are air conditioned, and have lighting levels well above the average – the main championship court having twice the normal number of fittings, all placed parallel to side walls. The latter have been finished with fibre-reinforced plaster which is considered to be an improvement to other plasters on the market although time will no doubt confirm this view. Maple strip flooring has been left deliberately unsealed to provide a better foot grip (many players consider seals to be a potential hazard), and to give a whiter appearance for optimum contrast with the ball.

Four of the courts are glass-backed and have been provided with microphone points for competition matches or instruction from outside the court. Padded benching is provided behind each of these courts, and heating is at skirting level in the form of very compact square section radiators. Upper level viewing balconies are either glass fronted or in brick, provided with a flat handrail or lectern on which scorecards can be kept, and match results recorded.

This attention to detail is obviously the result of years of feedback from experienced players, and illustrates many of the best features in court design at the present time and the confidence now being shown by entrepreneurs to invest in this particular end of the leisure market.

Golf clubhouses

Golf is similar to squash in being a rapid growth sport in many parts of the world. Some of the reasons for this are common to all sport – i.e. increased time for leisure and wide coverage by the media. But golf has now developed an image which has less social identification with the more affluent.

Provision has also been made for better all-round facilities both on the greens and in clubhouses. These take many forms. At one end of the scale can be seen the more lavish provision associated with American or Spanish clubhouses where the facilities frequently form part of a comprehensive leisure and commercial industry (including residential accommodation). At the other end, are the run-of-the-mill facilities for average members paying average green fees, while still serving a very necessary role in meeting demand.

Basic requirements for a clubhouse include a generous car park (most players come by car and, in many American clubs, by aeroplane), a golf professional's shop, locker and shower rooms, caddie store, control kiosk, administration offices, and social areas for members and their guests. In some cases a caretaker's flat or house is also provided. Any greenkeeping equipment should be stored well away from the public areas of the complex. The refreshment lounge or bar frequently overlooks the 18th hole which traditionally finishes at the clubhouse. Practice greens and putting areas are often sited between the last hole and first tee.

In many cases, in the UK, the average club has found it necessary in recent years to invest in other income-producing elements, including squash courts, sauna suites, keep-fit rooms, additional bars for non-members, billiard and snooker tables, and fruit machines.

The recent trend to use farmland for this purpose has resulted in many excellent courses, and equally excellent conversions of farm buildings including former barns. An interesting example is at Harlow in Essex, (page 9) which is typical of this type of sympathetic treatment; in this case of a grade two listed tithe barn and ancillary farm buildings acquired for this purpose by the new town development corporation in the early 1960s. Administration of the club comes under the aegis of the Harlow and District Sports Trust which also controls the affairs of the town's main sports centre (see page 77).

The eighteen hole course was laid out by Henry Cotton on land running between the north west periphery of the town and western industrial estate for which it forms a perfect landscape setting (and from which it has attracted many members). Conversion of the farm buildings took the form of a courtyard surrounding a pitch and putt area, and entered through an old archway framed by existing rose bushes and ornamental shrubs. Locker rooms and the professional shop were added to the tithe barn on one side of the courtyard, and refreshment facilities and a new clubhouse on the other, each designed to blend with the existing character of the barn. The latter is frequently used for ladies' nights, dances, meetings and receptions, with open rafters and roof trusses giving very much the impression of a mediaeval banqueting hall.

Artificial ski centres

The development of artificial ski slopes is comparatively new and stems from the considerable interest in skiing and ski holidays generated by the media and tourist trade in recent years. The shortness of such holidays, or the risk of bad weather, has made pre-ski training practically essential especially in low lying countries, or countryside.

One of the largest groups of users are schools, where pre-skiing preparation is usually expected to take at least eight weeks prior to school party excursions to mountain resorts mainly during the Easter vacation

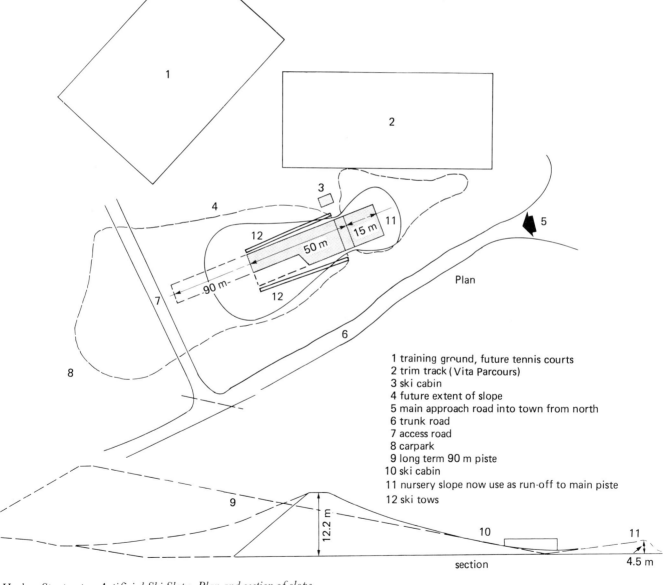

1 training ground, future tennis courts
2 trim track (Vita Parcours)
3 ski cabin
4 future extent of slope
5 main approach road into town from north
6 trunk road
7 access road
8 carpark
9 long term 90 m piste
10 ski cabin
11 nursery slope now use as run-off to main piste
12 ski tows

Harlow Sportcentre, Artificial Ski Slope. Plan and section of slope formed from excavated material from building sites elsewhere in the town. (Architects: Perrin Associates)

23

(at least in Europe). Parents often take a keen interest in this preparatory work and frequently arrange to take separate instruction either during the evenings under floodlights, or at weekends. Many of both age groups become very proficient and continue to visit such centres for recreation or to give instruction to beginners.

The basic requirements of the average ski centre revolve around these user groups and their particular needs. For example the minimum length of piste for recreational skiiing is considered to be at least 50 m, by 12 to 15 m high, for which a ski tow is essential for all groups if they are to get the most out of each training session. Training slopes for beginners are generally half these dimensions and should be sited parallel to the main piste and never at the end. Experience has shown that the latter arrangement leads to accidents and some teaching problems at the intersection of both slopes. As mentioned earlier, low level floodlighting is considered desirable for after dark instruction. This should be just high enough to illuminate the matting surface and pick out any 'moguls' or dips and mounds sometimes provided for added interest.

The nucleus of any complex however, should be the ski hut or cabin. This houses management staff (essential for the efficient promotion of such centres), skis and ski boots, a repair workshop, changing space, toilets, and preferably some form of refreshment facility – a milk bar for youngsters, and bar for adults. If possible an outdoor terrace should be provided for spectators in good weather.

The ideal situation for this type of project may be seen at Sandown Park Racecourse, where natural slopes have been used to good advantage, and mature landscaping provided the right environmental atmosphere from the moment the centre opened. An alternative is to create an artificial mound with the advice of an experienced civil engineer and soils expert as experience has shown all too clearly in the past that where short cuts have been taken with the type of fill is usually disastrous. An understanding of the type of spoil and its natural angle of repose is essential as is good drainage laid in herringbone fashion down the sides of the main piste, and at the foot of the run-off, which together with grassing do much to prevent erosion. Tree planting in the form of conifers (to avoid leaf fall in the autumn) is often part of any planning consent in such circumstances.

The Harlow Ski Centre is a typical example of the latter type of development, which with good management has proved successful and financially viable after three years of operation. With hindsight the nursery slope would not now be positioned at the end of the main piste, and future plans allow for alternative sitings adjacent the ski tow. Apart from this and some initial problems with the original matting, the project has worked well and has become a popular meeting place for the young, parents, and – on Sunday mornings – the disabled. One-legged skiers and the blind using these slopes regularly has are a feature of the centre for many local disabled people.

The alpine cabin forming the administrative headquarters of the Ski Centre is faced internally and externally with boarding. This is stained externally to catch the eye of passers-by on the adjacent main road entering the town from the north. Inside, the atmosphere is one of ski racks, ski posters, benching, and a small refreshment bar, with bright colours throughout against a pine boarded background. Due to its isolated position, all windows can be shuttered up (Swiss style) when not in use and natural lighting is via burglar-proof rooflights.

Harlow Sportcentre, Artificial Ski Slope. View from top of main 50 m long piste (Photo: Gerald Perrin)

A fail-safe system is incorporated into the Swiss-manufactured ski tow, but care is required at all times at the foot and head of the tow to ensure the safety of all users – even experienced skiers can get their skis caught in the matting. Other types of tow now on the market also give a much more positive 'hold' on the gradient which skiers tend to prefer.

From a planning viewpoint such slopes cause problems of scale, siting, and landscaping. In this case the sponsors (Harlow & District Sports Trust) were called upon to 'ripple' the banking to give an apparent reduction in overall massing, and to plant what amounted to a 'forest' of small trees, many of which have since been vandalised or have died. The survivors give a more natural look to the mound and also help break up the scale to blend with surrounding landscaping. The low-level floodlights give no problems to passing motorists. After five years the project now forms a well-known and liked landmark at one of the key entrance points to the town and its continually busy appearance has attracted many users from nearby towns.

Other examples of ski slopes are at Folkestone Sports Centre (see page 68) and Dunstable Recreation Centre.

Provision for the handicapped

Sport is being enjoyed by a growing number of handicapped people due partly to a more sympathetic understanding by those associated with the development of sport generally, and partly to recent legislation designed to encourage improved access to such facilities. The various types of handicapped user include the ambulant amputee, wheelchair confined disabled, blind and partially-sighted, sufferers from arthritis, the mentally handicapped, and the deaf.

The Paraplegic Olympics held in 1980 at Papendal, Holland, illustrated the range of activities now regularly undertaken at various levels of disablement. These include sprinting, archery and rink bowls by the blind, volleyball, basketball, weight-lifting and sprinting by amputees, fencing by victims of poliomyolitis, and basketball, athletics, field events and swimming by those confined to wheelchairs.

At a recreational/therapeutic level many other forms of active involvement are also available where provision has been specifically included among management objectives during the design and briefing stage. As already described, recreational skiing is regularly undertaken by amputees and the blind at the Harlow Ski Centre (see page 24) and golf for both forms of handicap is played at many courses.

Swimming is perhaps the commonest form of provision where access to the water has been assisted by such details as wider than normal doors, direct access from public circulation areas, handrails, sonic devices, ramps, duckboards in pre-cleanse areas, and a deck level system in the pool itself. In some cases additional aids may be provided in the form of hoists and ramps into the pool from the surrounds – as in the example illustrated in the case study of the Washington Therapeutic Centre, in the adjacent column.

Large signs around pools are another form of help for the partially-sighted, or those who cannot wear contact lens in the water. While coloured warning lights are essential for the hard of hearing. Non-slip surfaces give added confidence to those with a walking disability.

Other general points of detail include the omission of matwells at all entrances, and door closers which may create a problem for wheelchair users; handrails on both sides of all public staircases; steps of uniform height and width with the nosings clearly identified by a change in colour or texture and ramps with gradients of not more than 1:12. Toughened glass should be used in all screens to public viewing areas, with all access points clearly identified, double width cubicles for wheelchair users and toilets with special provision for access by the same type of user, and low-level urinals for men. Lifts should have a minimum internal dimension of 1400 mm by 11100 mm, with a door opening of not less than 800 mm. The top control button should not be higher than 1300 mm above floor level, and slightly raised for the benefit of partially-sighted users. However, in the UK, no lift may be used during a fire.

These and many other design guide features are listed in the publications *Data Sheet 22.1* (Technical Unit for Sport, 70 Brompton Road, London SW3) and *Designing for the Disabled* by Selwyn Goldsmith (Architectural Press, Queen Anne's Gate, London SW1). Most developed countries have national advisory centres. In the UK the Stoke Mandeville Centre for the Disabled contains many of these details in sports facilities built on the campus during the late 1960s and its staff have become recognised at international level for a considerable period of time.

Therapeutic recreation centre, Washington, DC, USA
The purpose of this project was to meet the specific needs of mentally retarded and physically disabled users from a wide catchment area (served by special bus service). It was the intention that the centre should serve as a model and feedback source for future projects of a similar nature.

The centre opened in April 1977, and the client was the city Department of Recreation Special Programmes Division. The preparation of the brief took ten years, in order to ensure a successful start to what is even today a unique concept in terms of recreational services for the disabled. These include the blind and partially-sighted, hearing impaired, epileptic, cerebral palsied and paraplegics. Key features referred to in the brief were 'barrier free circulation areas, a non-institutionalised and human scale, and finishes that were to be vandal resistant without resulting in a fortress-like appearance'.

The resulting solution to these basic requirements consists of two highly articulated buildings linked by covered way, and surrounded by outdoor play spaces and leisure areas. The area was once a favourite picnic

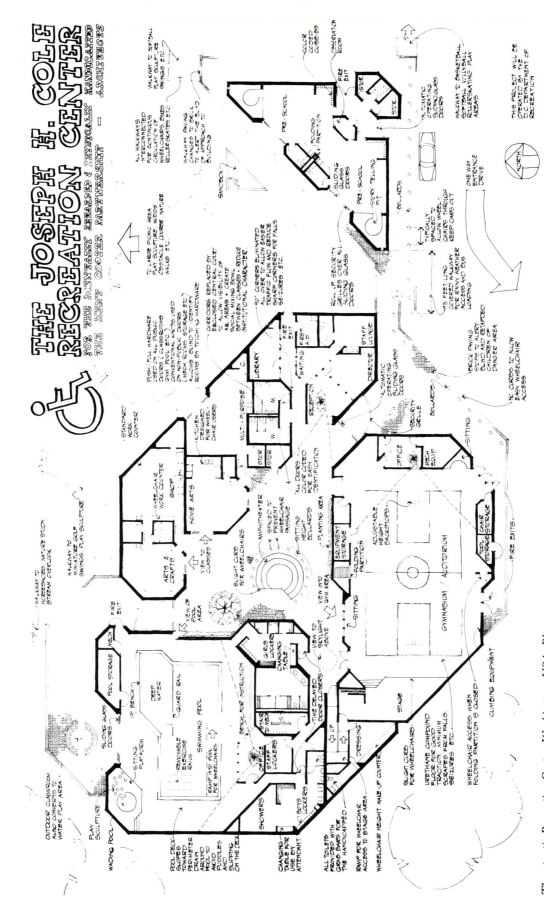

Therapeutic Recreation Centre, Washington, USA. Plan (Architects: Kent Cooper Partnership. William P. Lecky, partner in charge)

Therapeutic Recreation Centre. View of main reception area showing small sunken 'refuge' section used by mentally handicapped, or for meetings and 'events'. (Architects: KC Partnership)

Therapeutic Recreation Centre. The swimming pool can be entered by ramp or steps, and is divided into activity zones according to various levels of infirmity. (Architects: KC Partnership)

spot for local residents, set among mature mulberry and oak trees which provide both scale contrast with the buildings, and shade in summer.

The larger of these buildings is the Therapeutic Recreation Centre and the smaller a pre-school nursery. These two groups of users have been kept apart, but share common facilities for parking, catering, and library resources. One of these meeting points is the entrance which is covered by a form of porte cochere large enough to accommodate several cars and buses simultaneously. Low level bollards allow access by wheelchair users while excluding cars. Steps have been excluded except where emphasised as features. Automatic sliding glass doors lead into the main entrance area which is treated with materials and textures different in colour and composition from the entrance hall and other activity areas. This gives visual identification for the mentally retarded and a change of texture for the blind or partially sighted.

Once inside the main entrance, users enter a large well-lit inner hall in which all corners have been softened by 45° angles to give improved orientation and easier cornering for those in wheelchairs. (Sharp corners are also a hazard to epileptics when falling at the onset of a seizure). The arrangement also gives the director a clear view from an office sited at the entrance to this area. All doors around the hall have been colour-coded for easy identification, and a light metal space frame painted grey-green, allows the unimpeded entry of natural daylight through high level clerestories provided for this purpose. This area is large enough to be used for group activities such as discos and parties and refreshments for up to 150 participants.

A feature is a small sunken amphitheatre partially surrounded by bollards and kerbing to prevent entry by wheelchairs, which serves as a popular meeting place during break time, or as a retreat for the mentally retarded who feel they must come to terms with the larger hall space. They are encouraged to adjust by the informality of their surroundings, and by hanging vines, trees, and a large aquarium. This concept of small protected areas is repeated in the gymnasium and swimming pool.

The pool is accessible by both ramp and a ladder for ambulant users and the gradient of the ramp is designed to eliminate gravity roll into the water. The pool is separated into several user zones with a deep water alcove for those who can swim, and a small wading pool is sited away from the main pool for those who are reluctant to go into the latter. Temperature levels are well above normal public pool levels, and essential for users who may suffer from muscle spasms, while being more pleasant for all users. A one to one system of instruction and supervision is maintained at all user periods.

The floor finish in the gymnasium has a special rubber base and urethane top designed to minimise injuries, and warm enough to sit upon during coaching sessions. A stage at one end provides a facility for further instruction and 'in-house' performances (mime and dance are especially popular as a means of expression). Ancillary rooms associated with these areas contain many special design features, including basins with wrist action taps, large size toilet cubicles, backbars to all benches for paraplegic use, counter heights adjusted for wheelchair users, and colour coded doors for those who cannot read.

The smaller of the two buildings is also smaller in scale to reflect the young age of the users, and space inside the large teaching unit can be sub-divided by a full height partition. Sliding glass doors around the periphery of this area lead outdoors to external play and learning areas which come into use during fine weather. Metal roller shutters behind these doors serve as a security barrier when the building is closed.

Both buildings are served by arts and crafts areas, home arts and manual arts rooms, and a library which is a resource centre for the neighbourhood. Outdoor play areas include a miniature golf course, basketball court and softball field linked by continuous walkways for skateboarders and wheelchair users, to picnic and barbecue areas retained from the old site.

The vastly improved quality of life facilities such as these bring to users has more than endorsed the original research work and careful detailing which has gone into the project, while removing them from isolation which in itself is a handicap. Such recreational facilities have introduced many handicapped people to a range of experiences otherwise denied then and they serve as a model for all developed societies to aim at in the immediate future.

Chapter 3

Sports halls and indoor sports centres

The history of community sports halls in the UK is relatively short, dating back to the experimental projects explored in schools during the late 1950s when attempts were first made to widen games period curricula. The traditional $18 \times 12\,\text{m}$ gymnasium was an obvious constraint to the teaching of basketball, netball, and many other activities introduced at that time. It was not long before some of the more adventurous authorities had built alternative indoor solutions, within the same cost limits as the gymnasium,

for example, the 'three-sided barns' of Nottinghamshire, the 'sports-workshops' of County Durham and Sunderland, and the 'sports dome' at Wharrier Street Youth Centre in Newcastle upon Tyne.

All these had their limitations. Open-sided halls were no inducement to groups being coached in winter. Unheated sheds provided a similar problem, and introduced another problem – condensation. Hard dirty floors, and similar primitive finishes to walls and ceilings were little more successful, even

Lightfoot Centre, Newcastle-upon-Tyne. An early two-court sports hall intended primarily for youth service use. The circular plan and plastic clad dome supported on laminated Baltic Spruce beams was cost effective but gave rise to many environmental problems including acoustic control, glare, and heat loss. (Architects: Williamson, Faulkner Brown and Partners)

allowing for these particular generations being the last prepared to rough things. In summer it was difficult to keep facilities cool enough to play in and in the winter they were often unbearably cold. Glare and acoustic conditions were equally a deterrent to satisfactory playing comfort if measured by today's standards.

Historical background

It was the so-called 'red brick' universities of the early 1960s which began to set the design and performance criteria followed to this day, often as the result of individual research studies carried out by a group of highly innovative directors of physical education. Hull, Keele, Sussex, Kent, St Andrews, Liverpool and Birmingham were among those which produced solutions still considered from a design point of view at least, to be among the best in the country, if not in Europe generally. (In passing it is perhaps worth noting that in very British fashion, none were entitled under extant regulations to build a sports hall as such, and that they were only approved as large examination halls, for which they served several times a year). Cost limits were strictly enforced, but on what basis they were agreed was not very clear at the time, and it is interesting to compare the results here with those of a similar Dutch university project – Enschede – built in the early 1970s.

However, few universities allowed their facilities to be used by the public at large, apart from one notable exception at the University of Lancaster where joint use policy was written into the original brief. It was still a problem therefore in the early 1960s for young people leaving school to continue playing, even if they were lucky enough to find a suitable club accommodating their particular activity. This problem had been identified in the 1960 Wolfenden Report, but it was not until 1964 that a number of independent sports trusts led by that at Harlow, took the initiative by building the first 'community' sports halls offering

St. Andrews University Indoor Sports Centre, Scotland. View of the main sports hall designed a few years after the Lightfoot Centre by the same architects, showing their response to the problems of environmental control. Deep V-shaped roof members minimise glare from light sources in the apex of the structural frame: dark buff brickwork gives good background contrast for most activities and can be used for rebound practice, and the resilient floor finish (PVC carpet on ply panels on foam pads) gives excellent playing conditions involving a minimum amount of maintenance. (Architects: Williamson, Faulkner Brown and Partners)

University of Enschede, Holland. Natural rock built into the fabric of the sports hall wall cladding provides many alternative training programmes for climbing practice.

something for everyone, including schools on whom they were initially heavily dependent for support during the day.

Once the ice had been broken however, it was only a short time before local authority projects appeared in quantity with those at Bracknell, and Billingham Forum attracting considerable attention at the time. Towards the end of the 1960s however, it was the turn of 'joint use' community school projects, such as those

at Carlton Forum, Nottingham, to attract the limelight, especially by the introduction of other major elements into these complexes. These included theatres, swimming pools and, at Sutton in Ashfield built later in the 1970s, an ice rink and bowls hall – a miniature Billingham Forum in fact.

By 1972/3 when local authority reorganisation gave many older councils a last chance opprtunity to build 'dream' projects, the stage had been set for second

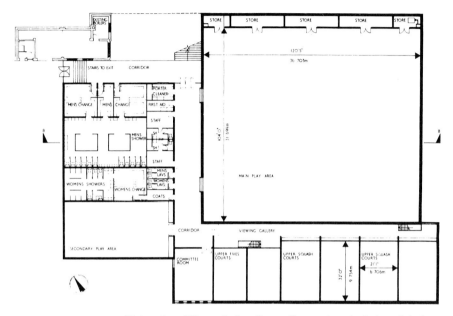

University of Exeter Indoor Sports Centre. A typical plan of the late 1960s later copied by local authorities as a model for community sports provision. (Architects: John Crowther Associates)

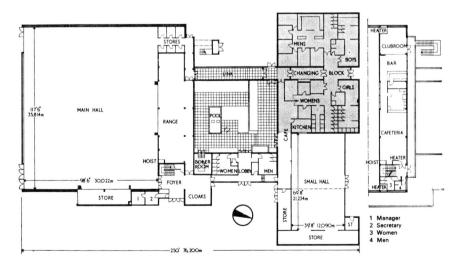

Bracknell Sports Centre (Stage 2). The two-court sports hall on the left was linked to an existing pavilion on the right by means of a landscaped courtyard in 1968. Built by the local authority for community use it has since had several subsequent stages added including a swimming pool. (Architects: John Rice and Partners)

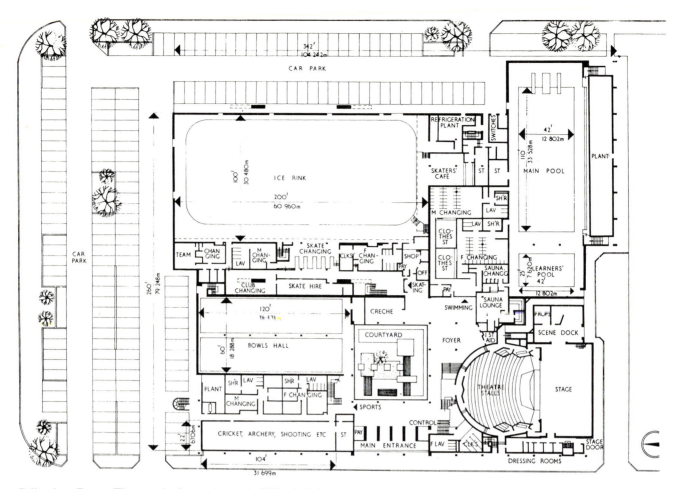

Billingham Forum. This was the first project in the UK to include other major elements to a one-court sports hall built above an indoor bowls hall. It was also the first to include facilities for the arts in the form of a 650-seat theatre. After initial teething troubles it has since become a popular focal point for leisure in the north east of England. (Architects: Elder and Lester)

generation facilities which heralded the change to 'recreation' and 'leisure' centres which has continued to this day. It can be seen however, that already the 'sports hall' of ten years earlier had grown enormously in size and administrative complexity.

Even in those cases where large scale elements such as swimming pools had not been added, most projects now included at least several squash courts, an ancillary hall (for all those activities not easily accommodated in the main sports hall, such as climbing and cricket), a martial arts room, weight-training room, refreshment lounges, and management offices. To acknowledge this situation the national Sports Council defined these projects as 'indoor sports centres'. This was done to differentiate between these and other examples as at Harlow, where the Centre formed part of a larger complex including sports pitches, still referred to as 'sports centres'.

Of these later examples it was largely the swimming pool element which generated the true 'leisure' use so frequently referred to today. The sports hall remained very much the same as two generations earlier, although its use was often widened during the 1970s to include non-sports activities such as car shows, dances, concerts, circuses and many other activities intended to bring in a much larger income and subsidise those areas of sport such as training with its low-income rating. To design for such multi-purpose use has proved incredibly difficult and, where carried out properly, very expensive. Where else in Europe, if not the world, for example, would architects be asked to design with the needs in mind of sports such as badminton, tennis, basketball etc, in addition to orchestral and choral concerts, string quartets, live entertainment, large scale spectator events, circus elephants, vintage cars, civic receptions and dances.

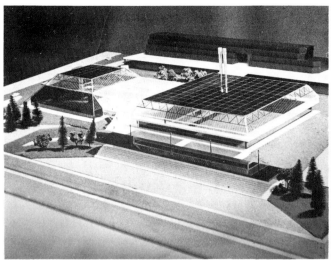

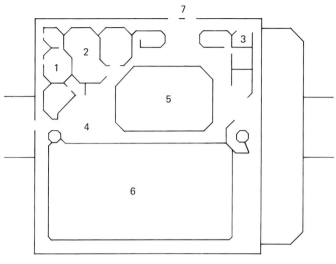

1 offices   5 learners' pool
2 club room   6 main pool
3 plant   7 entrance
4 cafeteria

Washington Sports Centre, Northumberland, (model and plan). By the mid-1970s dry sports hall elements had been replaced by swimming facilities in many indoor sports centres, as in this example. Most planned to build sports halls however as a second stage, although the high running costs associated with swimming often postponed further development indefinitely. (Washington Development Corporation)

Northgate Leisure Centre, Chester, (right). By the mid-1970s most UK sports halls were being used for other non-sports uses such as in this example, where motor shows are frequently staged, along with dances, and entertainment. (Architects: Building Design Partnership)

The solutions have been a series of compromises, which in many cases have often been to the disadvantage of the sports user. Floors are frequently unresilient, leading, it is claimed by the Otto Van Graff Institute at Stuttgart, to the onset of arthritic conditions in early middle age. Heating and ventilation costs are out of all proportion to those in 'pure' sports halls (sometimes adding as much as a third to the total capital cost of the entire project), lighting is based upon common denominators instead of individual requirements (units are often unprotected against probable damage from footballs), and wall linings are often the means for some highly colourful examples of artistic licence required by the overall razzamatazz looked for by some management personnel as part of the leisure scene of today.

Apart from these items, many halls are closed to sports use from midday Friday until midday the following Monday, while equipment is set up for one of these extravaganzas. What started as a daily 14 hour programme, 7 days a week has often been reduced to a weekdays–only sports involvement.

There are probably many who would see little wrong with this position today, until they realise that few of these extra-mural activities actually net any real added income, and that the additional staff required to organise, plan and arrange these events add considerably in the medium term to running costs. Low cost buildings and high cost management and maintenance charges are now commonly seen as one of the root causes of high deficit costs peculiar to the UK.

Development outside the UK

By way of contrast the development of European sports halls has remained firmly rooted in a 'sports only' tradition, with most the envy of many overseas visitors especially from the UK. Examples may be seen throughout this book, with particularly interesting projects described in chapter 6.

One of the many areas of contrast may be seen in the use made of automated equipment to minimise staffing duties, reduce the time taken between activities to set up apparatus, and to lower running costs. Another is the general acceptance of central sports offices to organise the day to day running programmes of several indoor sports centres, a feature which has in many cases led to medium sized facilities being run by at most three or four 'caretakers', the very opposite in fact to the British approach. Standards of finish are generally higher, and the number of specialist centres greater.

Because the range of activities in Europe differs from those in the UK, resulting in a bias towards 'large ball' games such as handball, volleyball and basketball, the need for glare-free conditions is that much less, and the appearance of completely fenestrated window walls is quite common. It goes without

Landskrona Sports Hall, Sweden. By sinking the playing area 4 m into the ground and surrounding it with seating and podium space, the apparent height of the building has been reduced considerably. Horizontality has been further accentuated by the deep overhanging fascia which, with curtaining has minimised the problem of glare while giving a 'glass-box' external cladding solution rarely seen associated with this building type. (Architects: M. A. A. Jacobson)

Deutz Halle, Cologne. General view of a multi-sport hall many times the average size for community use, but typical of most large West German cities at the present time. Automatic devices reduce most of the labour involvement in setting up equipment between events.

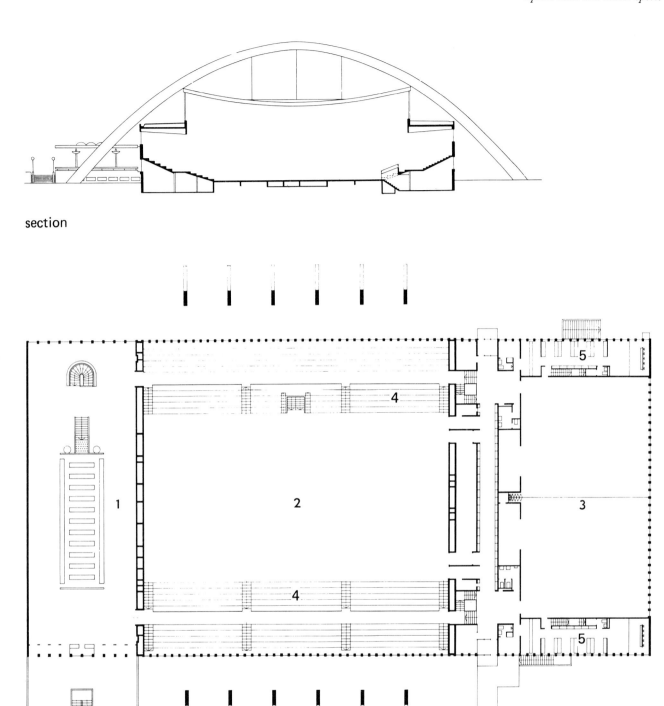

section

plan

1 entrance hall
2 athletics hall
3 gymnastic hall

Maserhalle, Børlange, Sweden. Section and plan. A typical arrangement for a European Sports Hall used frequently for competitive events.

saying that elevations are less stark, massing and scale relationships easier to control, and the general environmental quality much improved in consequence. Nevertheless the British trend towards 'black box' or completely artificially lit halls, is finding much favour at the present time, despite the higher running costs involved. (On the other hand, where other facilities such as swimming pools are attached, heat recovery systems often compensate for this factor).

The division of sporting activities

The process of natural selection is also much more in evidence in those areas not confused with multi-purpose use. For example, there has been a natural sieve process leading to the exclusion from the main sports hall of all those activities found from experience to be non-compatible with the main group of activities. Climbing practice has now been confined to outdoor or ancillary hall locations, as has cricket practice. Table tennis is much better sited in the same hall where it can be lit more positively and yoga classes are also much more private in a separate room. On the other hand, trampolining has recently reached such high standards that it can only be housed in the main hall.

Similarly, services standards have also increased in quality and variation, with 350 lux being the generally agreed lighting norm for recreational play, 500 lux for competition, and 750 lux for activities such as boxing or wrestling. If colour television is required however, provision must be made up to 1500–2000 lux. The number of air changes (3 per hour) still remains acceptable in the majority of cases (but not for multi-purpose use), as does warm air heating to 12–15°C.

Various means of dividing the hall into playing segments have become well established, including full height netting, roof-mounted plastic screens, push-button controlled, and movable screens such as that seen in the Papendal Sports Centre in chapter 6. Some examples of space permutations can be seen in the case study of the University of Kent sports hall. Audio systems to serve this area are more frequently located in the roof today than on side walls where they often lead to distortion and can be easily damaged.

Various court permutations are shown in the diagram below.

Two Court Hall. Court permutations

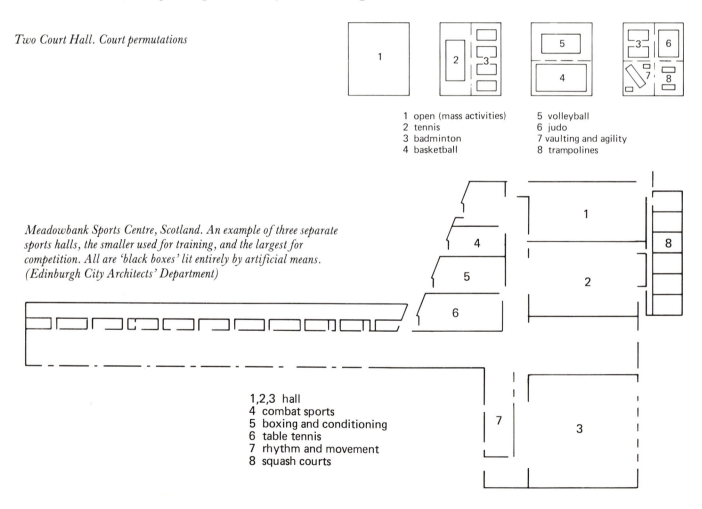

1 open (mass activities)   5 volleyball
2 tennis   6 judo
3 badminton   7 vaulting and agility
4 basketball   8 trampolines

Meadowbank Sports Centre, Scotland. An example of three separate sports halls, the smaller used for training, and the largest for competition. All are 'black boxes' lit entirely by artificial means. (Edinburgh City Architects' Department)

1,2,3 hall
4 combat sports
5 boxing and conditioning
6 table tennis
7 rhythm and movement
8 squash courts

Future trends

Future trends can be identified among the many variations seen in this chapter and in also in other chapters. It is probable, for example, that sports halls *per se* will become increasingly located in central area shopping precincts as part of the planning gain system seen at Eldon Square, Newcastle (chapter 7). Unlike swimming pools, sports halls can be made to be profitable, and as we have seen, can be used for other

Crawley Sports Centre, Sussex. The main hall arranged for a boxing tournament. Peripheral 'bleacher' seating units fold back into surrounding walls to give a flush surface for other activities to play off. The absence of automatic controls make this type of event very labour intensive, and the hall is closed for half a day while equipment is being placed in position. (Crawley District Council)

purposes. It is also probable therefore that the type of design solution described in chapter 7 at the Karregat Centre, Eindhoven, will find much attraction for sponsors wishing to provide a more loosely-knit planning solution than that associated with conventional halls.

On the other hand, the Eastleigh Sports Centre proposal to build a second hall specifically for multi-purpose use to relieve pressure from sports clubs on the first, existing hall, could be an equally acceptable solution. Until the number of facilities are as thick on the ground as in other parts of Europe, it is clear that 'optimum use factors' will continue to distort the development of sports halls in the UK. In the view of many, it will be left to the few 'centres of excellence' to continue the development and evolution of these facilities for general dissemination, although the opportunity to achieve the high technological factors now appearing for example in most West German and Dutch examples, has already been ignored on grounds of economic astringency.

One thing however is clear, and that is demand shows little sign of falling away except in those facilities which have not stood the test of time, or with little management imagination. The next decade should see much of the ground discussed here consolidated, with the appearance of third generation halls of much higher design standard, environmental quality, and finishes. In the UK there will be less emphasis on multi-purpose use, while on Western Europe there will be a trend to specialist facilities, automation and energy-saving methods.

Carlton Forum, Nottingham. Judo event in the main sports hall. Training facilities however are normally positioned in a separate martial arts room where equipment can be allowed to remain permanently in position. (Nottinghamshire County Architects' Department)

Practice Hall, Eastleigh Sports Centre. One of several smaller rooms around the main sports hall for multi-sports use. The full length mirrors on the end wall have stimulated a strong local following for ballet classes. (Architects: Perrin Associates. Photo: Peter Simpson)

Case studies

Sports Hall, University of Kent, Canterbury
The first generation of sports halls built during the 1960s in the UK resulted in many reports of operational difficulties, which if not corrected showed every sign of being repeated on the many subsequent projects then being considered. Feedback had been collected by the Regent Street Polytechnic Recreation Research Unit, who with the cooperation of the architects and university, applied these findings to this project as a live research and development exercise.

Three priorities were identified as being fundamental to the most efficient performance required for enjoyable participation up to international skill levels. These were:

1 The provision of a glare-free 'box' to minimise or prevent the recurring problems found in early halls where windows and clerestories had been included on south and west walls.

2 To provide as large a free space as possible within the current University Grant limits, in order to provide management with maximum flexibility when programming simultaneous activities.

3 To provide a floor finish which would be as near ideal as possible for sport and non-sports use, bearing in mind that the hall was to function as an examination hall several times a year.

It was agreed that a visit to existing continental halls would broaden the basis of the pre-brief investigations, and contact was made with the West German Sports Advisory Service in Cologne, who were the centre of a considerable development programme at that time associated with the first ten year Golden Plan for German sport.

The resulting building took shape around these performance requirements. Windows were excluded entirely, to be replaced by rooflights admitting natural light evenly over the whole playing area below. Deep V-shaped roof members formed from steel tubes lined with fibreboard were provided to give excellent cut-off sight lines for badminton and tennis players in particular, with courts placed at right angles to these roof beams. Walls were finished with smooth warm buff-coloured facing brickwork for the full height of the hall, to give good background contrast for most activities, and at the same time give a warm and inviting appearance considered to be essential in such a confined space.

The floor colour was kept a neutral shade of grey, and was the first in the UK to be designed along West German standards (based upon the now internationally accepted DIN norms), which placed strong emphasis upon resilience (or elasticity as described in the DIN performance specification), low glare factor, monolithic form of construction, good play characteristics (non-slip, and confidence when turning), and relatively low cost. PVC sheet formed the upper surface, which after thirteen years use, including roller skating, shows little or no sign of wear.

The $36.60 \times 34.70 \times 7.60$ m hall (now referred to as a 2-tennis court hall) was divided by full height netting with canvas along the bottom 2 m to give better visual definition between courts. This can be arranged as shown in the diagram to give many permutations of play. Warm air is blown at low

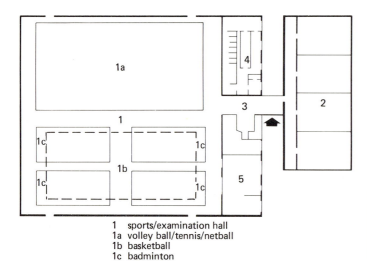

1   sports/examination hall
1a volley ball/tennis/netball
1b basketball
1c badminton
2   squash courts
3   entrance hall
4   changing rooms
5   superintendant and stores

University of Kent, Sports Hall. Plan

University of Kent, Sports Hall. General view of hall divided in four activity segments by full height netting. Nets on far left are for cricket practice. (Architects: Williamson, Faulkner Brown & Partners). (Photo: Sam Lambert by courtesy of The Architects' Journal)

velocities down perimeter walls as an air curtain, which is extracted in the centre of the hall at high level.

Other playing units in the form of squash courts are attached to the hall by a low level link, which also leads to the changing rooms, shop and supervisor's office. A large equipment store completes the ground floor accommodation, while upstairs are further changing rooms, staff rooms, and a balcony/lounge. Above these is the plant room linked directly with the heating and ventilation system installed at roof level.

The external mass of the hall has been played down by the steel supports forming part of the building frame, capped at the top by a deep overhanging dark coloured fascia, and standing on a well-detailed brick plinth. The same idea is repeated internally by a deep brick on end arrangement which gives the appearance of a plinth for walling above.

It says much for the original concept that this particular example has served as the model for two generations of sports halls in the UK, with few alterations being made to size, roof design or floor finish. The extra cost of roof construction if compared with a 'black box' solution is more than offset by the saving in annual running costs although there is a strong school of thought which believes natural lighting is more beneficial for the average situation encountered at community level.

De Meerpaal Hall, Dronten, Holland

Dronten is one of several small new towns of between 25 000 and 30 000 inhabitants built on reclaimed polder land in what used to be the Zuider Zee north of Amsterdam. It is linked by straight roads to Lelystad and Amsterdam across low lying agricultural land which can present a bleak appearance in poor weather, and it is not surprising to find most recreational facilities indoors where they can be well used throughout the year.

The Meerpaal Hall was designed to break fresh ground in this respect, and was the first of several experimental halls to be built by the Buro Van Klingeren (another, the Karregat in Eindhoven is described in chapter 7).

The site stands facing the town's main shopping centre, and the brief called for a building which could serve as a meeting place, in much the same way as the traditional town high street, and also as a market place, cinema, theatre, restaurant, arts centre, and 'events' centre, all in one. In fact, a modern day equivalent of the ancient Greek Agora.

The design solution takes the form of a large multi-purpose hall 191 × 19 m in floor area, and 9 m high, in which only the circular theatre is freestanding. Overlooking this area is a restaurant and administrative offices with a distinctively-shaped elevation to the street.

The floor of this hall has a dense bitumastic finish able to stand up to the heavy wear and tear generated by market stall holders and their supply vehicles, while also being suitable for general recreational play arranged informally whenever this area is not required for other uses. It is covered with special matting as elsewhere when large scale spectator events are held, such as one of the sponsored tennis circuits.

The structural frame is called upon for many uses,

De Meerpaal Hall, Dronten, Holland. External view of hall. (Architects: Buro Van Kilingeren. Photo: DLW (Britain) Ltd)

De Meerpaal Hall. Informal play in main hall

one of which is a ceiling-mounted cinema screen supported on trackways which can be swivelled in several directions. At other times it is used to support apparatus required to mount exhibitions. Part of the walling is reserved for large scale murals, otherwise it is largely glazed from floor to ceiling, a fact which appears not to interfere with recreational-standard play, or that of the better players. For major events, screens can be drawn behind play – which goes some way to disproving the widely held assumption that 'black-box' (windowless) conditions are essential in sports halls.

The principle behind the design concept that 'as all life is a series of compromises, therefore all architecture should build these into the design solution', has been strongly criticised, especially when simultaneous events are held in the hall and theatre, always to the disadvantage of users in the latter due to the noise factor. On the other hand the 'theatre-in-the-round' approach to its design has made possible many programmes involving audience participation, and it has often been used as a television studio, and intimate cinema, for example during the 1974 World Cup series when wide screen television brought matches into almost lifelike reality for audiences of six hundred or more at a time.

The free-for-all use of the Agora has led to the inevitable conflict of interests, apart from those concerned with the theatre, and towards the end of the 1970s other purpose built sports facilities were being built elsewhere in the town. Indoor tennis for example is now well provided for in a purpose-built hall. When the Lelystad indoor leisure centre opens in 1981, ice skating and swimming facilities will become available less than 40 km away (see page 72).

Long term projections for the hall are therefore difficult to assess, although it is clear that sport will figure less than before. The flexibility of the concept however, as at the Karregat Centre, is such that new uses can be accommodated without major disruption to those now *in situ* – a message which is only slowly reaching designers in other countries.

Perhaps one of the lessons learned in this case other than the design input, concerns the need for some form of professional management (this also applies to the Karregat project) and for the original concept to be less inclined towards 'the inevitability of compromise'. After all, an additional 3 m of walling would transform the use made of the theatre, and be of benefit to all users elsewhere in the building.

De Meerpaal Hall. Informal play taking place during an outside TV broadcast from the theatre to the left of the photograph. The large ceiling-hung screen on the right is for cinema shows. (Photo: DLW (Britain) Ltd)

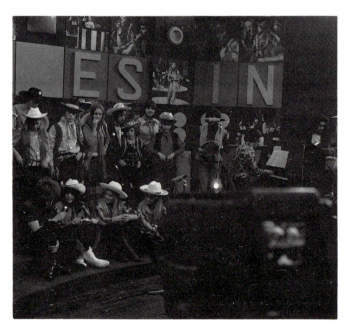

De Meerpaal Hall. Part of theatre in the round during TV broadcast. (Photo: DLW (Britain) Ltd)

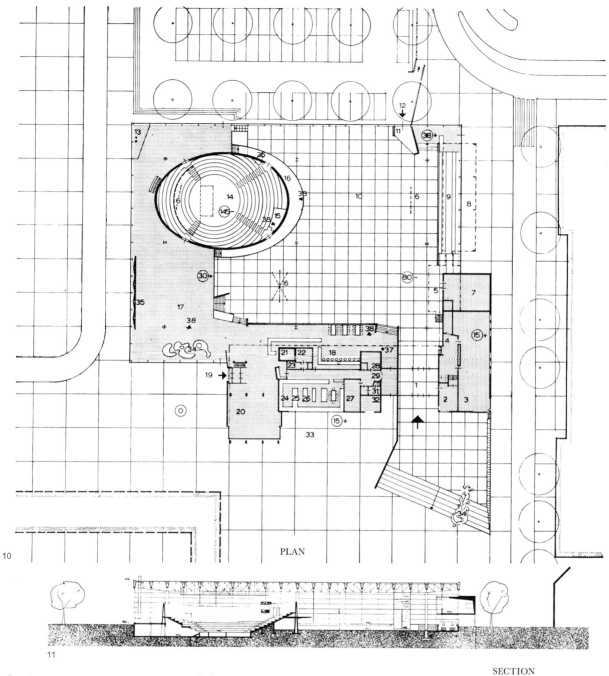

PLAN

SECTION

1 entrance	17 foyer
2 office reception	18 bar
3 changing rooms	19 entrance to cafe/restaurant
4 changing rooms	20 cafe/restaurant
6 overhead film screen	21 beer store
9 bowling	22 food store
10 hall for games: indoor market:	23 linen store
meetings: films	24 to 28 kitchen and food
11 shop	preparation
12 car access	29 administration
13 ventilation plant	30 toilet
14 theatre	31 cloakroom

De Meerpaal Hall. Floor plan and section of the whole project
(Courtesy of DLW (Britain) Ltd)

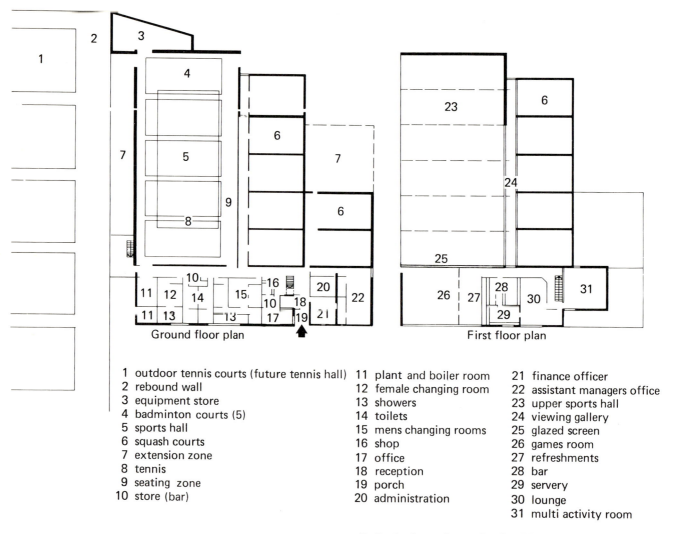

Ground floor plan

First floor plan

1 outdoor tennis courts (future tennis hall)
2 rebound wall
3 equipment store
4 badminton courts (5)
5 sports hall
6 squash courts
7 extension zone
8 tennis
9 seating zone
10 store (bar)

11 plant and boiler room
12 female changing room
13 showers
14 toilets
15 mens changing rooms
16 shop
17 office
18 reception
19 porch
20 administration

21 finance officer
22 assistant managers office
23 upper sports hall
24 viewing gallery
25 glazed screen
26 games room
27 refreshments
28 bar
29 servery
30 lounge
31 multi activity room

Redbridge Sports Centre, London. Floor plan showing stages in development since opening in 1972. (Architects: Perrin Associates)

Redbridge Sports Centre. Sports hall showing rooflight arrangement between each badminton court to ensure no overhead shots are played into a light source. (Photo: Torvale Building Products Ltd)

Redbridge Sports Centre, North London

This project is of interest on two counts. It has consistently run at a profit, which makes it almost unique in the UK, and it has become recognised as a centre of 'rackets excellence' for south east England.

The idea of building an indoor sports centre took shape in the late 1960s when the North Ilford Lawn Tennis Club were notified that their ground was required for other purposes. The search for alternative facilities eventually identified the present site which served as an anti-aircraft base during the last war; and a peppercorn lease was agreed with the Greater London Council. At this stage it was decided to restructure the Club in the form of a charitable trust company in order to widen the base for fund-raising purposes: a method which enabled the executive board to approach would-be sources of finance in local and central government, private industry and benevolent organisations such as the Wolfson Foundation who were the first to contribute towards the capital cost of the project.

The original brief called for 5 outdoor shale tennis courts, 1 indoor tennis court and 5 badminton courts, with ancillary facilities in the form of 4 squash courts, a bar and refreshment lounge, games room, and the usual changing and administration areas. At the time it appeared to be an ambitious target for the Trust to set, but by means of much hard work involving sponsored runs, long negotiations with the local authority and regional Sports Council, the money was raised within 18 months, and the Centre opened 12 months later in 1972.

From the outset facilities were strongly biased towards the raquets group of sports – tennis, badminton and squash. Finishes, spatial requirements and colour schemes were orientated towards these particular games. The result is a 36 × 18 × 9 m sports hall accommodating 5 badminton courts, 1 tennis court, five-a-side football, indoor hockey, and many small group activities such as vaulting and agility classes, and trampolining.

Special attention was paid to the needs of badminton players, as members of the English national squad wished to train at the Centre. Surrounding wall finishes were selected in the form of grey/green sand-lime brick panels to give a good background contrast to shuttlecocks, and purpose-made light fittings were installed which could be lowered between courts for match play events. Courts were off-set to allow spectator seating down one long side. The same floor finish as at the University of Kent sports hall was provided to give the correct degree of resilience and confidence on the turn. This floor was requested by players after a short tour of other centres. Yellow PVC was selected as the surface material to provide these conditions and to act as a relief to the darker wall colours. White tape line markings were provided for both badminton (across the hall), and tennis (down the hall).

Natural lighting was provided by means of roof-lights constructed between badminton courts so that no overhead shots would be played into a light source. The woodwool slabs forming the roof cladding were left exposed for acoustic reasons and spray painted light grey/green. A channel was provided at mid-point in the wall to house a straining wire which could be moved up or down with netting for tennis, badminton or volleyball. In practice however, this has been little used.

Elsewhere, finishes are in honey-coloured facing bricks, timber (for ceilings), and quarry tiles or PVC tiles to the floors. The exception is in the bar where good quality carpet was laid, in lieu, and walls were finished in hessian.

Each year additional facilities have been added, paid for out of the profits from the previous year's operations. These include a large equipment store (which most managers find essential), three squash courts (two of which have glass-backed walls and an individual microphone system for scoring), a dojo (or martial arts room), and further office accommodation to house the increase in staff needed to run the larger centre.

The financial viability of the project has been attributed to several factors. Tight budgetry control monitored regularly to ensure that cash flow is on target; no loan repayments; a staffing structure which requires each member to undertake at least two duties, for example, administration and coaching. In addition the inviting atmosphere on entering the building is backed up by in-house maintenance of an exceptionally high standard. All these factors are believed to have contributed something towards the obvious success of the venture.

Additional income is derived from occasional dances and festivals, when the floor is covered (as all floors should be at such times) with hardboard panels taped together. The Centre is heavily used by local schools and it says much of the standards provided that many pupils return on leaving school as fully fledged members. Vandalism has been minimal, and the original finishes look as good today as when first installed.

The project has been the subject of many seminars arranged by the regional sports council and has attracted many visitors from the UK and elsewhere in Europe.

Chapter 4
Swimming pools

The design of public swimming facilities has undergone many radical changes in the past decade. This has been due as much to attempts by a new generation of 'recreation managers' to give swimming a new image far removed from that of the 'municipal baths', and partly to improve the number of adult attendances in order to increase revenue, and lower annual deficits.

It is common knowledge that the public use of swimming facilities has several irreconcilable factors affecting present-day standards of provision. On the one hand swimming is undoubtedly one of the most consistently popular activities in any community. It usually has the strongest lobby of supporters and the most vociferous pressure groups of any, and with good reason. Swimming exercises every part of the body; it has excellent therapeutic qualities for the disabled. Swimming can be a fun attraction in good weather and a training ground for young and old which could stand them in good stead should they ever get into difficulties at the seaside or on inland waterways and lakes.

On the other side of the coin however, swimming facilities are among the most expensive to run, are the accepted loss leaders of the leisure market, and (in the UK) have a long tradition of use by very young people charged a fraction of the real economic running costs of such facilities. It therefore requires a considerable commitment on the part of any sponsor to provide a public service along these lines, and it is inevitable that it should be left largely to local authorities to shoulder this burden. Even so the challenge has been met albeit on a lesser scale in the UK than elsewhere, and few communities today are without facilities of one kind or another, or have reasonable access to nearby provision.

Development of facilities

Changes have been universal although it is probably worth tracing development over two decades in the UK as one example of this process. The main form of provision by the early 1960s usually consisted of a single multi-purpose pool 33.33 m long and 12.5 m wide, with a deep end and a shallow end, and 5 m, 3 m and 1 m springboard diving boards. It also had seating for 500 to 600 down one long side, and a ceiling line selected to give ample clearance over the 5 m board, maintained over the whole building. It was highly expensive to run, became overcrowded in the summer, and established the now familiar pattern of coloured armbands, and call-out systems still in use in many parts of the country today.

By the mid-1960s strong pressure was brought to bear by central government, the national Sports Council, and Baths Institute, to phase out such facilities, and replace them with smaller 25 × 12.5 m pools and separate facilities for diving and learning to swim, similar to those at Eastleigh and Folkestone (see chapter 5). These were later to omit all diving provision except in 'areas of regional significance', with the result that most now consist of 'standing depth' water for at least two thirds the length. Spectator accommodation was often reduced to around 200 and in many cases was omitted completely in favour of informal high level viewing galleries, and 'parent seats' beside the learner pool.

Although this policy achieved savings in construction costs over previous examples, it led to considerable overcrowding in the main pool at peak periods, and the elimination of many traditional activities such as water polo, sub-aqua diving, and life-saving classes. It did however encourage alternative uses such as

Dunstable Park Recreation Centre. Main pool hall showing irregular shaped 25 m pool. Competitions are held down the length of the pool; training across the pool. One metre springboard diving is in far left of pool. (Architects: Perrin Associates. Photo by Reed Harris Ltd)

Saar Louis Pool, West Germany. View across deep end of irregular shaped 25 m pool. Landscaping seen through far windows had been planted two years when photograph was taken. (Architects: Traub and Prokopowitsch. Photo: Gerald Perrin)

Saar Louis Pool. View down pool hall towards far learner pool, showing strongly textured low acoustic ceiling. (Photo: Gerald Perrin)

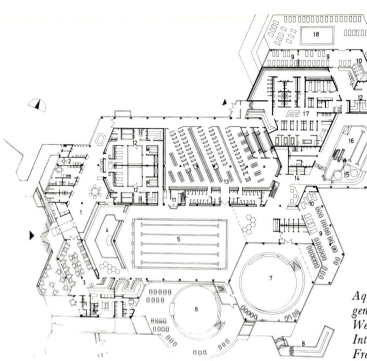

1 entrance hall
2 administration
3 restaurant
4 children's pool
5 swimming pool
6 external brine pool
7 brine excercise pool
8 Kneipp department
9 rest room
10 solarium
11 first aid
12 sauna
13 changing rooms
14 solar cubicles
15 hot whirl pool
16 childrens, aged and
   handicapped pool
17 therapeutic pool
18 external diving pool

Aquadrome, Hockenheim, West Germany. Plan of typical new generation thermal (brine) leisure pools now appearing throughout West Germany, as part of a continuing research programme for the International Aquatic Board (IAB). (Architects: Dieter Arnold and Freier)

Northgate Leisure Centre, Chester. View of Leisure pool, artificially lit to simulate 'daytime' conditions. Underwater lighting and concealed units in the ceiling can also provide 'evening' conditions when required. (Architects: Building Design Partnership)

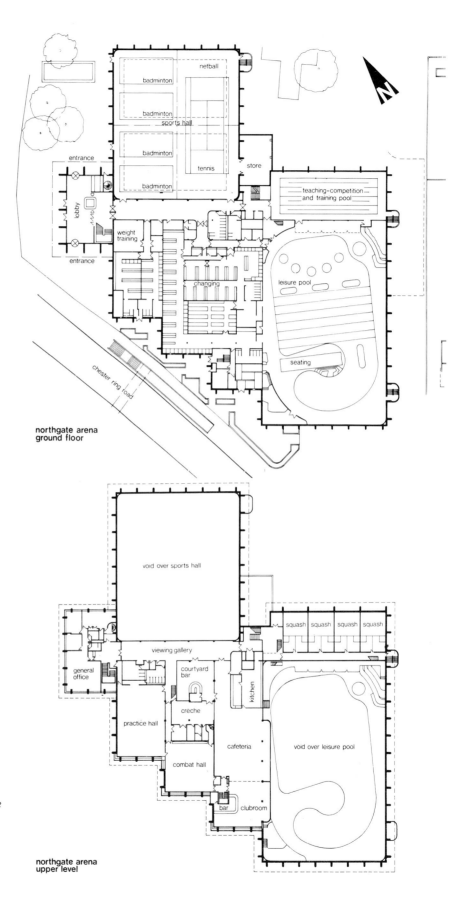

northgate arena
ground floor

northgate arena
upper level

Northgate Leisure Centre, Chester.
Plan of complete complex showing prominance
given to Leisure Pool area. (Architects:
Building Design Partnership)

kyak training, capsize dinghy practice, and other non-swimming activities at the side of the pool, for example, trampolining. There were many however who lobbied strongly for a return to larger pools, either of 33.33 m length or 50 m, or of 'equivalent water area' to both, in irregular-shaped pools similar to the example at Dunstable Recreation Centre (see page 45).

By this time however the eye-catching appeal of Bletchley Leisure Centre pool (see chapter 5) had caught the imagination of all those wishing to break away from the 'competition straitjacket' system. The race was on to see who could outdo the other (often in the most unlikely places), to provide illusory South Sea paradises, Mediterranean beaches, or tropical islands complete with wave pools, palm trees, waterfalls, cascades, and whirlpools. Examples of these at the Mirandabad, Amsterdam, Wester Hailes, Edinburgh and Broxbourne Lido can be seen on pages 104 and 115).

The design quality varied considerably. The 'fly's eye' construction of the Bletchley pyramid, and the highly coloured expression of service ducts above the same pool still attract much favourable comment after almost a decade in use. The way in which the lower half of the dome at Swindon's Oasis Centre, has been landscaped showed much initiative, although it would probably have been better applied to the attached multi-purpose hall, and its uncompromising mass. The diffused lighting above the pools at Sunderland and Southwark in London, gives excellent visual conditions below, although the starkness of the brick-faced surrounding walls is almost barracklike in appearance, although probably considered a good foil for the water and landscaping in the central area. The carpeted surrounds, play pits, and poolside sunshades and chairs, however, all contribute to the general process of relaxation, comfort, and of 'being on holiday a bus ride from home'.

Attractiveness to the user

Despite all these new facets of pool development, the average age of users rose only fractionally above the 85% previously reported in conventional pools. Yet during the same period the number of adults who could swim had risen from 55% to 70% due largely to school based training facilities. Why then were they not part of the leisure market appearing in these new surroundings. The answers may lie in feedback from continental pools, and in particular the research projects developed by the International Aquatic Board to study changing user needs during the 1970s.

It would seem from these that adults respond most to a completely different management approach than that seen in traditional pools in the UK. A system which is designed to exploit the long-stay use of adults by offering them a range of alternative options which include fashion shows, hairdressing and manicure facilities, shops, sunbathing and sauna areas, and many other 'sales points' much in line with the 'sports hypermarket' approach now being franchised in recently completed tennis halls in Holland and West Germany.

In order to do this however, adults have to be attracted into the building, and this can only be done with any degree of success apparently by adding considerably more to the traditional range of environmental services provided in public swimming pools. As part of this process, ozone has replaced other systems of chemical water treatment; air-conditioning has been improved (not least by computerised controls), and finishes up-graded to those resembling the foyer area of the average four-star hotel.

One result of these methods has been to free the designer from many previous planning constraints. For example, meals can now be served beside pools with none of the smell associated with conventional water treatment systems. Finishes do not necessarily

Huddersfield Sports Centre. View across pool hall, with the separate diving pool on the right, and dry land training area with trampoline on the left. (Architects: Faulkner Brown, Hendy, Watkinson, Stonor)

need to be so carefully protected against corrosion and plants appear to flourish. The emphasis has been taken out of the water and placed on dry land and the spaces that can be enclosed as sales outlets.

How far these outlets go is a matter for fine judgement. The underwater jets seen at the Zeist pool described in chapter 6 appear reasonable for practice in swimming 'against the tide', but of superficial use as body-toners for fat people. Similarly, waves are an attraction for young people, but a bore for older generations once they have experienced them. The capital costs on the other hand are considerable.

Cost-in-use

The cost-in-use feedback from these research projects is also of interest, especially for those anxious to improve on the present system of high overheads and low income. Each member of staff was made responsible for at least two duties, for example poolside supervisor and plant engineer.

All plant was fully automated with computerised controls programmed to sessional needs (as in the Zeist example). Heat recovery systems were used in association with ozone purification treatment, with up to a 50% saving in fuel costs reported from most examples. Each service element was monitored in order to achieve a fine tuning of the day to day running sequence.

Another means of improving income involved not only the alternative spending options previously mentioned but also the extended use of outdoor facilities, which unlike those in the UK are rapidly increasing. Indoor/outdoor pool complexes as they have been called have captured the adult support needed to make them viable, by the provision of linking canals between the main indoor pool and outside 'freetime' pools, landscaped sunbathing areas, and outdoor games courts, maintained to a very high standard.

In some cases the formal means of enclosure associated with indoor pools has been replaced by tent coverings which can be taken down in good weather; in others, notably in France, sliding roofs and walls have been installed to achieve much the same objectives.

Any attempt at indicating which of these planning concepts is the most suited to present day needs, would be highly unreliable in view of the present volatile state of evolution. Water is undoubtedly a 'generator' of public interest but has not been handled in the past as a highly marketable commodity. The options now accompanying the swimming programmes of an increasing number of leisure pools, are a step in the right direction. The example at Rhyl in

Variable depth pool, Holland

North Wales with its nightclubs and casino among indoor pools, reached by overhead cable car goes further than most, although for how long these will attract visitors to the town remains to be seen.

The Interbad range of pools illustrated later in this chapter on the other hand, give much more to the swimming public by providing a complete range of separate pools (competition, diving, sunbathing *et al*) even down to small village communities of 5000 or less. Perhaps the latter approach has the 'something for everyone' ingredient lacking in the former concept but whatever the outcome, public swimming pools entered an era which will see many similar ideas put to the test before a clear 'best buy' emerges.

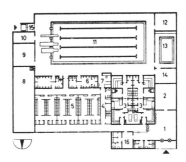

1 entrance hall	9 fitness room
2 cafe	10 apparatus
3 sauna	11 variable depth pool
4 dressing/sanitary unit for handicapped and families	12 lounge
	13 pool for children/aged/handicapped
5 dressing unit	14 childrens playroom
6 showers	15 ventilator
7 swimming instructor	16 staff
8 plant	

Internorm type plans. Indoor pool type 1 for 10 000 inhabitants

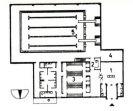

1 entrance
2 swimming instructor
3 changing area
4 apparatus
5 variable depth pool

Internorm type plans. Indoor pool type 1a for 10 000 inhabitants

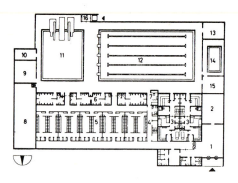

1 entrance hall	9 fitness room
2 automatic cafe	10 apparatus
3 sauna	11 diving pool
4 dressing/sanitary unit for handicapped and families	12 swimming pool
5 dressing unit	13 lounge
6 showers	14 pool for children/aged/handicapped
7 swimming instructor	15 children's playroom
8 plant	16 ventilator
	17 staff

Internorm type plans. Indoor pool type 2 design for 20 000 inhabitants

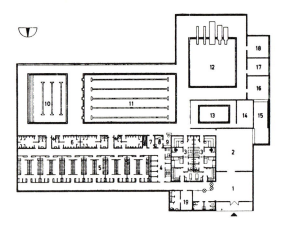

1 entrance	10 non-swimmers pool
2 restaurant	11 swimmers pool
3 sauna	12 diving pool
4 clothes changing and sanitary unit for handicapped and families	13 children's/aged/handicapped
5 changing area	14 children's playroom
6 showers	15 kitchen
7 detergent	16 lounge
8 swimming instructor	17 apparatus
9 first aid	18 fitness room
	19 staff

Internorm type plans. Indoor pool type 4 for 40 000 inhabitants

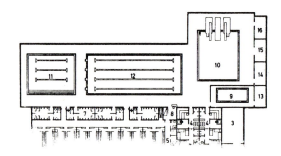

1 entrance	8 swimming instructor
2 staff	9 children's/aged/handicapped pond
3 restaurant	10 diving pond
4 sauna	11 non-swimmers pond
5 clothes changing and sanitary unit for handicapped and families	12 swimmers pond
6 changing area	13 children's playroom
7 showers	14 lounge
	15 instructor

Internorm type plans. Indoor pool type 3 design for 30 000 inhabitants

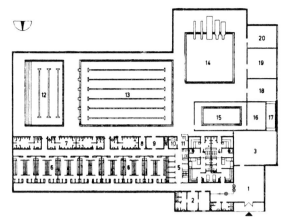

1 entrance	11 swimming instructor
2 staff	12 non-swimmers pool
3 restaurant	13 swimmers pool
4 sauna	14 diving pool
5 clothes changing and sanitary unit for handicapped and families	15 children's aged and handicapped pool
6 changing area	16 children's playroom
7 showers	17 kiosk
8 wash room	18 lounge
9 apparatus	19 fitness room
10 first aid	20 solarium

Internorm type plans. Indoor pool type 5 for 50 000 inhabitants

1 entrance	9 apparatus
2 staff	10 first aid
3 restaurant	11 swimming instructor
4 sauna	12 variable depth pool
5 clothes changing and sanitary unit for handicapped and families	13 diving pool
6 changing area	14 children's, aged and handicapped pool
7 showers	15 lounge
8 wash room	16 children's playroom
	17 fitness room

Internorm type plans. Indoor pool type 5a for 50 000 inhabitants

1 entrance hall
2 restaurant
3 terrace – visitors
4 lounge – bathers
5 terrace – bathers
6 children's playroom
7 children's aged and handicapped pond
8 swimming instructor
9 variable depth pool
10 sauna
11 clothes changing and sanitary unit for handicapped and families
12 clothes changing area
13 staff
14 apparatus
15 fitness room
16 swimming channel to outside pools
17 non-swimmers pool – adults
18 non-swimmers pool – children
19 diving pool
20 swimming pool
21 swimming instructor
22 children's playground
23 clothes changing and sanitary unit

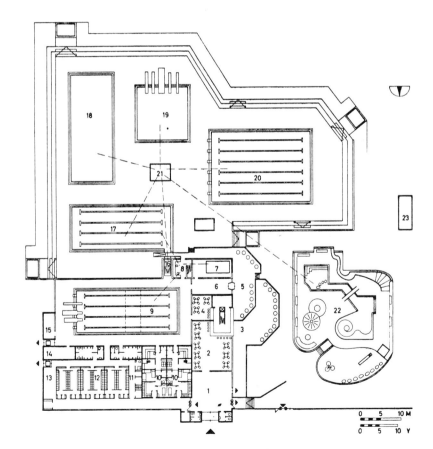

Internorm type plans. Type 1 indoor/outdoor pools

51

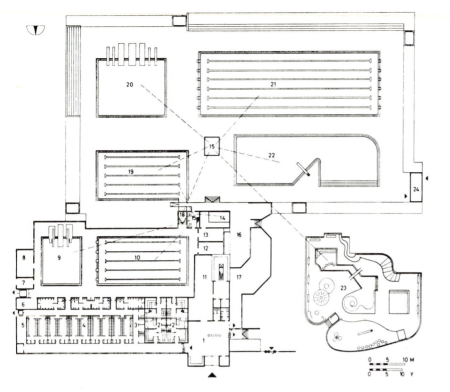

1 entrance hall
2 sauna
3 clothes changing and sanitary
   unit for families and
   handicapped
4 clothes changing area
5 staf
6 apparatus
7 outdoor apparatus
8 fitness room
9 diving pool
10 variable depth pool
11 restaurant
12 lounge – bathers
13 children's playroom
14 children's aged and
   handicapped pool
15 swimming instructor
16 terrace open air
17 terrace – visitors
18 swimming channel to outside
   pools
19 nonswimmers pool – adults
20 diving pool

Internorm type plans. Type 2 indoor/outdoor pools

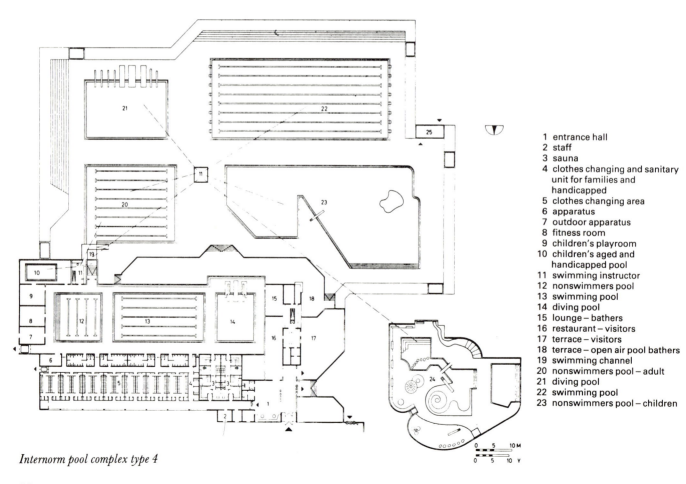

1 entrance hall
2 staff
3 sauna
4 clothes changing and sanitary
   unit for families and
   handicapped
5 clothes changing area
6 apparatus
7 outdoor apparatus
8 fitness room
9 children's playroom
10 children's aged and
   handicapped pool
11 swimming instructor
12 nonswimmers pool
13 swimming pool
14 diving pool
15 lounge – bathers
16 restaurant – visitors
17 terrace – visitors
18 terrace – open air pool bathers
19 swimming channel
20 nonswimmers pool – adult
21 diving pool
22 swimming pool
23 nonswimmers pool – children

Internorm pool complex type 4

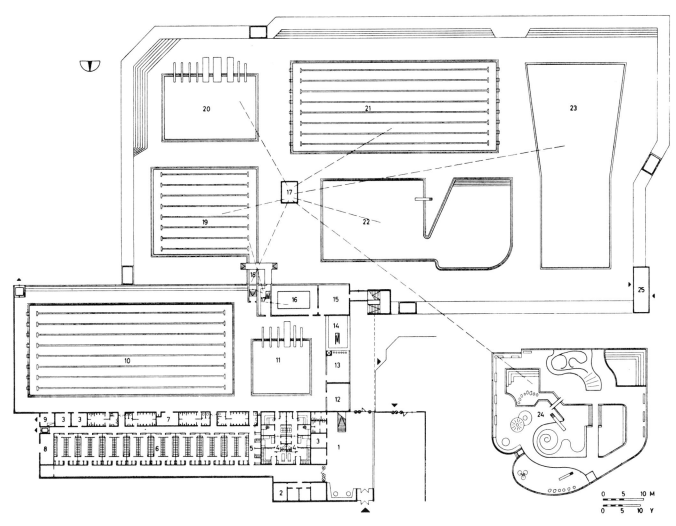

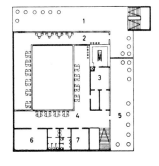

ground floor
1 entrance hall
2 administration
3 staff
4 sauna
5 clothes changing and sanitary
   unit for families and
   handicapped
6 clothes changing area
7 apparatus
8 outdoor apparatus
9 first aid
10 variable depth pool
11 diving pool
12 fitness room
13 lounge – bathers
14 kiosk
15 children's playroom
16 children's aged and
   handicapped pool
17 swimming instructor
18 swimming channel
19 nonswimmers pool – adults
20 diving pool
21 swimming pool
22 nonswimmers pool – children
23 wave pool
24 children's playground
25 clothes changing and sanitary
   unit

upper floor
1 terrace – open air pool bathers
2 restaurant – open air pool
   bathers
3 kitchen
4 restaurant – visitors
5 terrace – visitors
6 clubroom
7 staff

Internorm pool complex type 5a indoor/outdoor pools

Case studies

Royal Commonwealth Pool, Edinburgh

This pool complex was completed in 1970 to accommodate the aquatic events held in that year's Commonwealth Games. It gained considerably from a pre-briefing study tour undertaken by the manager and the architectural team, which identified three common faults in pool design and planning up to that time. These were:

1 too much specular reflection on water surfaces due to excessive fenestration;

2 too much volume inside pool halls where the height of the hall had been set by the clearance needed above the 10 m high diving tower;

3 too great a water volume in 50 m pools where they were to serve mainly as recreational pools between large scale international meetings.

The planning concept of the building therefore developed from these findings, influenced by the slope down the length of the site, and the magnificent setting behind provided by Arthur's Crags – a well-known local landmark consisting of hills and rough pastureland. As a foil for this jagged skyline the building was designed as a long horizontal, white coated ground-hugging mass, with the main access located at the highest point of the site where the scale becomes single-storey and very human.

The pools inside are 4.8 m below this level at natural ground line, and are immediately overlooked on entry through a well-organised control system which takes swimmers (or those using the rowing apparatus in the basement) downstairs, and leads spectators to refreshment rooms running down the length of the main hall, seen through windows lining the cross secton of the same hall. Orientation is quickly established therefore with all major elements – something all too frequently ignored or forgotten in many cases.

The first implementation of the fact-finding tour may be seen by the way in which all pools have been surrounded by seating. This acts as a buffer zone between the water and the outside, reducing specular glare and heating costs. Fenestration has been limited to narrow high level clerestories, and lower level walkways requested by the fire officer as a secondary means of escape from adjacent spectator seating.

The diving zone has been offset from the main hall to give divers an uninterrupted view of the water, further aided by a sprinkler system which ripples the surface when required. At this point, the roof line is raised to house the 10 m diving tower, in marked contrast to other Olympic pools where the same height has been extended across the whole building, as at Coventry and Crystal Palace, London. The saving

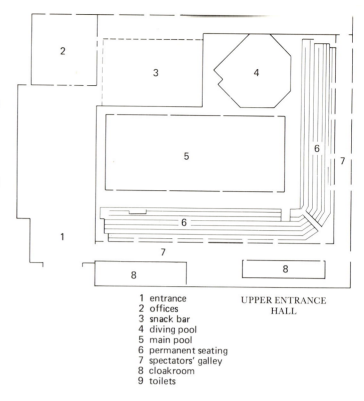

1 entrance
2 offices
3 snack bar
4 diving pool
5 main pool
6 permanent seating
7 spectators' galley
8 cloakroom
9 toilets

UPPER ENTRANCE HALL

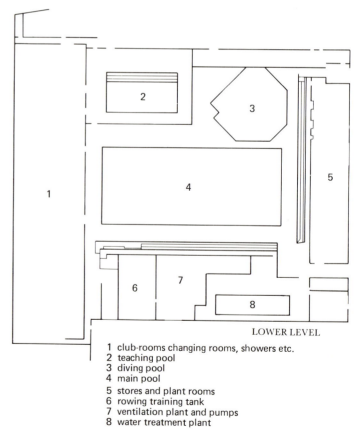

1 club-rooms changing rooms, showers etc.
2 teaching pool
3 diving pool
4 main pool
5 stores and plant rooms
6 rowing training tank
7 ventilation plant and pumps
8 water treatment plant

LOWER LEVEL

Royal Commonwealth Pool, Edinburgh. Plans at ground and upper floor levels. (Architects: Robert Mathew, Johnson-Marshall and Partners)

*Royal Commonwealth Pool. Competition event in main pool hall.
Tha main entrance is to the left of the far screen*

*Royal Commonwealth Pool. Diving tower and separate pool off the
main pool hall. (Photo: Henk Snoek)*

in volume between the 15.20 m high hall at the latter, and the 11.50 m here is considerable, as are the running costs of heating and ventilating this space. The diving tower is of interest in that it is constructed of concrete filled stainless steel columns each carrying its own diving board, in order to minimise interference by other users.

Seating around the main hall encloses changing rooms, plant space and the rowing practice area below. This contributes a good deal towards insulating ambient temperatures in the hall from the outside, and lowering fuel running costs.

In the same context the depth of water in the 50 m pool has been reduced from a constant 2 m normally provided for international competitions, to a gentle slope 1.067 m deep at one end, and 1.98 m at the other. More than two-thirds of its length is therefore at standing water depth, which again has led to a reduction in heating and purification costs if compared with previous examples. It has also allowed management to programme much greater recreational use for the pool when not required for large scale competitions or training purposes, and in so doing has increased annual revenues. Recreational use has since been further increased by the provision of an equally well-considered sauna suite, described later.

A further effect of reducing the height of the pool hall has been to achieve a much greater acoustic control over this area – 2.2 sec at 500 Hz – although recent standards now recommend reverberation times of 1.5 sec and less if possible. Fluorescent strip lighting is mounted flush with the acoustic ceiling, and is arranged longitudinally to assist backstroke swimmers to maintain their lane position. Lighting levels however, considered at the time to be suitable for colour television transmissions, have long since been upgraded fivefold.

Criticisms such as they are, have been relatively minor. Divers were distracted by people moving about the adjacent refreshment room, and blinds are now provided when required to screen off this area. Low setting sun causes a few problems at certain times of the year in controlling glare in the same location. Space about the main pool is minimal for large scale events and complaints have been made that the lockers are too small.

On the other hand the building is generally well liked by all who use it regularly, and it can in every sense be described as a success. Comparison with the latest continental Olympic facilities, or those at National Centres of Excellence would be invidious, as one would need to be a clairvoyant to predict at the present time the type of facilities which may be in use in 1990, or to have a client prepared to back such judgement financially. Suffice it to say that in its day

this project was instrumental in raising pool design standards considerably in the UK, and has since continued to function more than adequately within the context of the original brief.

Royal Commonwealth Pool, Sauna Suite extension
Following the completion of the main building in 1970 a strong recommendation was subsequently made for the inclusion of a sauna suite in line with trends in this direction which are common throughout Europe. When the opportunity came therefore in 1973 to replace the worn-out Turkish Baths in another part of the city, this extension became one of the first purpose-designed public saunas to be built in the UK (although others had been included some years earlier as en suite units at sports centre such as Harlow, Bracknell and Guildford).

A glance at the site plan indicates the care taken in relating the extension to the pool on the quieter side of the site, where it can be reached either from an adjoining car park, or from the main circulation path in the pool entrance area. Access from the independent reception hall to the two suites beyond is via an

Royal Commonwealth Pool (Sauna Suite). View of ladies rest lounge overlooking internal landscaped court yard. (Architects: Robert Mathew, Johnson-Marshall and Partners)

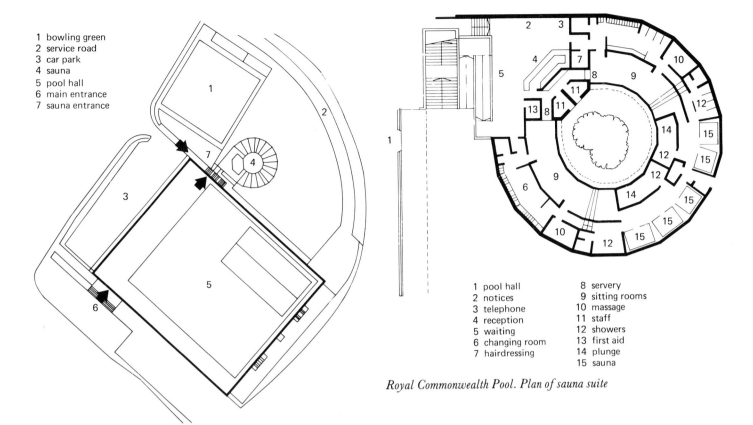

1 bowling green
2 service road
3 car park
4 sauna
5 pool hall
6 main entrance
7 sauna entrance

1 pool hall	8 servery
2 notices	9 sitting rooms
3 telephone	10 massage
4 reception	11 staff
5 waiting	12 showers
6 changing room	13 first aid
7 hairdressing	14 plunge
	15 sauna

Royal Commonwealth Pool. Plan of sauna suite

Royal Commonwealth Pool. Plan showing close relationship between sauna extension and main building

Royal Commonwealth Pool. Internal courtyard screened and planted to provide interest and limit sight lines

outer band of changing rooms, toilets and showers and then to an inner core of relaxation rooms. These overlook a courtyard screened and planted to create small zones of interest immediately outside the full height windows provided for this purpose.

The character of the circular plan is essentially inward looking and much trouble has been taken to heighten the feeling for Finnish authenticity by the liberal use of timber for wall and ceiling finishes. This is augmented by a colour scheme consisting of dark brown (carpets) and oatmeal (lounge chairs). Spotlights have been used to emphasise ceiling colour and texture, while recessed fittings elsewhere add to the atmosphere of warmth and comfort in both sitting rooms.

Although subsequent examples have gone considerably further to attract up-market attention by the inclusion of facilities for manicure, hairdressing, sunbathing and massage, this project remains a good shop window for sauna promotion in the UK and it is well worthy of its 1974 RIBA Design Award Commendation.

De Mirandabad, Amsterdam

With the appearance of so many free-form public swimming pools in the UK during the 1970s it was perhaps inevitable that the trend would spread sooner or later to the mainland of Europe. In particular, to Holland with its long close association with Britain and British sport.

At first glance this project resembles the Oasis Centre at Swindon, and its large acrylic-panelled dome over the indoor pool complex. Inside there is a distinct likeness with the Bletchley Leisure Centre, its palm trees, colourful background, and free-shaped pools. Having said this, De Mirandabad is one of the best examples in Europe at the present time, especially when the outdoor pool complex is taken into consideration as part of the total package offered the public at the height of the swimming season.

Access to the indoor pools is via a spacious and well-organised entrance hall at ground floor level, which also leads to three glass-backed squash courts and a small refreshment gallery overlooking play which appears to absorb ambient heat from the pool area without entering the actual courts. Spectators are separated from users at this point by a staircase leading to first floor level and a glimpse of the swimming area before leading to an open restaurant at the end of the main wave pool. This is 936 m² and leads to two interlinked pools with water slides and a toddlers' zone.

Around these pools are other 'fun options' in the form of a separate whirlpool which is snail-shaped and filled with spiralling bubbles forced under pressure

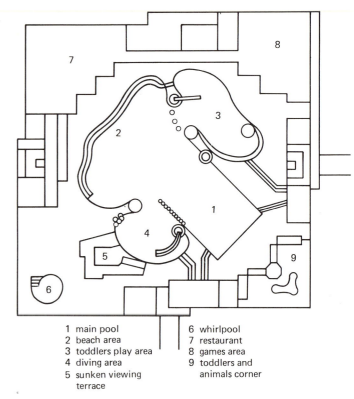

1 main pool
2 beach area
3 toddlers play area
4 diving area
5 sunken viewing terrace
6 whirlpool
7 restaurant
8 games area
9 toddlers and animals corner

De Mirandabad, Amsterdam. Plan at Upper level. (Architects: Architektenburo Baanders, Frenken)

De Mirandabad, Amsterdam. Detail of play slide to 'jump pool', 2.5 m deep. (Photo: Philips International)

De Mirandabad, Amsterdam. Central 'lookout tower' which serves as focal point of total pool complex. Announcements are relayed by four loudspeakers on mast. (Photo: Philips International)

from the pool floor to the surface. A small zoo and aquarium are also included. An enclosed games room filled with space age fruit machines of the kind one finds in any amusement arcade stands in another corner, while in another a zone has been reserved for dry land instruction.

The whole area is covered by a 45 m double glazed translucent dome which gives a considerable transmission of natural light to the water area and its oasis-like planting, which includes several 100 year old palm trees imported from Algeria. A sunbathing 'beach' is provided at the shallow end of the main wave pool, and the colours selected for the floor of the pool resemble the same pattern as those found around coral reefs when seen from the air. A 'pelican' slide, 'stepping stones' and many individual pieces of play sculpture add to the the total feeling of seaside, without any of the design excesses one would probably expect to see in real life.

A balcony links each of these zones around the building, while overlooking the outdoor pools and

landscaping which is still slowly maturing. A 'look-out' tower in the centre cluster of pools indoors serves as their focal point and main supervisory point, especially during wave sessions.

After dark, the area is lit by recessed fluorescent strips let into the underside of the dome base, and by secondary luminaires mounted on posts around the waterside. A maximum illumination of 500 lux is reached over the main pool by a combination of high pressure mercury fittings and sodium lamps with diffusers. Lower levels of lighting have been provided down to 150 lux over the restaurant and toddlers pool.

Plant rooms, administration offices, changing rooms and storage space have been located at ground level, where they can be closely related to the main surge of use which comes on fine days in the summer. Ample car parking is provided in front of the building, although many of the regular users live within walking distance.

The project goes much further than those of a similar concept in the UK, by the provision of outdoor swimming facilities when they are most needed, i.e. in good weather. This is in marked contrast with trends in the UK which have seen the rapid decline of outdoor pools over the past two decades, although many are much further south than this example.

It also illustrates the much wider range of options available to continental users in recently completed projects (this building was opened in 1979), and the strong bias placed on attracting many more adult users and their higher spending power. It also demonstrates the part that automated computerized plant is now playing on the European continent in reducing staff and running costs.

Herranalb Thermal Baths, Black Forest, West Germany
This spa and health resort in the Black Forest has become a well-known tourist centre for West Germans, who in addition to taking the 'Trinkkur' are offered tennis, riding, golf, fishing, and swimming packages while holidaying in the surrounding district. Among these facilities, the thermal bath has become a popular focal point for meeting other people and for enjoying one or more of the services it offers. It is therefore a good example of a highly organised commercially-run pool complex catering for an up-market type of user at the other end of the scale from the run-of-the-mill municipal pool described elsewhere in this section.

The users are predominantly well-to-do adult tourists who expect, and receive, more than normal attention, in better surroundings. In short, the facilities and attention that one would expect to find in a four or five star hotel. It is interesting to note therefore the importance placed in the general hierarchy of provision on ancillary features such as the solarium, gymnasium, rest rooms, sauna and massage suites and landscaped viewing areas, which together equal the area occupied by water facilities.

Environmental conditions are on a par with these surroundings, with pool water (heavily salted) heated to between 30°C and 35°C, and acoustic levels dramatically reduced by the use of carpeted floors and specially treated ceilings. The normal smell associated with public swimming pools is again absent, due to the use of ozone in the purification system. In addition most of the social facilities are open to the pool hall.

The decor is bright and attractive and unified by a colour scheme consisting of chocolate browns, orange, buff and white. This blends well with the blue of the pool water as a background.

A design feature of note in the main pool hall is the electrically-operated window panel which can be raised when required to allow swimmers to pass outdoors into the heated recreation pool provided for fine weather use (including that in mid-winter when pool surrounds are high with snow). It is possible in fact for users to pick up skis at this point and take a ski lift up into the surrounding hills, before skiing back to the poolside.

The capital cost of the project was proportionately high, but so has been the revenue. A clear indication that, given the right mix, and facilities designed to

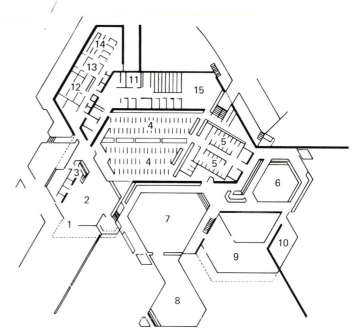

1 entrance
2 foyer
3 cash desk & information
4 changing rooms
5 showers and w.c's
6 medicinal pool
  bath heated to 30° C
7 main thermal bath
  heated to 30°C
8 outer recreational pool
  reached by swimming
  through sliding window
9 rest and sunbathing area
10 solarium
11 sauna
12 massage
13 rest area
14 underwater massage
15 gymnasium

Herrenalb Thermal Baths, West Germany. Plan at ground floor level. (Architect: Karl Heinz Angst)

Herrenalb Thermal Baths. Heated outdoor pool is separated from the indoor pool by electrically operated sliding window. (Photo: DLW (Britain) Ltd)

Herrenalb Thermal Baths. View of irregular shaped indoor pool. (Photo: DLW (Britain) Ltd)

appeal strongly to an adult market (almost to the total exclusion of young people unless accompanied by parents), swimming pools can approach break even point within two or three years of coming into use. It is an interesting proposition which appears to have escaped the attention of many seaside resorts or spa towns in the UK who have seen their clientele attracted away to other options over the past decade.

Seefeld Sport and Congress Centre, Tyrol, Austria
The growing relationship between sport, tourism and leisure can be seen at many recently completed hotels throughout the developed world. Few are as comprehensive however, as this example at Seefeld, 1200 m up in the Austrian Tyrol.

The resort caters for visitors all the year round in the centre of countryside well known for its lakes,

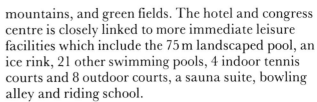

mountains, and green fields. The hotel and congress centre is closely linked to more immediate leisure facilities which include the 75 m landscaped pool, an ice rink, 21 other swimming pools, 4 indoor tennis courts and 8 outdoor courts, a sauna suite, bowling alley and riding school.

Easy access is provided between these and nearby golf courses, cross country ski trails, fishing and sailing areas, and 40 alpine curling rinks. For those who are not so sports minded, ten nightclubs and a gambling casino are also provided.

The indoor pool has captured the local alpine character of waterfalls, whirlpools, grottos, cascades, all in an artificial environment complete with underwater lighting, and access to an outdoor heated pool via an electrically-operated sliding window. The panache with which this has been carried out makes it

Seefeld Sport and Congress Centre, Tyrol, Austria. Internal view of leisure pool. (Photo: sponsors)

Seefeld Sport and Congress Centre. View of swimming area seen in the winter

Seefeld Sport and Congress Centre. View of heated outdoor pool reached via a sliding window seen in the background

Seefeld Sport and Congress Centre. Detail of 'rocks' in the main pool with 'cascade jet' between the two segments

Seefeld Sport and Congress Centre. The whirlpool with a detailed view of the elaborate eggcrate ceiling over

without doubt one of the best examples of a leisure pool anywhere in Europe – although obviously one aimed at a well-to-do clientele, with commercially orientated objectives firmly in mind throughout.

Central Swimming Baths, Mönchengladbach, West Germany

Technical innovation is never very far from many recent European swimming pools, and this example is unique for the method devised to accommodate both waves and a deck level system in the same pool. (For those not familiar with either system, a wave pool requires walls along both long sides high enough to contain each wave. A deck level pool is one where the water level inside the pool is the same as the surrounding walkway).

These two formerly irreconcilable objectives have been achieved by the introduction of a variable depth sub floor to the shallow end of the main pool, operated by electrically-controlled hydraulic supports located in the principal floor of the pool below. Water displaced by the floor when in the raised position is taken to a holding tank positioned between the main and learner pool as shown in the accompanying section. The whole operation takes only a few minutes, and users are warned by klaxon when it is about to commence.

Variable depth floors may be seen frequently in this part of Europe, where they provide management with a number of options ranging from shallow depth teaching sessions, to water polo competitions requiring deeper water. This particular arrangement however has far-reaching implications for all those interested in the provision of wave pools and suitable 'beaches' (where water has so often been lost to surrounding areas in the past).

For those wishing to note the extent of other sports facilities in this typical industrial town of approximately 262 000 inhabitants, the following had been provided by the mid 1970s:

   3 large outdoor leisure pools
   1 large indoor leisure pool complex
   7 ordinary swimming pools
   2 school training pools
   4 indoor tennis halls
   58 sports halls and gymnasia of various sizes
   2 sports stadia, seating 45 000 and 35 000 respectively
   1 horse-trotting course
   1 gliding school
   1 target shooting range

In addition to these, recreational facilities are available for fishing, boating, and riding, with a zoo and nature park also within the town's boundaries.

Greenbank Pool, Street, Somerset

With the trend towards 'indoor/outdoor' pool complexes now well established throughout Europe, the

Mönchengladbach Central Baths, West Germany. Section showing arrangement in main pool used to accommodate both deck level and wave pool conditions. Variable depth pools are to the right of the section

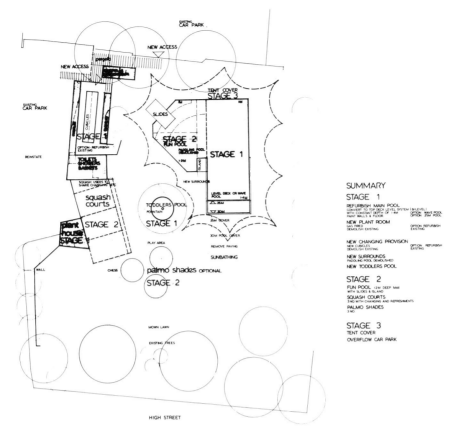

Greenbank Outdoor Pool, Street, Somerset. Long term master plan proposals

number of outdoor pools declines every year in the UK. This is attributed to the weather, and the attraction of overseas beaches, although many outdoor continental swimming centres are much further north than those now being closed in England. More probable reasons for this decline could therefore be unimaginative design, unheated water, poor surroundings, and a tradition of closure on the first of September, irrespective of weather conditions.

The Greenbank Pool illustrates one attempt to reverse this process, and of suggested treatment intended to attract back the traditional family groups which have been long associated with Street and the Clark Trustees of the pool. The site is a green wedge in the centre of the main shopping area of the town, surrounded by mature trees and well-kept lawns much admired by the many visitors to the area (which includes Glastonbury Tor nearby). The two pools were originally built in the 1930s serviced by changing cubicles and a reception area very reminiscent of the architecture of Voisey, Mendelssohn and early Locke.

Inevitably it now has a run-down look and less than satisfactory ablutions if measured by present-day standards. The outdoor sunbathing areas on the other hand are still attractive, but not sufficiently so as to persuade users not to bother going to Weston-super-Mare for the day, or to the local indoor 25 m pool less than 2 km away. Attendances have steadily declined, income has fallen, and the future looks fairly bleak, despite the fact that annual subsidies are much less than for any other outdoor pool in the country.

A feasibility study identified three possible courses of action, which could lead to a return of interest. In so doing the study suggests a model which could be followed by many other projects at the same stage of indecision.

The obvious first step suggested the complete renovation of changing facilities and plant room, including a different system of heating and purifying the water similar to that seen throughout the continent. The second stage would be to rehabilitate the existing pools, and convert them into either a deck-level system (ideal where leaves and grass cuttings fall onto the water surface), or a wave pool which would almost certainly have an attraction for local people in an essentially rural area. Fun chutes, and even a flume ride could be considered in this context, together with 'stepping stones' and play sculpture similar to that found in almost every fun pool complex today.

Associated with these facilities would be other long stay options in the form of giant chess sets, sandpits, and childrens play areas, protected by tent covers and giant umbrellas. Eventually the whole central water area could also be covered in the same way, the water heated, floodlighting provided and the user period extended considerably beyond its present level.

All this would require a considerable capital investment from mainly private sources. But it could form the basis of a live research and development experiment between the Trustees and central government, to illustrate the range of possibilities which exist to bring into public use considerable resources now being allowed to disappear through disinterest and lack of imagination.

Chapter 5

Sports centres

As their name implies, sports centres are an extension of scales of provision associated with one-off sports halls or swimming pools, provided basically to make more impact on the communities they are called upon to serve, and to optimise shared services, car parking facilities and management. In many cases they are the main location for sport in the area, the place where inter-town competitions are played, school days held, or local cup finals decided.

In the UK they have developed from the stadia plans of the mid-1950s when provision largely centred around the town athletics track, the central arena, and any support facilities considered necessary to service these elements. The New Towns around London were a particular vehicle for long term proposals indicated on master plans of the period, as in the example at Harlow described later in this chapter. This was in fact one of the first to be built in 1959 (although in many parts of western Europe, especially West Germany, projects along the same lines were already much in evidence). Other sports centres were built at Cwmbran, Wolverhampton (Aldersley Stadium), and Stockport. Together these formed the basis of considerable national interest at a time when the mood for change was strong and decisions were being taken which were to alter the whole of the former structure of sport for many years to come.

Use of sports centres

The feedback from these early centres proved a major factor in this process. From the outset it became clear that conventional running tracks and central sports fields fulfilled the needs of only a very small minority of sports people in any community. Most were only used during daylight hours or at the weekend. Some required ground staff to maintain both track and field in reasonable condition, and few could justify either the expense of this upkeep, or the land values associated with several acres/hectares of prime land, often very close to the main shopping centre in each of the towns under scrutiny.

At first a concession was made to those wishing to train after dark, by the installation of floodlighting, and at a later date, hard porous training grounds. The latter were to attract many users not connected with either athletics or soccer, including hockey, basketball, and tennis, which together with other pitches designated for cricket, hockey and childrens play, laid the foundation for the multiple units forming the sports centre of today.

Increasing use brought with it the need for some form of coherent management, both to organise and coordinate regular training programmes and fixtures. Also to promote the centres to a much wider public than anything seen in the past.

The cost v size problem

It was soon self-evident however that the cost of such management, together with the growing cost of ground staff and maintenance costs could not be supported by the income alone from those using these facilities. The same kind of Catch 22 situation as that facing management today in the UK developed almost overnight – either the centres needed to grow very much bigger and attract more users to generate a much larger income, or they could linger on indefinitely as loss-leaders providing the sponsors concerned were prepared to subsidise costs in perpetuity.

Some centres opted for the latter course, and remain unaltered (and underused) to this day. Others decided to go the whole way along the opposite course led again by the Harlow Sportcentre project which became the first community based centre to provide a large indoor sports centre in the summer of 1964, the details of which are described more fully in the later

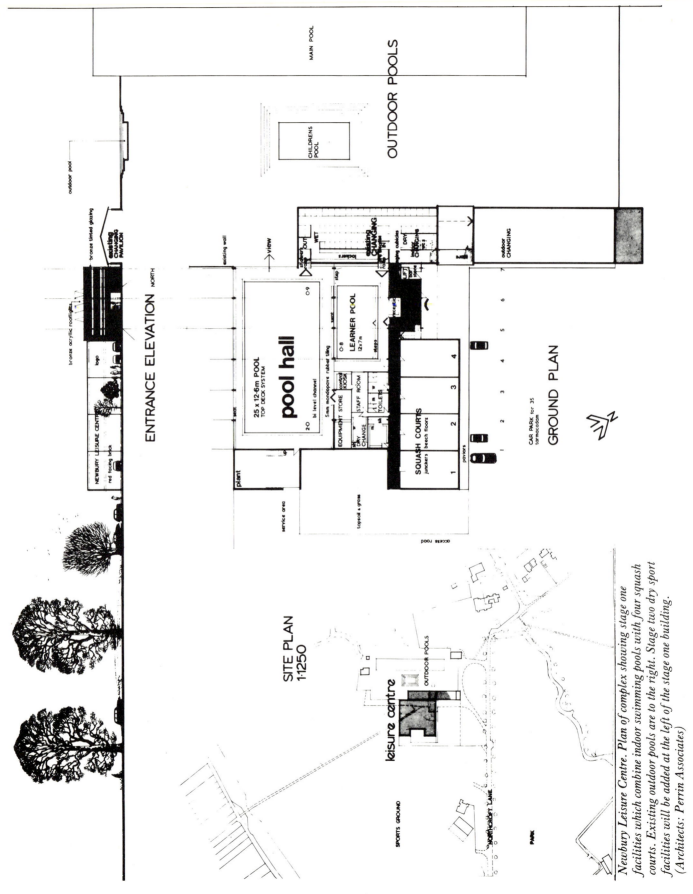

MAIN POOL

OUTDOOR POOLS

CHILDRENS POOL

outdoor pool

ENTRANCE ELEVATION NORTH

bronze acrylic rooflights

bronze tinted glazing

existing CHANGING PAVILION

logo

NEWBURY LEISURE CENTRE

red facing brick

view

existing wall

WET

existing CHANGING

DRY CHANGING

outdoor CHANGING

lockers

step

pool hall

25 x 12·6m POOL
TOP DECK SYSTEM

5mm mondopave rubber tiling

bi level channel

LEARNER POOL
12 x 7m

steps

EQUIPMENT STORE

control KIOSK

STAFF ROOM

DRY CHANGE

TOILETS

plant

service area

topsoil & grass

pavions

SQUASH COURTS
junckers beech floors

1   2   3   4

CAR PARK for 35
tarmacadam

1   2   3   4   5   6   7

GROUND PLAN

access road

SITE PLAN
1:1250

leisure centre

SPORTS GROUND

OUTDOOR POOLS

NORTHCROFT LANE

PARK

*Newbury Leisure Centre. Plan of complex showing stage one
facilities which combine indoor swimming pools with four squash
courts. Existing outdoor pools are to the right. Stage two dry sport
facilities will be added at the left of the stage one building.
(Architects: Perrin Associates)*

Newbury Leisure Centre (left). View of 25 m pool used for Kayak training. (Photo: Gerald Perrin)

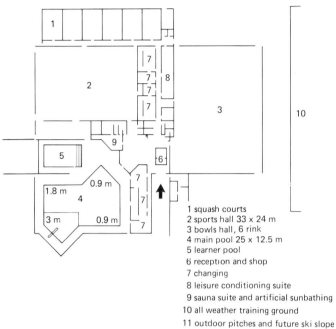

1 squash courts
2 sports hall 33 x 24 m
3 bowls hall, 6 rink
4 main pool 25 x 12.5 m
5 learner pool
6 reception and shop
7 changing
8 leisure conditioning suite
9 sauna suite and artificial sunbathing
10 all weather training ground
11 outdoor pitches and future ski slope

Dunstable Park Recreation Centre (right). Plan of indoor sports centre. The 25 m competition pool has the same water area as a 33.33 m pool. First floor circulation space is used as a refreshment area where main footpaths meet, and part overlooks the pool hall. The six rink bowls hall often remains empty in summer months as elsewhere, and new uses have since been found for this period.

Dunstable Park Recreation Centre (right). Site plan of centre which serves a town of some 30 000 people. Chalk excavated from the pools and basement plant room was used to form the artificial ski slope. (Architects: Perrin Associates)

case study. Within one year use of the centre rose from around 3000 to 250 000, and income *pro rata*, which due to the voluntary nature of the project had to meet expenditure to keep functioning. It was not long before the success of this example triggered off very similar centres throughout the country, particularly in other New Towns.

Subsequent feedback however indicated the disproportionate costs involved between running indoor and outdoor sports facilities, the latter often subsidised by the former. It was sufficient to convince many would-be sponsors of the time to reconsider proposals for the form and siting of future projects, with the result that many like Bletchley decided to opt for an indoor only solution favoured by a great many clients at that time in the late 1960s and early 1970s.

Although this achieved greater efficiency it led to problems of flexibility and future expansion. Obviously it did not meet the needs of those requiring outdoor facilities, for whom subsequent sports centres with changing and refreshment pavilions were provided at less economical rates than those maintained by the all-in-one type of sports centre. It did lead however, to much discussion as to whether policies should be aimed at the provision of one major centre or several for the same amount of money, scattered among town neighbourhoods or associated with secondary schools.

This particular concept coincided with current European practice generally but with one major difference. Spending in Europe was on a far larger scale than in the UK, and provision was often made on the basis of four or five centres being provided simultaneously, managed from one central sports office essentially concerned only with the needs of clubs.

Lack of finance precluded many UK towns from following this pattern especially after it was found that the first of these projects exhausted all available finance – with little prospect of further funds appearing for a very long time. Construction in stages became common in the late 1970s.

On the other hand the pattern of indoor provision in the UK has diversified considerably more than on the continent. This has led to the inclusion of large scale elements such as bowls halls, ice rinks, and roller skating halls, commonly seen in many parts of the country (see the Magnum Leisure Centre, Irvine, page 116).

Urban rest and leisure parks

The appearance of urban 'rest and leisure' parks, described in chapter 8, has opened up a further dimension to the future growth and development of sports centres as we now know them. Why, it is argued,

provide sports pitches on valuable inner urban land, when these could be resited elsewhere, and their place taken by a landscaped setting for many other recreational facilities including those associated closely with the arts. Provision along these lines would bring together sections of the community rarely in contact with each other, so the argument goes, to their mutual benefit, and would again optimise valuable assets more fully.

Tentative studies along these lines are being given consideration by a number of authorities, and it would not be surprising to see examples appearing within the next decade. Whether they eventually supercede conventional forms of provision described later in this chapter time alone can tell – all the indications point however in this direction.

Case studies

Folkestone Sports Centre, Kent
Plans for the project were discussed in the late 1960s when land was made available near the town centre by Earl Radnor, who played an active role as chairman of the Board of Trustees formed to administer the work through each stage of early development.

A preliminary feasibility study had indicated the advantages to be gained by joint sponsorship, especially where the provision of a public swimming pool was envisaged. One result of this recommendation has been local authority responsibility for the capital and running costs of this element – the most expensive in the complex.

A feature of early development was the role played by an existing two storey Victorian house standing at

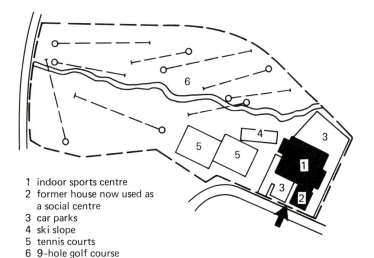

1 indoor sports centre
2 former house now used as a social centre
3 car parks
4 ski slope
5 tennis courts
6 9-hole golf course

Folkestone Sports Centre. Site plan (Architects: Dahl & Cadman and Perrin Associates)

one corner of the site, which became the centre for subsequent administration and fund raising activities. It also provided the nucleus around which Stage I facilities in the form of three squash courts were built to launch the project. With the conversion of ground floor rooms into a bar and social facilities, fund raising for the major part of the project began in earnest. By the early 1970s, government and local authority funds had become available for the construction of the sports hall and swimming pools, and external works in the form of tennis courts, an artificial ski slope and a nine-hole golf course.

The steeply sloping site adjacent to the Stage I clubhouse and squash courts led to the final plan form taken by the building. This brought users into a reception area at second floor level, and channelled them to the swimming pools at first floor level, and the sports hall at lower ground level.

This arrangement has many advantages over conventional flat sites. The mass of the building was minimised, especially from the road (access) frontage where it is the same height as other two storey property adjoining. Users can look down on the swimming pools immediately upon entry and can therefore orientate themselves without further reference to members of staff or complicated signposting systems. Spectators can stay at this level (unless taking seats at sports hall floor level for special events) without having to negotiate further staircases or unsupervised corridors.

The appointment of a manager before final planning commenced proved a considerable asset to the client and architects, as all pre-contract discussions centred around the way the final project was to be run.

This, in turn, determined circulation and control systems, the relationship of major elements to each other and to ancillary facilities, and the points at which further stages of construction could be added without considerable disruption to users.

Completion of Stage II took place in the summer of 1972, and since then Stage III ancillary halls have been added, and adjoining property acquired for leisure conditioning provision.

Roller dance, and roller discos have become a popular part of the user programme, while specialist provision in the form of climbing walls, and the artificial ski slope have declined in use. Squash and

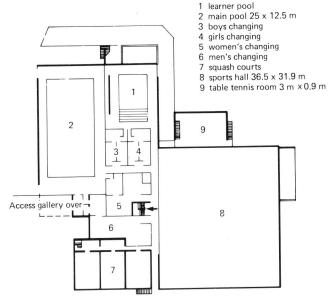

1 learner pool
2 main pool 25 x 12.5 m
3 boys changing
4 girls changing
5 women's changing
6 men's changing
7 squash courts
8 sports hall 36.5 x 31.9 m
9 table tennis room 3 m x 0.9 m

Folkestone Sports Centre. Intermediate plan of centre

Folkestone Sports Centre. Main 25 m pool used for water polo match. The upper viewing gallery and refreshment room overlook the pool behind. (Photo: Folkestone Sports Centre)

Folkestone Sports Centre. Steps at one end of learner pool allow the very young to acclimatise themselves slowly to the feel of water. (Photo: Folkestone Sports Centre)

badminton have retained their early popularity however as in most other sports centres, and the original bar facilities continue to be the centre of attraction for players and non-players alike. Many of these are continental visitors who have come to use the centre as they would their own.

Bletchley Leisure Centre, Buckinghamshire

Bletchley is a victorian suburb of the new city of Milton Keynes in the southern midlands of England. Until recently most of the working population were involved either in the brick-building industry or in light engineering and agriculture, and the town had a somewhat run-down image.

When plans were first drawn up to redevelop the town centre during the 1960s ideas began to be discussed concerning the inclusion of a sports centre on land previously designated as town park on planners maps, but which in reality was little more than a collection of tennis courts and bowls greens surrounded by grass used largely as a dog exercise area. The sole concession to some form of indoor sports provision was a somewhat spartan 25 m outdoor swimming pool covered over with plastic sheeting which in a short time had been badly vandalised, and gave little benefit to the users in terms of warmth or comfort.

Discussions with the Regional Sports Council at that time led to the suggestion that a short list be drawn up of architectural practices experienced in sports centre design and construction. This led to the eventual appointment of a practice responsible for the steady progression of ideas from its first experimental project – the Lightfoot Centre, Newcastle – in 1965, to the highly sophisticated Huddersfield Leisure Centre which immediately preceded this project.

Armed with this feedback the practice was able to argue convincingly for a general change in direction of the brief from its 'sports' image to one of 'leisure'. Emphasis was placed less on 'activity' areas and more on social and cultural facilities, with considerable attention to good finishes, pleasant colours, and the use of interconnecting areas as meeting places rather than corridors.

The building was completed in three stages – the main hall, bowls hall and ancillary rooms in 1972, the leisure pool and sauna in 1974, and the theatre, bowling alley (Kegelbahn) and snooker room in 1975. Administration for the centre was transferred from the old District Council to Milton Keynes in 1974.

The most striking feature of the Centre is the leisure pool and its pyramid roof, clad with bronze tinted

Bletchley Leisure Centre. View from side of free form, figure-of-eight pools, towards palm trees imported from North Africa. (Photo: Gerald Perrin)

Bletchley Leisure Centre. External view of pool hall with its distinctive pyramid shape clad with bronze acrylic 'fly's eye' panels. (Architects: Faulkner Brown, Hendy, Watkinson & Stonor. Photo: Gerald Perrin)

acrylic panels in marked contrast to the largely un-fenestrated massing of adjacent areas of the building. Glimpses of this may be seen from the nearby shopping centre and through the multi-storey car park which provides free parking space for users. Access is by a high-level, train-like, passage which crosses landscaped lakes around the southern part of the centre serving the dual function of amenity feature and moat, thereby restricting public access to within 50 m and minimising problems of security and vandalism.

Once inside the building, the two storey terraced housing outside is quickly shut away behind bronze tinted windows, and the atmosphere becomes air-conditioned, landscaped, carpeted, and rather 'Mediterranean'. In the pool hall, two palm trees form the focal point of figure-of-eight deck-level swimming pools. Elsewhere concealed roof lighting within the V-shaped ceiling units (which have become an in-house trade mark of this practice), and white wicker-work chairs reinforce the feeling of spaciousness and sunshine which are fundamental to the leisure philosophy established in the initial brief.

Apart from these elements of specific composition, the overall standard of detailing is among the best in the UK. Glazing is generally direct to brickwork, plate glass doors and screens around the licensed bar sitting-out area hardly interrupt the transition from

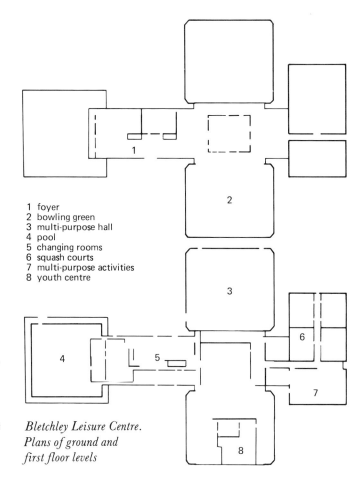

1 foyer
2 bowling green
3 multi-purpose hall
4 pool
5 changing rooms
6 squash courts
7 multi-purpose activities
8 youth centre

*Bletchley Leisure Centre.
Plans of ground and
first floor levels*

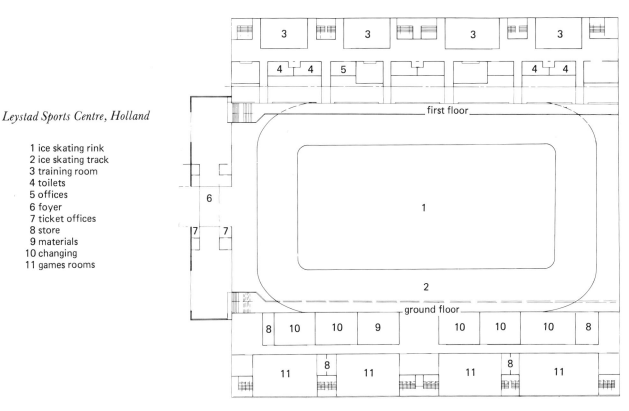

Leystad Sports Centre, Holland

1 ice skating rink
2 ice skating track
3 training room
4 toilets
5 offices
6 foyer
7 ticket offices
8 store
9 materials
10 changing
11 games rooms

non-licensed to licensed space. Electrical fittings are recessed with none of the lines of exposed conduit often seen elsewhere, and frequently vandalised. Curtaining features prominently around the discotheque area and bowls hall where it forms an attractive backcloth along one end of the green.

The V-shaped ceiling in the main hall is a replica of earlier prototypes tried out by the practice at the University of Kent (1968) and Huddersfield Sports Centre. This is now generally accepted as one of the best methods of giving good glare free lighting conditions in sports halls.

The same type of ceiling but without roof lights is seen in the bowls hall, where the need for daytime natural lighting is not as great as in the sports hall. In any case most bowls players prefer to play out of doors from late April to early October if the weather is reasonable.

The small hall can be divided into two by means of an electrically-operated partition mounted in the ceiling, and the floor is resilient for the many sports uses programmed in this area. One wall of the hall has been designed for climbing practice, an arrangement better suited to a small hall like this than in the main sports hall.

It is the leisure pool however which strongly influenced the trend in the UK during the 1970s away from conventional pools. For virtually the first time no concession was made to competitive sizes, depths or racing lanes. The old 25 m pool nearby was demolished on completion of the new pool, and the transformation to the leisure image was heightened by the importation from North Africa of two mature palm trees which have fruited every year since being planted. Traditional non-slip ceramic tiling around conventional pools was replaced by green carpet, a slide was introduced, and a childrens play pit included at the side of the shallower pool. Smooth brickwork replaced conventional wall tiling, and ductwork was exposed and painted bright colours.

These ideas have been repeated and enlarged upon since by many more recently completed leisure pools – the Wester Hailes pool is a typical example – but the Bletchley example will continue to be a source of interest to users and visitors alike for many years to come.

Lelystad Sports Centre, Holland

Lelystad, like its neighbour Dronten, is one of several new towns built on land reclaimed from the Zuider Zee in the polder region of north Holland. Its exposed position and relative isolation have made the development of indoor sports facilities more than usually essential, and the largest of these, the town sports centre, was commenced in 1980.

When fully operational the centre will contain several unique features including a 20 × 20 × 20 m deep indoor diving pool. An ice hockey rink has been designed to provide top class playing conditions for one of the country's major ice hockey teams, with additional space around for recreational skating by townspeople and local clubs. Ice skating, not unnaturally perhaps, is a primary growth sport in Holland where it has a long tradition, and this particular stadium will become a centre for first class events with seating provided for up to 15 000 spectators. The sponsors have sensibly made provision however for the daily use of 250 × 10 m additional recreational ice space around the main rink, from which it is hoped future talented players will emerge.

The 20 m deep diving pool has been designed to provide what might be called a diving centre of excellence which combines diving for sport with specialist facilities for professional off-shore divers, working on oil rigs, and for the Dutch navy and fire brigades. Submarine escape technique is one of the courses made possible in such conditions which enable instruction to be carried out in safe, clear water. The idea has already aroused considerable interest in surrounding countries, particularly Britain and Norway.

Monitoring facilities are provided in an adjacent 'technical room'. An aquarium is a feature of another part of the same space, reached from a central meeting space also serving as a large indoor restaurant.

A large sports hall, 80 × 30 m, completes the main elements inside the building. Outdoors there is a second large diving pool surrounded by other sports areas, including tennis courts, in landscaping planted in the mid-1970s in anticipation of this project.

Squash courts – now beginning to attract much attention in Holland and West Germany – and a rifle range are also provided. Hostel accommodation in the form of 120 bedrooms, lecture and bar facilities will eventually complete the centre.

It is of interest to note that the planning of this building follows more or less conventional lines, and has departed completely from the experimental ideas tried out at Dronten and Eindhoven (Karregat Centre) in the mid 70s. This is an indication that the compromises involved in the latter have not met with the success considered possible when first discussed and that flexibility may have its limits when it comes to managing these extremely loose-knit units.

Heureid Leisure Centre, Zurich, Switzerland

Heureid is one of a number of freetime or leisure centres built in Zurich in the 1960s which has since served as a model layout typical of many subsequent centres elsewhere in Switzerland. It is administered by

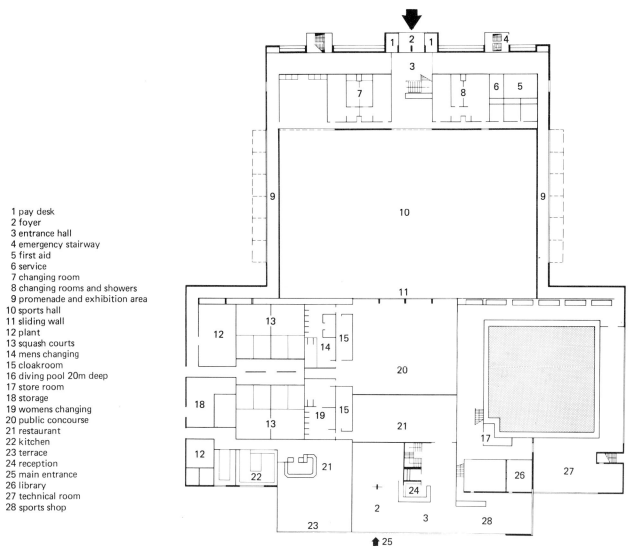

1 pay desk
2 foyer
3 entrance hall
4 emergency stairway
5 first aid
6 service
7 changing room
8 changing rooms and showers
9 promenade and exhibition area
10 sports hall
11 sliding wall
12 plant
13 squash courts
14 mens changing
15 cloakroom
16 diving pool 20m deep
17 store room
18 storage
19 womens changing
20 public concourse
21 restaurant
22 kitchen
23 terrace
24 reception
25 main entrance
26 library
27 technical room
28 sports shop

Lelystad Sports Centre, Holland. Plan. (Architects: Fred Balm BV)

Lelystad Sports Centre, Holland. Photograph of centre model, with 15 000 seat ice stadium behind foreground aquatic centre which includes a 25 m deep diving research underwater training pool. (Photo: Fred Balm BV)

the Pro Juventute organisation based in the same city which receives financial assistance from many sources including the national sale of special postage stamps and posters, and is similar in some respects to the National Playing Fields Association in the UK.

Heureid was one of the first european projects to base the provision of facilities on what is now known as an 'indoor/outdoor' yearly programme. Summer facilities include four large open air heated swimming pools, roller skating rink, tennis courts and sports pitches floodlit for evening use. Winter provision is in the form of ice skating rinks, and indoor sports and arts facilities including a library, restaurant, and disco room sited in the mandatory nuclear fall-out shelter in an underground basement. A school and kindergarten share the same site, separated from other areas by tree and shrub planting established well before development commenced.

The indoor centre occupies the highest part of the site and is a natural focal point for all newcomers to the site, and houses, in addition to the library and craft rooms, a general administration suite of offices. Attached to this centre is a Robinson Crusoe adventure playground where children can imagine they have been shipwrecked on a desert island and are encouraged to build themselves survival shelters, and keep animals for eggs and milk supplies – a concept now widely copied throughout Europe.

The centre is arranged around an internal courtyard which also serves as a sunken stage for fine weather performances with steps as seating around all four sides. Construction is typically Swiss – board marked concrete finishes internally an externally, and timber, with deep overhanging eaves as the traditional protection against snow in winter.

The outdoor pools are well landscaped with shrubs arranged in such a way that entry to the poolside can only be gained by passing through one of several precleanse areas. The depth of the main 'swimmers' pool is a constant 1.80 m with a diving bay 3.6 m deep and that of the 'non-swimmers' pool from 0.00 m to 1.20 m deep. Changing cabins for individuals and families are arranged between these and two 'learning' pools used mainly by school classes.

The restaurant has a large terrace for summertime use when it can accommodate up to 300 overlooking the swimming pools and ice/roller skating rink (66.30 × 63.60 m in area). Car parking is located in the familiar 'maze' method of planting arranged in bays of shrubs which considerably reduce the apparent number of cars visible to other parts of the site, avoiding the unsightliness of average rectangular car parks and the mass parking which they encourage.

Since completion of this project more than twenty others have followed in other parts of the city, some catering for specialist activities in the form of swimming centres, ice skating rinks, and roller skating cenres. Many have a teaching element attached to relate some aspects of play to learning very similar to joint use projects in the UK which followed a decade later.

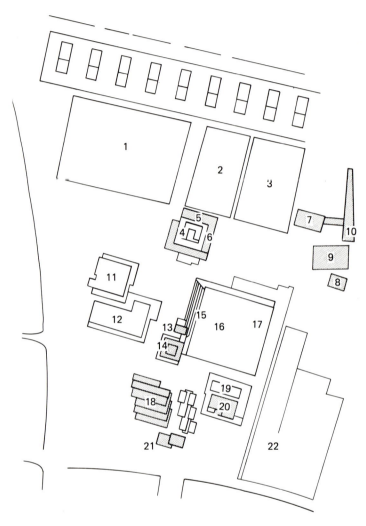

1 games courts/play areas
2 'Robinson Crusoe' adventure playground
3 school play areas
4 club room
5 offices and workshops
6 library
7 training hall/gymnastics
8 school
9 kindergarten
10 school facilities
11 non swimmer pool
12 swimming pool
13 kiosk
14 restaurant
15 seating
16 roller skating, floodlit
17 ice skating, floodlit
18 changing rooms
19 training pool
20 schools changing
21 offices
22 parking

Heureid Lesiure Centre, Switzerland. Site plan of centre, one of twenty-five in Zurich provided and managed by the Pro Juventute organisation

Eastleigh Sports Centre, Hampshire

Eastleigh is a rapidly growing town 5 miles from Southampton in the centre of what has been called the south Hampshire 'corridor'. This is an area linking the busy port of Southampton and the Solent estuary, with the hinterland of Hampshire to where it joins the M3 motorway and East West transportation systems.

It served for many years as a large depot for Southern Railway rolling stock, employing many people living around the station and marshalling yards, in two-storey red brick terraced houses. More recently factories and light engineering industry has diversified employment in the town, and new housing estates have encouraged the growth of a large commuter/young executive community on the outskirts of the town. It is therefore well-balanced politically, socially and economically, and typical of many towns of similar size in England showing the same rate of growth of the past decade.

In the 1920s an area of land near the town centre known as Fleming Park was given to the town as play

11

1 sports hall
2 swimming pool
3 bowls hall
4 car park
5 redgra training area
6 tennisquick area
7 ski slope (future)
8 miniature golf
9 former tennis courts
10 bowls including artificial turf green
11 golf course (18-hole)
12 future expansion

Eastleigh Sports Centre. Site plan of complete project which utilises an existing park complex first provided in the 1920s (Architects: Perrin Associates)

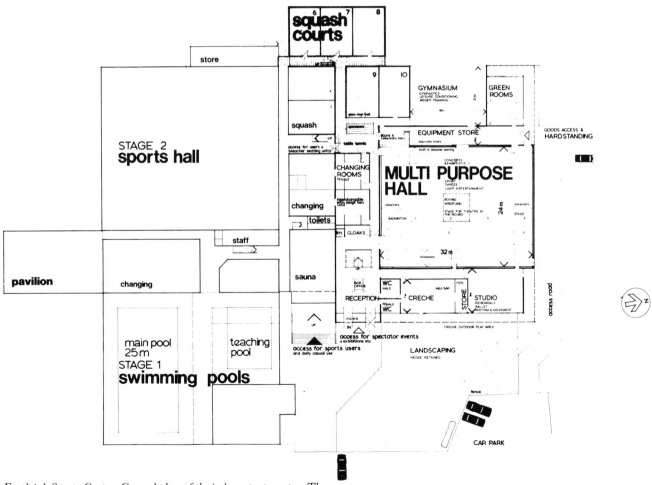

Eastleigh Sports Centre. Ground plan of the indoor sports centre. The Phase 3 multi-purpose hall on the right remains to be completed

space, and this has since become the home of several cricket, football and hockey clubs, as well as providing facilities for tennis and bowls. In 1969 plans were discussed for the inclusion of a large indoor sports centre to accommodate three primary elements, swimming, dry sports, and indoor bowls. Their size and phasing were determined by means of a feasibility study which took into account predicted growth rates, transportation assessments, socio-economic factors, surrounding catchment areas and the provision they were making for indoor sport, and possible contributors to the various phases of construction proposed.

Impetus was given to swimming facilities as the first stage of development (in preference to the dry sports recommended in the feasibility study) by the offer of capital from the county education authority. Their researches had revealed that it would be cheaper to provide one central pool complex serving the six secondary schools in the area, than several smaller pools in each school.

Construction commenced in 1972 and the first phase consisting of one 25 m × 12.5 m pool, one 12.5 m × 9 m learner pool, three squash courts, bar and refreshment lounges, and a sauna suite, was opened by Mary Peters (the modern pentathlon Olympic gold medallist in Munich) in 1974. Outdoor provision was made for a hockey pitch size hard porous training ground, and a landscaped sunbathing terrace at the side of the main indoor pool.

Eighteen months later phase two had also been completed comprising a two court (36 m × 32 m) sports hall, multi purpose games/meeting room, projectile gallery, two additional squash courts, a weight training room, and general changing and administrative areas. Outdoor facilities also included all weather tennis courts, but plans for an artificial ski slope were abandoned following objections by nearby residents.

At this point a mid-development reassessment was made of the original proposals, and discussions with user committees and management revealed a growing demand for a second large hall for clubs and multi-purpose use, and additional squash courts and ancillary rooms.

The provision of an all-weather synthetic grass surface on one of the existing bowls greens met most of the needs expressed by bowls players, and resulted in the substitution of a multi-purpose hall for the original bowls hall as phase three development. The additional squash courts were completed by 1980, but plans for the main proposals were held in abeyance during government restrictions on public spending at that time.

Long term proposals were also agreed during mid-development discussions for phasing out the sports pitches (by siting them elsewhere) and restyling the

Eastleigh Sports Centre. Entrance hall where dry sports users, spectators, and swimmers are separated at the central control kiosk, which also operates the lighting and loudspeaker systems throughout the building. (Photo: Wimpey News)

Eastleigh Sports Centre. Sauna rest lounge and solarium. (Photo: Wimpey News)

site as a 'rest and leisure' park (see page 111. This includes the existing golf course to the west of the site, and a small lake for boating (similar to that in the Gruga Park example on page 111), canoeing, and fishing. When completed in the mid-1980s the project will be one of the most advanced in the UK.

Lessons learned from this particular phased building programme suggest the positive advantages to be gained from phased construction (such as keeping in touch with changing user needs), while pointing out the problems of allowing for future requirements within the first stage. For example, should services include those for later stages; also drainage, car parking and the management structure; how is the building to be constructed to allow for future extensions without seriously disrupting use; and how is momentum to be maintained over a 10 to 15 year programme.

The big advantage of this site over those with no outdoor facilities has been its ability to expand and consolidate its position as the focal point for major sports and leisure facilities both in the town and in the surrounding catchment area.

Harlow Sportcentre, Essex

Harlow is one of eight original New Towns designated after 1945 to house overspill population from London less than 30 miles away. During its early development it pioneered many experiments in the field of social and community planning, and is particularly well known for its three tier system of provision for sport and recreation.

Tier 1 consists of 'round the corner' sports facilities serving local needs, which have been situated in green

Harlow Sportcentre. Photograph of original model made in 1955 which anticipated the final form of the project mainly as a 'sports stadium', with the grandstand the major building on the site. (Architects: Frederick Gibberd & Partners for Stage one. Perrin Associates for all subsequent stages).

wedges running between each of the town's four major neighbourhood units, each made up of approximately 22 000 people. Tier 2 is based upon the shopping centres and secondary schools in each neighbourhood, and consists largely of small training indoor pools and sports halls, and in one unit, a bowls hall. Tier 3 however is the main event area for the town – the Sportcentre described here – where minor county cricket is played, local derbys are held, and the top coaches are accommodated.

As the original model shows (see below) early conception was very much along the lines of a traditional stadium, with a grandstand serving the needs of spectators watching events on the running track or central grass arena, and few other facilities included apart from cricket, hockey and tennis for each of the existing town teams or clubs playing at this level of competition. In 1958 pressure to implement the project came from local industrial and commercially-based sports organisations, with strong support from the Development Corporation who at that time were one of the biggest employees in the town . The

Harlow Sportcentre. Internal view of sports hall with under 10's session in progress, watched by parents from high level viewing galleries.

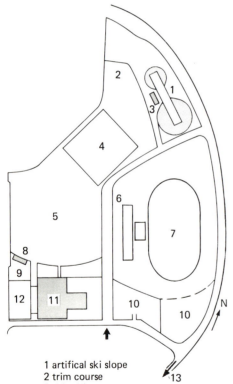

Harlow Sportcentre. Plan of 11 hectare (28 acre) site

1 artifical ski slope
2 trim course
3 ski cabin
4 training ground
5 cricket and hockey
6 stand and changing pavilion
7 soccer and athletics
8 pub
9 cars
10 car park
11 indoor sports centre
12 all weather tennis courts
13 to train centre 400 m away

Harlow Sportcentre. Hall used for a darts competition

opportunity to begin site work came with the decision to construct a link road across land liable to flooding, requiring spoil excavated from the site designated as the stadium.

With the banking to the stadium completed as a result of this work, it was logical to continue with the formation of the running track, central grass arena, and adjacent cricket and hockey pitches and to build a small changing pavilion to service these areas. It then became clear that a sponsoring agency was required to take over the responsibility for running these facilities, and after considerable discussion an umbrella organisation in the form of a charitable Sports Trust was formed in 1959, followed shortly afterwards by the appointment of a full time manager to coordinate activities, and promote the aims and objectives of the Trust.

It was quickly seen that additional facilities would be needed if better use were to be made of the Centre, especially in the evenings when people were free to train or take part in limited competitive activities. A subsequent decision was therefore taken to instal a floodlit hard porous training ground slightly larger than a hockey pitch, which resulted in not only improved use but also a more diverse range of activities being accommodated, in the form of tug-of-war events, basketball, five-a-side football, netball, tennis and athletics field event practice sessions.

At weekends the ground was often used for major hockey matches or tournaments, especially when poor weather precluded use being made of the adjoining grass pitches. During the annual town show less than 400 m away, the area was also used as an overflow car park (although this was soon discouraged due to the damage caused to the top surface).

Growth continued to flourish and brought with it a demand for more facilities, to the point where in the summer of 1963 the decision was again taken to expand with the construction of the country's first community sports hall, financed by funds provided initially by the Wolfson Foundation, local councils, the Development Corporation, local people (through 'buy a brick' campaigns), and the main contractor.

It says much for the original brief that the size and shape of the main hall, and disposition of rooms around this space, were the model for many subsequent projects. This remains one of the norms recommended for the present generation of sports halls (or indoor sports centres as they have since become called).

Within the first year of use attendances rose from approximately 3000 to 250 000, and have since been maintained at around 350 000 per annum. Coping with such large numbers required considerable management skill and much dedication by the small band of largely volunteer helpers. With considerable goodwill a daily pattern of use was established which again became the norm for similar projects elsewhere in the UK. This consisted largely of school use during the day, lunchtime squash and five-a-side soccer matches, early evening and Saturday morning under 10s clubs, and evening and weekend peak time club and individual bookings. The main hall, 36.50 m by 30 m, has been used frequently for choral and orchestral concerts – for which the acoustics have proved quite acceptable – dances, Christmas parties, fashion shows, and large scale sports events including 'Its a Knockout', and 'Top Town' competitions.

The grounds have gradually been developed to include an artificial ski slope (which is profit-making), a trim-track (for keep-fit and jogging exercises), tennis courts (on an all-weather porous surface), and large scale additions to the original sports hall. These include two squash centres (making 16 courts in all) and a sauna suite.

Today the centre receives considerable support from the local council and the regional sports council, and continues, with the aid of a thriving lottery, to expand in many directions dictated by local needs. The voluntary involvement in the early days has been replaced by more formal staffing appointments tied to local government salaries and grades, although the spirit of self-help still exists through the special relationship between the centre and its ninety or so board members.

Decision-making is undertaken by an Executive Board on which local business people and local authorities are equally represented. Long term planning is carried out by Development and User Committees interpreting the views and opinions of playing and social members.

From a design point of view the original concept of the sports hall as being a 'sports workshop' with basic hard wearing surroundings and few concessions to 'refinement' particularly in respect of the services elements, has worked well in practice – although far more attractive examples have since been built at much higher cost (the contract sum for the building in 1964 was £120 000). The policy of maintaining an in-house maintenance team to deal with day to day renovations to services and the building fabric has also proved highly economical.

The main lessons to have been learned after twenty-one years of operations include the need for loose-fit planning in and around all major indoor facilities, good management, a close relationship between users and all decision-making committees, the need for a sustained injection of capital funds to promote growth, a balance between loss-leader facilities and high income-producing elements, good car parking, and a diverse programme of activities with 'something for everyone'. A fine balance is also something to be struck between long term club use and individual use as the former has been known to 'freeze space' for long periods at a time. Perhaps the Eastleigh approach to this problem also described in this chapter has much to offer in this respect.

Ahoy Centre, Rotterdam, Holland
This is one of the larger projects to have been completed by the early 1970s as a major attraction for the south west region of Holland. It is linked by motorway to the surrounding countryside, and by overhead walkways to adjacent areas of the city and to the Rotterdam Metro system. The airport is 15 minutes drive away.

It is similar in size to the Deutz Halle in Cologne, or the Wembley Conference Centre, with seating for between 6000 and 9000 spectators in the sports hall. A feature of the latter is a 200 m cycle racing track permanently installed for major international events. In addition to the main hall there is anice skating hall (60 × 30 m) which can be adapted by means of portable flooring for many other types of sports and non sports activities. These include mass meetings, conferences, concerts, shows and festivals. The lighting system is suitable for colour television transmissions,

and scoring is recorded by a 6 × 4.5 m electronic scoreboard.

In an adjacent part of the site, four exhibition halls 12 000 m² in area are provided to attract international events. Air conditioned meeting rooms, and underground technical facilities have been installed for this purpose, and one of the halls serves as the main refreshment and social centre for the site. Telex, Press, telephoto, dark rooms, and a VIP suite are included as part of the impressive range of facilities made available for users.

Ahoy Centre, Rotterdam. General view of the complex from one of several high level walkways which link the centre to nearby shopping precincts and a large theatre/arts complex. (Photo: Gerald Perrin)

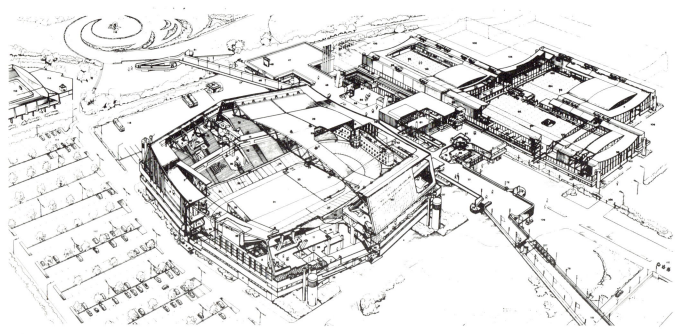

Ahoy Centre, Rotterdam. Cut-away perspective of one of the largest projects to have been provided for sport, congresses and exhibitions in Holland, by the early 1970s. Seating for between 6000 and 9000 spectators is provided in the sports hall, which also has a 200 m permanent indoor cycle racing circuit. A 60 m × 30 m ice skating hall has an adaptable floor which allows other uses to be accommodated including mass meetings, conferences, concerts, shows, and festivals. Lighting is suitable for colour television broadcasts. Telex, telephoto, and darkrooms are available for use by the media. Similar-sized projects can be found in many European cities where they are regarded as a sound investment for prestige reasons

Chapter 6

National training centres and centres of excellence

The rapid growth of community orientated sports facilities over the past decade has made little concession to the gifted player or performer, many of whom have gained sports scholarships overseas in order to attain the skill levels necessary to compete at international level today. In recognition of this fact many countries have recently initiated the construction of national training centres, or specialist centres of sports excellence which offer many unique features of design and construction not normally found at local levels of provision.

The philosophy behind this movement appears to be common throughout the world. Anyone showing above average ability is encouraged to attend coaching sessions lasting one or several weeks, in an environment designed to improve personal performances, and to prepare users mentally for future events both in the long and short term. Not only are the playing conditions the best of their kind, but they are normally backed up by an impressive range of ancillary facilities including body-monitoring laboratories, video and computer recording devices, lecture theatres, bio-mechanical testing apparatus, and residential facilities on a par with any to be found in five star hotels.

This is a far cry one may feel from the more laissez faire attitudes which existed twenty years or so ago, but essential in the field of top class competition today. The results speak for themselves. Individual performances have improved beyond barriers previously considered to be unobtainable, and group training has taken teams such as the Dutch national soccer squad to the forefront of all recent international competitions.

Choice of location

The siting of each example has generally been in or close to an established sports complex, and often involves the research capabilities of a nearby university, as in the case of the Canberra National Training Centre, Australia.

In one or two cases however, where a suitable estate has been offered for this purpose as at Zeist, Holland, new facilities have been built to include specialist research and laboratory conditions, on site. Hostel accommodation, lecture and video theatres, a resource library, and relaxation areas form a major proportion of general schedules of accommodation, in addition to activity spaces.

National characteristics are reflected in many examples. The present East German drive to become the top sports nation is very apparent at the Leipzig National Training Centre, which has become 'home' for several generations of talented performers first assessed for ability at primary school age. Coaching and research methods are among the most thorough in the world, and the rewards for good performances often bring with them privileges of status, travel, and generally a quality of life normally reserved for the elite.

In France, Holland and West Germany on the other hand, equally excellent standards of provision are often made available for the local community at large when not required for national training purposes. The Font Romeau centre in the French Pyranees has one of the largest camping sites in the region, and encourages tourism to the area by holding regular open air pop concerts and exhibitions each year. The equestrian centre is a popular focal point of the site, but its main role is that of a high altitude training camp originally provided prior to the Mexican Olympic Games in 1968.

A similarly relaxed atmosphere can be found at the Papendal National Training Centre near Arnhem in Holland, the site of the 1980 Paraplegic Olympics. The Zeist training centre placed at the disposal of the Dutch national football squad since the early 1960s has been reserved almost entirely for this purpose, although recent policy has encouraged public re-creational use of all facilities.

The secondary role of the Sporthochschule in Cologne as a national sports advisory centre, has encouraged considerable contact with the outside world, and is an open house for many visitors each year who come to study the high standard of facilities provided for teaching, research and competition. So far, nine other centres have been provided in West Germany, specialising in specific groups of related activities, for example racquets centres, martial arts and swimming. All have been built to the highest standards.

Some international solutions

Two British examples may be seen at Lilleshall in the West Midlands, and Bisham Abbey south west of London, where former country houses and their estates have been developed as national training centres initially by the Central Council of Physical Recreation and more recently by the National Sports Council.

Features of both are large indoor sports centres, essential for bad weather training and regular competition. Both may be used by local clubs when not required by national training squads. The University of Loughborough has provided many of the research facilities required for these centres, including the use of student physical education teachers as in Cologne for the monitoring of human performance characteristics.

One of the finest facilities currently being constructed and due for completion in the mid 1980s, is the National Training Centre at Canberra (see page 95), which in addition to the activity areas being provided will also include a centre for sports research and feedback for the whole of Australasia. The Jubilee Centre in Hongkong will complement these facilities in Asia when completed about the same time. The architectural appearance of both projects has created considerable interest worldwide with the latter, like Munich's Olympic Games centre, the result of an international competition.

The home of the Danish Sports Associaton at Brøndbyvester (see page 92) is another sports project with a strongly modelled external appearance, reflecting the four use zones inside available for teaching, learning, administration and residential accommodation.

The trend is therefore well established in this direction of sports excellence, and has produced already a number of facilities generally considered to be the best of their kind in the world. Inevitably they have become the Mecca for visitors from overseas anxious to carry back with them many points of detail for inclusion in future projects yet to get past the hurdles of finance and internal politics. Like their users they have already advanced the quality of sports architecture considerably further than at any previous time in history, and established many design and construction trends certain to be seen many times between now and the end of the present century.

Case studies

The KNVB National Football Training Centre, Zeist, Holland

Much of the success of the Dutch national soccer team in recent World Cup series has been attributed to the excellent training facilities provided on this 25 hectare (63 acre) site on the outskirts of the small town of Zeist known for its close association with the Dutch Royal family.

It was originally one of many large estates in the area which has been converted into the administrative and training headquarters of the Royal Dutch Football Association (KNVB), with a full time staff of 65 responsible for the 560 000 matches played each year in Holland, and the training of the national squad, referees, and coaches.

Development began in the early 1960s with the construction of the large sports hall, hostel block, medical centre, and administrative centre, with the most recent addition, the indoor swimming complex, opening in 1978. These are arranged in linear form in pine and beech woods closed to traffic (and to many of the media when the training squad is in residence), with open air sports pitches discreetly sited between. One of these pitches has been surfaced with artificial grass for intensive training in all weather conditions.

Royal Dutch Football Association Training Centre, Zeist, Holland. External view of 50 m × 30 m sports hall. (Photo: Gerald Perrin)

Royal Dutch Football Association Training Centre. Hostel block opposite sports hall. (Photo: Gerald Perrin)

Royal Dutch Football Association Training Centre. Recreation pools adjacent the main pool

Royal Dutch Football Association Training Centre. 30 × 25 m training pool. (Photo: Gerald Perrin)

Royal Dutch Football Association Training Centre. Underwater jet gives 'swimming against the current' practice, and can be used for slimming/massage sessions

1 swimming pool
2 dormitory pavilion
3 social pavilion
4 lecture pavilion
5 association office
6 sports hall
7 hotel
8 medical centre
9 artificial turf pitch

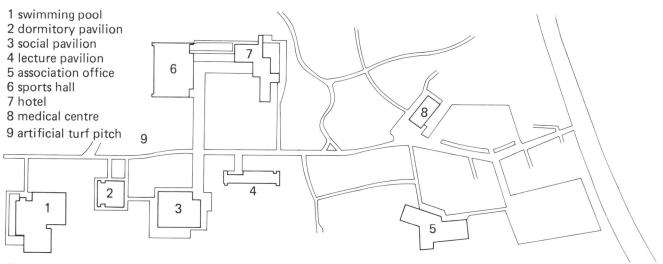

Royal Dutch Football Association Training Centre. Site plan

Landscaping is again of the highest standard between these facilities, and much of the indiginous wildlife of the district (which includes deer and red squirrels) has been left undisturbed.

Perhaps the building of most interest to sports hall designers is the large $50 \times 30 \times 8\,m$ indoor sports centre, which can be used for all major indoor games up to full international standard. It has special provision for indoor football training, including ceiling-mounted footballs which can be lowered to head height on steel wires push-button operated, for heading practice.

Flush-mounted bands of artificial lighting run lengthways down the hall, containing a mixture of fluorescent and tungsten fittings protected by grilles which can be operated to give localised or universal lighting at various levels of illumination, operated from a nearby console. The boarded ceiling, light brown cork lino floor finish, dark brown brick end walls and white brick long walls, give excellent background conditions for all activities played in this area, and an environmental quality much admired by the many overseas visitors to the Centre each year. The scale of this building has been minimised externally by its position in a natural hollow, allowing spectators to enter the viewing gallery on one side of the hall, at first floor level without the need for steps.

The swimming complex had the same restraint put on its size as its counterpart at Papendal, due to the sponsors (the Dutch National Sports Federation) request that it should be for training purposes only. The $30 \times 25\,m$ main pool therefore has ten training lanes and can be used for water polo practice and recreational swimming. As at Papendal, increasing use has come from local people and clubs interested in keeping fit for health reasons more than for competition training, and one of the most popular areas in the $20 \times 12/15\,m$ recreation pool adjacent is the fun slide, paddling/learning-to-swim pool, and specialist facilities such as underwater jets for massage purposes, and learning to swim 'against the current'.

Water temperatures can be adjusted for specific types of use: 26 to 27°C for training and recreational sessions, 24°C for water polo matches. Lane marking booms which can be pulled up and and onto the water surface when required, are stored in $2\,m$ walkways below the pool surrounds.

A single large filtration tank $3.2\,m$ high handles all the purification requirements of both pools in one of the plant rooms $10 \times 6\,m$, which also contains the boiler plant. All the services are automatically controlled, enabling the whole complex to be operated by two full time members of staff assisted by part time cleaners, and swimming coaches. A separate air handling plant room is positioned between the two pools, as are free-standing showers arranged on 'posts' to give 20 sec impulse sprays before and after entering the water.

Changing rooms are well removed from the pools, and are consequently relatively free from water. Finishes are immaculate with full height brown tiling on the walls and non-slip ceramic tiles on the floors in cream. Around the pools, walls are in brown brickwork above a $500\,mm$ tile plinth. Ceilings over the surrounds are in preservative treated timber slats, while over the pools they are finished in white acoustic 'planks' with inlaid flush fluorescent fittings to match the plank module. Air inlets are angled down to the pools at intervals around the hall.

Other elements are equally well finished in the hostels and social centre, the latter having an open fireplace with copper hood, enormous double glazed sliding doors leading out onto a patio, internal courtyards planted with small scale heathers and other sand-loving ground cover shrubs. Discreet lighting gives an atmosphere of comfort and relaxation similar to what one would expect in better standard hotels in some of the larger cities. Lecture facilities are equally well finished with pine ceilings, brick facings to all walls, deep window cills to display pieces of sculpture, and automatic devices for video demonstrations, slide shows and other teaching aids.

The facilities may be used by selection committees, youth leaders, and sports organisations other than football. The hotel has sixteen bedrooms, which can have 1, 2 or 3 beds as required, and all have their own toilet and bath, and are connected up for TV and telephone. It also has conference facilities for up to 150 people, and smaller rooms for not more than 16 people per room. The original dormitory pavilion accommodating 52 people using communal toilet and washing facilities, was refurbished in 1979 to bring it up to date in a much more sophisticated manner to meet present day needs.

As at Papendal, a camping centre has also been provided as a recreational area for young people where they can meet players, arrange their own competitions, and enjoy pop concerts and 'events' in and around a large 'hut' provided for this purpose. The medical centre has a permanent staff of two doctors, a physiotherapist, masseur, and two medical assistants responsible for medical examinations, and the treatment of sports injuries – including patients from outside the country. External claddings to the majority of these smaller buildings are of western red cedar allowed to weather to its natural silver grey, and white brickwork, with timber framed windows in dark stained finishes.

The recent decline in attendance at Dutch football matches, together with the apparent loss of form by

National Training Centre, Sporthochschule, Cologne. Administrative block on right leading to lecture hall, and covered way which links all facilities on the campus, see plan. The administrative building also serves as the centre for the West German Technical Advisory Service for Sport and Recreation

the national team, has led the sponsors to encourage more diversification at the Centre – hence the provision of swimming facilities – and the pursuit of recreational objectives within a centre of sports excellence. The result is that it is better used, and satisfies the needs of a much wider public market than hitherto; part of a general move in this direction throughout the western world at the present time.

Sporthochschule, Cologne, Germany

West Germany has played a leading role in sports provision for many years, and the focal point for much of the research underlying this development has been the sports college or Sporthochschule at Cologne. Situated in the Mungersdorf district of the city the

college was established along campus lines between 1960 and 1963 in a well wooded site forming part of a much larger sports complex used by the public at large.

During their training to become teachers of physical education, students are used to test many aspects of sports research including new ideas associated with the design and construction of sports buildings. Results are then disseminated for general public use in the form of the now well known DIN norms governing all sports development work in Germany, and since 1972, also in many other European countries.

The campus is based upon a series of experimental halls connected to a long covered way, with sports pitches between each consisting of different surfaces and background conditions. New facilities have been

National Training Centre, Sporthochschule, Cologne. Diving pool with a complete range of 1 m, 3 m, 5 m and 10 m boards. (Photo: Gerald Perrin)

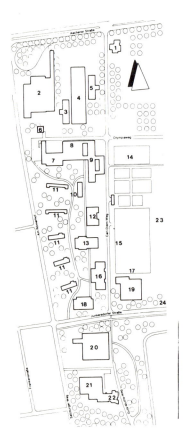

1 hostel
2 indoor athletics hall
3 small halls
4, 12, 16, 18 recreation halls
5 plant and services
17 football
18 recreation hall
20 aquatic centre
21 hockey and judo centre

National Training Centre, Sporthochschule, Cologne. Site plan

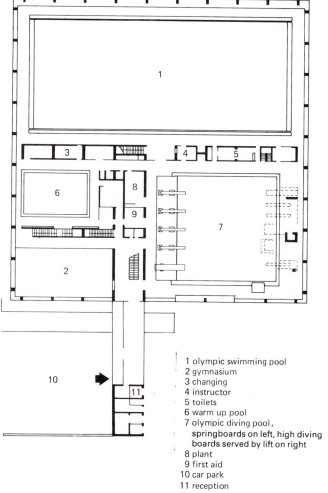

1 olympic swimming pool
2 gymnasium
3 changing
4 instructor
5 toilets
6 warm up pool
7 olympic diving pool,
   springboards on left, high diving
   boards served by lift on right
8 plant
9 first aid
10 car park
11 reception

National Training Centre, Sporthochschule, Cologne. Plan of aquatic centre

added periodically and now include a national aquatic training centre and athletics/hockey complex which are generally agreed to be among the best of their kind in the world. A multi-storey student hostel, five storey office block, and lecture theatre complete the accommodation provided up to 1980.

Each of the small halls is designed to assess player reaction to floor finishes, lighting systems, background colours, specialist items of equipment and methods of installation. For example in one of the halls used primarily for gymnastics, rhythm and movement and ballet groups, one wall is completely covered with mirrors for correct posture training, the timber floor is highly sprung, and audio equipment is cleverly concealed in one of the timber-lined walls. The floor system (Baltic spruce on cross battens) and acoustic ceiling were subsequently considered acceptable for inclusion in the DIN normen.

Another larger hall has a 'schwingboden' floor consisting of sheet PVC covered plywood on three rows of cross battens which can be tensioned to provide ideal playing conditions for basketball, volleyball, badminton, handball or gymnastics. Equipment in this case has been largely built into the fabric of the building and is push-button controlled. When required, footballs can be lowered on steel wires from the ceiling, telescopic posts raised from the floor (to slot into portable basketball backboards, or vaulting horses), and 4 m long, up-and-over doors leading to the secondary equipment store can be raised to allow access from the hall.

Between each hall, experimental surfaces – some synthetic, some hard porous – form the basis of further test programmes. Great care has been taken to soften their appearance with trees and shrubs.

A research laboratory is also included for physiological and psychological work with students using treadmills, video cameras, and computers in keeping with the school's status as a major national training centre.

The aquatic centre was inaugurated in 1972 at a cost of 13 million marks provided by the Federal Government, the State of North Rhine-Westphalia and the city of Cologne, who built the project. A feature of the external elevations is the stainless steel cladding which can be seen glinting through the thickly planted surrounding trees, even on dull days. The entrance courtyard is walled and landscaped, and enriched with pieces of sculpture, including a richly embossed set of entrance doors approached by a covered way reached after passing through a control kiosk. Inside, the building is compartmented into separate activity areas consisting of a main 50 m eight racing lane pool hall, diving hall with boards (up to 10 m high reached by hydraulic tower),

a warm-up pool (12.5 m by 8 m) with adjustable floor for teaching purposes, and an intensive training room. This latter room can accommodate twenty-five persons at any one time using wall bars, dumb-bells and other pieces of apparatus permanently installed in the room.

There are several features worth noting in the design and fitting out of the main pool. In addition to the underwater window, electronically-operated starting blocks, and training clocks, there is a novel pacemaker system which provides swimmers with a series of flashing lights on the pool bottom, and in the ceiling which can pace swimmers at desired speeds, for a total distance of 3000 m programmed over 15 sections at various speeds set by the trainer.

If required a gantry-hung instruction platform can be used to move down the length of the pool immediately above the swimmers wearing hearing devices, for closer observation, measurement and instruction.

Timing devices record performances to $\frac{1}{100}$ of a second, and transmit these to a digital indicator in the hall, while giving the finishing order, and intermediate times over every 100 m. During water polo matches the scoreboard gives in addition to the score, the actual playing time and penalty times.

Windows around the pool are partially glazed with white opaque glass, which together with the close tree planting outside, minimise specular reflection on the water surface to acceptable levels throughout. A slatted metal ceiling serves as the main acoustic control in the hall (1.5 s at 500 Hz). Vertical slats over the viewing gallery are used to conceal light fittings and give a well controlled lighting level to all upper circulation areas in the centre of the building. Continuous bands of light run down the length of the hall above the pool. Walls at this level and below are clad in orange tiling. A Weisbaden edge detail allows deck level water to percolate through to perimeter overflow channels covered with a white plastic channel grating.

The diving hall has the same external wall treatment on two sides of the 20 × 20 m pool which has a depth of 5 m. On one side of the pool are five 1 m springboards, and on the other side two 3 m boards. An hydraulic tower can adjust the boards between 1.20 m and 3 m. There is also a diving tower with platforms at 3, 5, 7,5 and 10 m, reached by lift. All springboards are similar to those used at the 1972 Olympic Games at Munich. The surface of the water is sprayed with fine jets of water during training sessions and competitions. This gives divers better visual definition of distances between board and water.

An observation pit at the side of the deck level pool contains a large underwater observation window. This enables instructors to see and record on film or videotape the underwater stages of a diver's performance, for subsequent analysis and comment. A trampoline and dry diving unit with soft foam rubber padding are available in the training room for diving practice away from the pool.

The use of an adjustable floor to the warm-up pool is in keeping with current International Aquatic Board recommendations for training pools. This can be raised or lowered hydraulically to suit the needs of a wider group of users than in conventional training pools, including young children, adult non-swimmers, the disabled, and water polo players. The higher than normal water temperature (36°C) makes the pool particularly suitable for the disabled.

The adjacent athletics centre was completed in 1976 in order to put into practice changes occuring about that time in training techniques and bio-mechanical research. The resulting specialist sports hall is still among the best of its kind both functionally and architecturally, incorporating many features and finishes which are the envy of would-be sponsors around the world.

The hall can be divided into three zones for running, jumping and throwing events, each of which can be used simultaneously by three or four training parties. Audio-visual aids relay performances to the lecture hall in the main body of the institute, and data can be processed for record and instruction purposes. The jumping zone has force platforms at take-off points to measure the pressures involved, mounted on special foundations mechanically separated from the remainder of the hall floor.

In the throwing zone circles can be recessed after use into the floor. A roof-mounted three-sided retractable net is used for javelin hammer and discus throwing. A special plastic floor has been installed to take the impact forces of shot put practice and competition.

Apart from the throwing zone, the sand-coloured synthetic floor is 13–18 mm thick, suitable for all types of needle-spikes and giving the same measure of resilience as experienced on every Olympic running track since the mid-1960s. A special grating around the long jump pit prevents sand from drifting onto the surrounding floor. In the vaulting zone the box can be adjusted to three depths to enable the pole to bend more easily.

The hall floor has been marked out to provide a 140 m sprint track, and one bend of a 400 m track for relay baton-changing practice. The centre of the hall has an area of 30 × 20 m for general training and recreational activity. Retractable seating units for 512 spectators are arranged in two sections, and ancillary accommodation includes (in addition to the usual changing and shower area) two saunas, conditioning room (18 × 10 m), lecture room, staff work rooms and a 'cold dip' pool.

The saw-tooth roof system is illuminated by recessed 3-lamp reflector covered fittings, giving three levels of illuminations (200, 300 and 400 lux) as required for various functions.

The low level ceiling above the track zone has the same arrangement arranged parallel to the track for near ideal running conditions. Clocks showing actual running times have been installed beside each 'slave' clock, with switches available to give eleven optional preset times with automatic stops and acoustic signals.

A further hall was completed nearby in 1976 to serve as a national hockey and judo training centre, to identify and select potential performers to take part in inter-European, Olympic and world championships. Part of this process involves the use of bio-mechanical and sports-related medicinal facilities already referred to, without which no national training centre is complete these days.

The hockey hall is 52 × 30 × 8 m high which is one third the normal outdoor pitch size. This stands above the judo hall located in the basement which is 34 × 16 m in area. Both halls have seating for spectator events, 340 in the hockey hall and 224 in the judo hall. Both have access to changing rooms, showers, sauna, massage room, lecture rooms and a Japanese 'warming-up' pool heated to 41°C. A hostel block for 138 is also provided.

A feature of the hall is the glazed treatment to all external elevations by means of hockey ball-proof insulation glass inset into frames without the use of putty. This is in marked contrast with halls in Europe generally which are often unglazed, much to the irritation of planners concerned with visual amenity planning considerations.

Other features include a special training room with synthetic grass floor finish (PVC sprung flooring is used in the main hall), retractable hockey pitch markings, equipment for measuring performances, as well as a photocell system for measuring ball speeds. Padding is provided on internal walls to minimise damage to both the building and players. Video cameras are used extensively for training and instruction purposes; as elsewhere relayed to a audio-visual centre consisting of picture/sound control desk, recording table and firm fixing equipment.

In the judo hall a spring floor has been laid to cushion impact forces, even where protective matting is laid over the top. The floor to ceiling height is 5 m. Lighting is by means of fluorescent fittings (mercury arc lamps are used in the hockey hall). Four digital clocks and an electronic scoreboard have also been installed.

Bisham Abbey National Training Centre. Internal view of sports hall, which is lit only by artificial means. Each activity has its own special lighting arrangement. (Photo: Rice Roberts and Partners)

Bisham Abbey, Bucks, S. England

The 11 ha estate is bordered to the south by the River Thames, and was previously run by the Central Council of Physical Recreation as a national training centre, before being taken over by the National Sports Council, enlarged and run as a 'sports workshop'.

The purpose behind the construction of the large $72 \times 37 \times 9.5$ m sports hall is to provide specialist indoor facilities for a limited number of activities – in this case soccer, rugby, cricket, tennis, hockey, squash and weight-lifting squads – where players can be trained up to international level. Additional activities such as volleyball, basketball and badminton, can also be played in this space, and the community is encouraged to take advantage of these facilities when not required by the national teams, although the site is somewhat remote for this purpose. Its nearness to Heathrow airport however makes it a convenient location for incoming and outgoing national players.

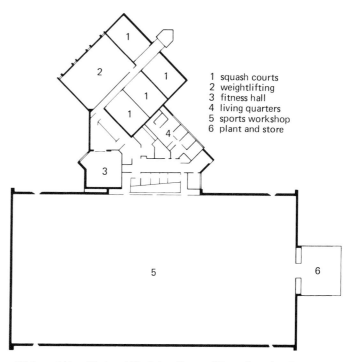

1 squash courts
2 weightlifting
3 fitness hall
4 living quarters
5 sports workshop
6 plant and store

Bisham Abbey National Training Centre. Floor plan. (Architects: Rice Roberts and Partners)

The 'workshop' has been designed to harmonise in colour and texture with the adjacent Abbey, and the scale relationship has been cleverly overcome by strategically placed mounds, trees and shrubs. Five residential units have been linked to the main building, which also includes ancillary accommodation in the form of social and refreshment areas, and an administration suite.

A feature in the main hall is the carpeted floor which has been taken up surrounding walls 3 m as a suitable backround and rebound surface. The latter are inclined at an angle of 10° to improve rebound characteristics.

No concession has been made for spectator seating, although a coaching gallery for 100 people has been provided on one long side. This position is also used for video camera research in addition to mobile cameras at floor level. A console mounted screen is used to play back film in front of this viewing gallery.

Lighting is entirely artificial and provides three levels of illumination by a combination of fluorescent tubes, and incandescent 'spots' mounted on ceilings and walls. Research has since been undertaken using this system to determine 'ideal' lighting mixes for different games, a difficult task when more than one activity is to be provided to these standards.

Air conditioning maintains inside temperature levels at a steady 13°C whatever outdoor temperatures may be; an important aspect of guaranteeing pre-match conditioning often found extremely difficult out of doors. The higher than normal ceiling in the main hall encourages this feeling however, although with hindsight it could have been even higher to accommodate tennis and badminton to internationally accepted conditions. A second floor bar and social room overlooks pleasant grounds. The main lounge can be sub-divided to provide a reception suite when required.

The centre is equivalent to those in central Europe but without the gadgetry as seen in the examples at Zeist or Cologne. Management is efficient, and better use is probably obtained of these facilities than one often finds elsewhere.

National Sports Centre, Papendal, Holland

The Papendal National Sports Centre is a 124 ha training centre standing on the outskirts of Armhem. Pine and beech woods form a tranquil setting for tennis courts, a nine hole golf course, a 5.3 km long road network for cycle training, a synthetic topped 400 m athletics track and artificial grass central area, a baseball field, sports pitches, a large sports camping centre, sports hall and swimming pools, an inflatable hall, a medical centre, a research station for turf and synthetic sports finishes, and two hostels with all the

Papendal National Training Centre. Indoor dry sports centre built in the early 1970s before the addition of the swimming complex.

Papendal National Training Centre. Part of the 80 × 24 × 9 m sports hall, arranged as a 'movement area'. This occupies only one third of the hall which can be divided into three segments by full height push-button controlled timber partitions

Papendal National Training Centre. The hostel serving the training centre is used by sports people when on short stay courses, and by non sports visitors, as during the 1980 Paraplegic Olympics

1 entrance
2 parking
3 social building
4 medical research centre
5 hostel
6 sports hall/indoor sports centre
7 aquatic centre
8 plant
9 office (ground staff)
10 sauna
11 tennis courts
12 grass pitches
13 hockey pitch
14 athletics track (synthetic surface)
15 golf driving range
16 handicapped golf course
17 train course
18 camping centre
19 sports testing laboratories
20 conditioning centre

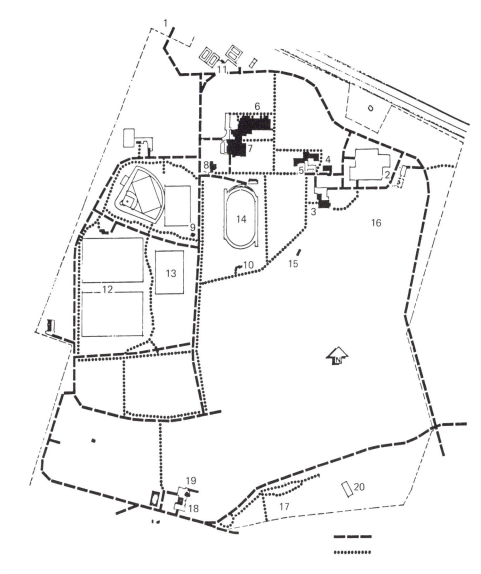

Papendal National Training Centre. Site plan

facilities associated with a good hotel. Finance was provided by money from national football pools and and the state lottery (TOTO). The centre is administered by the Dutch National Sports Federation.

User policy in the mid 1970s was originally aimed at encouraging gifted sports people to improve up to national and international standard, but more recently there has been a shift in emphasis towards encouraging greater use by local clubs and people, and in particular, paraplegics. As a result of facilities provided for the latter, the centre was selected in 1980 as the setting for the Paraplegic Olympic Games in association with the Rijhn Hall in Arnhem. Its strategic position in relation to West Germany and Belgium make it an ideal centre for regular European sports events.

The indoor sports centre was among the first buildings to be completed by the early 1970s and consists of a sports hall 80 × 24 × 9 m, meeting and lecture rooms, massage and medical facilities, fitness training room, a long gallery down the 80 m length used for equipment storage an paraplegic archery practice, and limited high level viewing space down the other side of the hall, which can also be used for video filming and instruction. A feature of the hall is the way it can be divided into three two-court hall size segments by full height timber-lined screens operated by push-button control, giving ideal training conditions for a wide variety of activities.

A large overhanging eaves minimises glare through the high level clerestory running down the north side of the hall. This is a design feature which was much used in the UK in the 1970s when built on south and west walls without the protection of a roof overhang. The cork lino floor (relaid in 1980), timber lined partitions, acoustically treated brick walls, and timber ceiling with inlaid bands of lighting, give excellent environmental conditions for training and occasional competitions.

The sports centre is linked by means of a generously large entrance hall to a new training pool complex completed in 1978, consisting of a main 30 × 25 m pool sloping from 1.8 m to 4 m deep in the 12 × 12 m zone associated with one and three metre high diving boards, and a 18 × 9 m training pool with a graduated depth of 0.49 m to 1.45 m.

The main pool corresponds in size to a similar training pool at the national football training centre in Zeist, both deliberately selected to emphasise their use for training rather than competition purposes. Three underwater windows have been provided to assist the teaching of correct swimming techniques, with radio communication also provided between instructors and swimmers. Video cameras can also be used to record swimming and diving techniques at these positions.

Hostel accommodation has twice been enlarged to cope with growing demand for short stay courses, and the main refreshment building has special facilities at ground level for handicapped users. A bar, lounge with open fireplace, covered terrace, and excellent canteen facilities match those provided at the Zeist training centre.

Research into various sports finishes has been put into practice throughout the centre. The central grass pitch inside the 400 m track has been replaced by artificial grass, the tennis courts have been resurfaced with layers of hard and resilient finishes, and an area of 45 × 30 m has been laid in artificial grass for basketball matches played by people in wheelchairs. Part of the cycle course has been finished with smooth asphalt to provide roller skaters with 'dry' training conditions.

The golf training course has 5 covered tees, a putting green, and midget golf courses around the refreshment building finished with eternit and concrete for paraplegic use. The inflatable hall serves as a tennis hall in bad weather for use by campers. A few artificial slopes have been formed around the running track for intensive condition training. Sports medical research facilities are provided to assist players before, during and after playing, and research data is made available to universities and research bodies worldwide.

The centre is administered by the Dutch National Sports Federation and many of the recent facilities have been provided as a result of funds raised from the TOTO national sweepstake and football pools.

Justification for the scale of provision seen on this site (bearing in mind the number of good indoor sports facilities elsewhere in the Arnhem district) has received a boost in recent years by the increasing use of facilities by local people wishing to keep fit, without going through the vigorous training schedules needed to reach national or international performance levels. At the same time the geographical position of the centre has attracted many gifted sportspeople from outside Holland to attend courses while living on site in the first class social facilities also provided.

Danish Sports Association Headquarters, Brøndbyvester, Copenhagen

This strongly articulated building is one of the few national training centres to include accommodation for the national body for sport, in this case the Danish Sports Association, and a number of subsidiary sports organisations. The resulting closely-knit liaison between each is claimed to improve administrative efficiency considerably, something sport has seldom managed to achieve in the past.

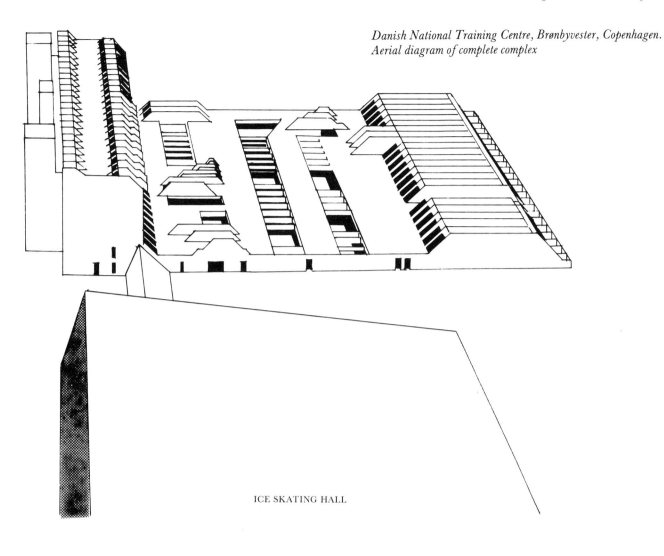

Danish National Training Centre, Brønbyvester, Copenhagen.
Aerial diagram of complete complex

ICE SKATING HALL

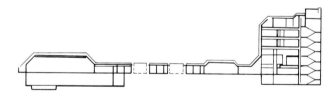

1 foyer	13 inspection flat
2 meeting rooms	14 instructor's room
3 reception/social area	15 bed-sitting rooms for students
4 chair	16 changing rooms with showers
5 congress hall	17 sauna
6 film room	18 sliding door store
7 group and lecture rooms	(for dividing the teaching hall)
8 courtyard	19 test room
9 auditorium	20 teaching
10 lounge	21 gymnastics room
11 library	22 small teaching hall
12 television room	

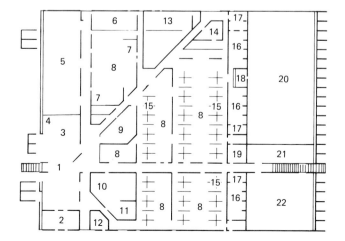

Danish National Training Centre, Brønbyvester, Copenhagen.
Sections and ground floor plan

National Training Centre, Canberra, Australia. Side elevation of model showing cable supports used to carry the 50 m × 40 m sports hall roof

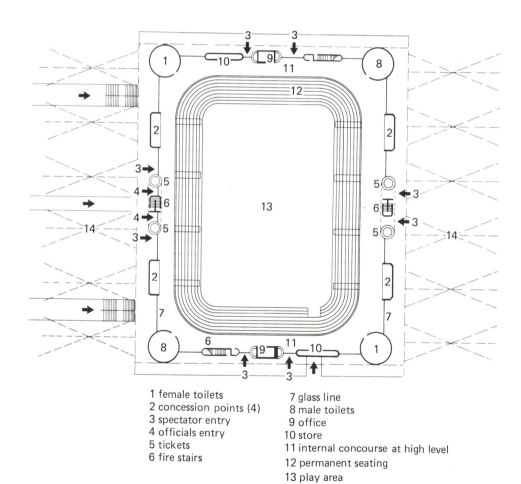

National Training Centre, Canberra. Plan

1 female toilets
2 concession points (4)
3 spectator entry
4 officials entry
5 tickets
6 fire stairs
7 glass line
8 male toilets
9 office
10 store
11 internal concourse at high level
12 permanent seating
13 play area
14 structural members as external feature of building

Standing just outside Copenhagen, the building can be easily identified by strongly modelled roofscapes overlooked by the five storey administrative unit bordering the entrance to the site. Instead however of looking down onto the usual roof finishes, the low level buildings have been broken up into a series of internal courtyards, giving views through into light and shade, and landscaping.

Each of the four uses undertaken in these buildings is expressed in parallel zones of spaces reserved for these purposes, linked at right angles to each other around the courtyards referred to earlier. These uses consist of playing and training in the large, timber lined and floored sports hall or outdoor pitches, attending lectures, using the resources provided by the centre (i.e. library, congress hall, film theatre and television room), relaxing in the first floor social rooms overlooking the double height entrance hall and ice skating in the hall to the south of the sports centre. The latter serves as the main orientation and reception space which leads to surrounding lounges, cloakrooms, a travel agency, and upper level canteen. Materials are traditionally Scandinavian, with concrete used in many forms to denote various circulation paths and reception/information points. Colour is also used for the same purpose to aid orientation, together with the lighting system. Thus reference points or changes in direction are picked out in strong colours and textures, and general circulation paths are kept subdued. This has resulted in a warm and inviting interior throughout the building in somewhat marked contrast to the grey anonymous appearance externally. This pleasant atmosphere is further confirmed by the treatment of the study bedrooms which face into landscaped patios through large double glazed picture windows and are equipped with worktops, excellent furnishings, and reading lights for further study and research.

National Training Centre, Canberra, Australia

The impetus needed to continue the development of this project came with the success of the 1977 Pacific Games. These were held in the first stage stadium, since used mainly for soccer and athletics matches, occasional pop festivals and sports carnivals.

Long term master plans have allowed for the inclusion of an indoor national training centre, an aquatic centre, a velodrome, human performance and sports research institute, a squash and tennis centre, special activity centre, and an all weather hockey field. Residential accommodation will be shared with the adjacent college of advanced education and national university, which will also provide additional research and computer resources. The first of these, the indoor training centre will be completed in 1981, to accommodate the complete range of 'dry' sports, and will be followed immediately afterwards by the national aquatic centre.

A feature of the indoor training centre is the cable structure carried on compression members supported by rows of peripheral pylons placed at right angles to the main axis of the building. As they pass over the pylons the cables become tension members which are taken to bed rock anchors beyond. Earth removed during the construction of the stadium has been used to form banking around the building to conserve heat and minimise losses through the fabric.

Spectators enter the arena at high level and circulate around a peripheral concourse before passing down to seating permanently located around the playing area. Players and officials enter at intermediate level below this seating before circulating to changing rooms and ancillary activity areas.

Refreshment rooms and mechanical services ducts have been sited in the four corners of the upper concourse level, with lifts at strategic points for use by the disabled. Media television coverage has been provided at high level with camera positions at predetermined points found by experience to be most suitable for each activity.

The main floor finish will be either in timber or PVC carpet laid on an 'air thrust' underfloor system to provide the necessary resilience for play at this level. Special matting and portable floors will be installed over this for events such as gymnastics or Olympic standard judo. Warm-up areas have been provided below the permanent seating, and storage rooms have been arranged in various sequences for greater flexibility. An access ramp has been provided for fork lift trucks if required in the main arena.

When completed the Aquatic Centre will provide Olympic swimming and diving facilities for national training squads, and recreational provision for the local community. Special features worth noting include the use of ozone for the water purification system (similar to West German and French practice), a movable boom in the main 50 m pool to provide two 25 m training pistes, a one second reverberation time at 500 Hz in the main pool hall, 10 to 15 air changes per hour, a deck level pool system throughout with raised touch pads at the ends of the 50 m pool, underwater lighting, and a dry land training area between the main Olympic standard pool and 25 m warm-up pool.

The National Centre will eventually become the focal point for sports research in Australasia, by the provision of additional lecture theatres, analytical laboratories. A national coaches' centre will publish up to the minute data affecting playing or training schedules.

Chapter 7
Sports grouping in community facilities

The principle of sharing social, educational and recreational services at community level has long been recognised in many parts of the world. This is particularly the case in western Europe where it has been the main means of provision in the smaller communities since the early 1930s.

The first experiments along these lines in the UK in the present century can be seen in the Cambridgeshire village colleges pioneered by Henry Morris between 1920 and 1939. These became the focal point for village life with the shared use of studios, workshops, recreation facilities, libraries, and many other aspects of community life. This was a forerunner of the present day resource centre concept such as the Stantonbury Centre at Milton Keynes (see page 106).

The combined conservatism of English educationalists during that period saw little progress along these lines elsewhere in the country, and it was not until educational progressives renewed these ideas in the late 1950s in Durham, Northumberland, Cumberland, Leicestershire and particularly Nottinghamshire, that further experiments in forms of 'joint use' policy were initiated.

The success of similar policies in West Germany and Scandinavia in the early 1960s, provided the necessary stimulus for a major programme of shared recreational facilities on school sites, strongly backed by the newly formed national Sports Council. Nottinghamshire led the way with projects at Carlton Forum, Worksop and Bingham, which were the subject of much interest both in the UK and in the Commonwealth. The early 1970s saw rapid progress in many other parts of the UK, with perhaps the Wester Hailes example in Edinburgh the most noteworthy from a design point of view (see page 104).

Somewhat surprisingly, the relationship between 'town and gown' use of university facilities over this period rarely extended to the excellent sports centres available for student use. A notable exception was Lancaster University where policy has encouraged joint use with excellent results for all concerned. To be fair to other universities however, it became obvious that student use at this level of provision often approached the same intensity as at comparable American universities, and the extension of extramural vacational courses left little time throughout the year for outside participation.

The development of joint uses

By the mid-1970s enough was known about joint use policy for further development to be implemented. This has been done at Milton Keynes and Sutton-in-Ashfield (Nottinghamshire), where the concept has been widened to include many other aspects of Henry Morris philosophy, including the involvement of medical and social services. At the same time it was generally recognised that many problems had occurred which required adjustment in these newer projects. These included problems of caretaking, joint management interests between headmasters and recreation managers which often led to open conflict, vandalism on school premises, and legal technicalities which required changes to Education Acts and legislation at the highest level. Today many of these barriers are removed, although the exclusion of the public during the day from sports facilities used exclusively by schools, still causes some concern, especially when compared to the open use of all outside community-funded projects.

The last problem, together with the increasing sophistication called for by the general public, had led to many of the earlier projects being regarded as 'second grade', or Tier Two in planning jargon. This implies suitability as training centres for sports clubs, where 'fun' and 'leisure' facilities feature little in the overall policy of provision. Notable exceptions, however, are the Wester Hailes and Sutton projects where it can be seen that these concepts can be

Sutton Centre, Sutton-in-Ashfield. External view of ice rink. (Nottinghamshire County Architects Department. Photo: Gerald Perrin)

Sutton Centre, Sutton-in-Ashfield. View of bowls hall adjacent the ice rink. (Photo: Gerald Perrin)

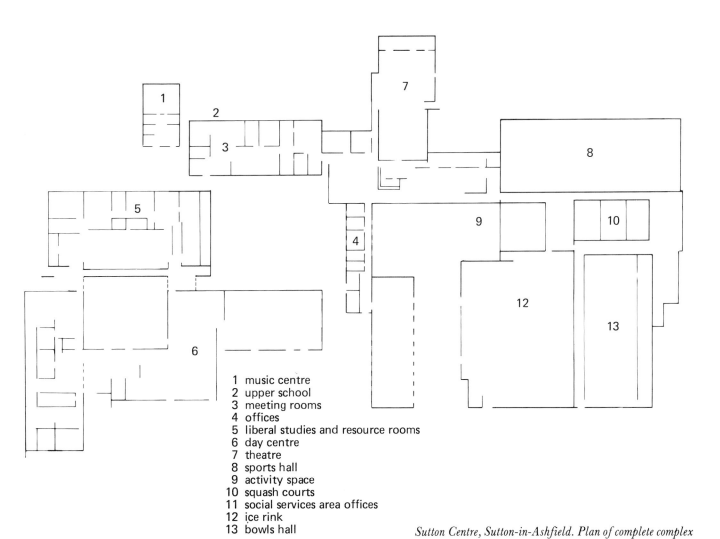

1 music centre
2 upper school
3 meeting rooms
4 offices
5 liberal studies and resource rooms
6 day centre
7 theatre
8 sports hall
9 activity space
10 squash courts
11 social services area offices
12 ice rink
13 bowls hall

Sutton Centre, Sutton-in-Ashfield. Plan of complete complex

incorporated on the school campus if the brief and management input are clearly organised with this in mind.

By the late 1970s other forms of joint provision were beginning to appear both on and off the school campus, throughout Europe. Experimental projects involving many aspects of community life, including the arts, and commerce emerged and were studied with much interest. The Karregat venture in Eindhoven described on page 98 attracted much attention, with the most recent results indicating the need for adjustment and further monitoring in order to gain a clear picture of the way ahead in this field. Comparisons have been made between this project and a similar concept at The Cresset Centre in Peterborough (UK), see page 102, where an even wider spread of community services, including those associated with the deprived and handicapped, has received much attention if only because of the way in which sponsorship has included local authorities, the church, and local business interests. This appears to be working well in practice and is showing a profit from the first year of operation.

Covered communal spaces

Many good examples using these principles, and adapting them to new forms of covered communal spaces have appeared during the same timescale elsewhere. Romsai in Oslo, the Kerpen High School near Cologne, and Bielefeld High School are among the best examples due to their excellent planning, and standard of finishes. Sable-sur-Sarthe in France is another where experimentation led initially to problems with the inclusion of a sixth form college, but with commonsense and new management policies it has achieved a remarkable turn round in mutual cooperation and workability (see page 107).

Eldon Square Shopping Centre in Newcastle, and the Hoog Catherijne project in Utrecht, have extensive sports facilities included to provide a strong recreational service where it is most in the public eye and where the commercial input can be used to subsidise this service. The Newcastle centre is – like The Cresset example – one of the few to achieve some form of viability in an area all too well known for its loss-making characteristics. The Catherijne project has also developed a series of public spaces at key changes in direction as 'event' points, used for impromptu busking, demonstrations, viewing television data programmes and special events such as the World Cup series, and many other happenings. This design feature has also been included in a similar development at the Kawasaki Plaza near Tokio,

where it has gone much further by including a 500 seat theatre, a 30 m 5-lane swimming pool covered by a retractable roof, provision for senior citizens, and 'meeting places' suitable for tea ceremonies, art shows, and exhibitions.

There can be little doubt that the next decade will take these ideas very much further. The scope for innovation and experimentation, given a sensible brief and good management back-up in practice, is considerable, and in the view of many will be the main avenue for progress in the field of both sport and the arts. For a contrasting approach, readers should compare this section however with that dealing with urban recreation parks described in chapter 8.

Case studies

The Karregat Centre, Eindhoven, Holland
This is the second of two experimental projects commissioned in the early 1970s to assess public reaction to new forms of community provision, and to monitor the subsequent interaction between various user groups in order to arrive at a point where this feedback could be used to frame future development policy in the Netherlands.

Designed by the architect/engineer Buro Van Klingeren, it takes the concept for a single large meeting place (or Agora) seen at Dronten, a stage further by the inclusion of two nursery and primary schools, shops, a supermarket, medical and social services, and recreational spaces. All these being grouped around a central open concourse intended for large scale meetings, events and concerts. The relationship of these elements to each other and their openness to the large central area, attracted much international attention when the centre opened in 1973, if only out of curiosity to see if they would work in practice. The building has been the subject of many subsequent revisits by architects, social workers, and those connected with the field of education worldwide.

Planning commenced in 1970 following consultation with neighbouring communities, bearing in mind that work on this new suburb for 5000 on the east side of the city had not then started. It therefore anticipated many of their needs in abstract, and made many assumptions which in practice were either found to be wide of the mark, or disliked by subsequent users. However, the framework provided for changes to be made to the original design without the need for major structural alterations within a very loose-knit planning concept which characterised its appearance, and shaped later patterns of use considerably.

Finance for the project came from two main sources. Commercial elements occupying 2100 square

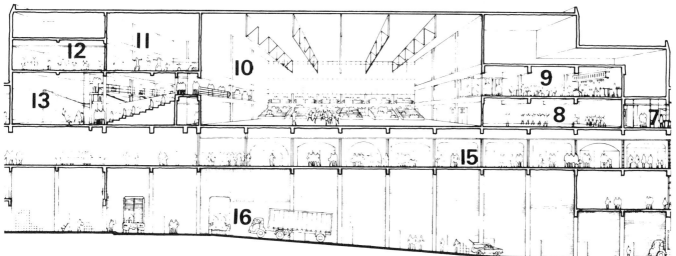

Eldon Square, Newcastle-upon-Tyne. Plan of sports centre sited above indoor shopping precinct. (Architects: Chapman Taylor & Partners)

7 administration	10 main sports hall	13 squash courts
8 fitness room	11 fencing gallery	15 shops
9 spectator bar	12 judo room	16 service road

Eldon Square, Newcastle-upon-Tyne. View towards 8 rink indoor bowls rink across shopping concourse. (Photo: Gerald Perrin)

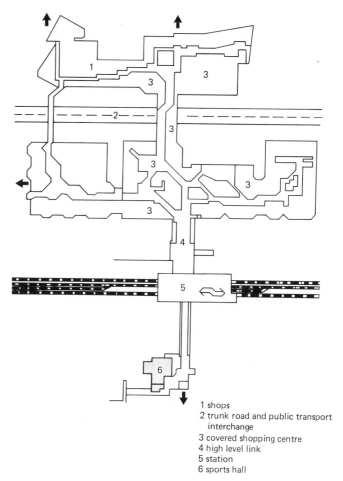

1 shops
2 trunk road and public transport interchange
3 covered shopping centre
4 high level link
5 station
6 sports hall

Hoog Catherijne, Utrecht, Holland. Plan of indoor shopping precinct over the city's main traffic interchange (road and railway), with Sports Centre at bottom left

metres of floor space were provided by the Amro Bank of Holland, and the remaining 4650 square metres by the Municipality of Eindhoven. The total mix comprised two nursery and primary schools, four shops, a bank, branch library, pub-cum-cafe, a youth and social centre, medical centre, music school, community areas and a meeting room. A later addition was the petrol station on the north side of the building adjacent the supermarket service area.

The long low external appearance was given human scale by the formation of a 2.5 m high mound on which the building sits, surrounded by extensive and attractive landscaping. Interest was provided both externally and internally by a series of glazed pyramids which stand on a framework of steel struts cantilevered from central clusters of supports as seen in the diagram, each colour coded to denote different user areas and activities inside the building. Construction took less than ten months to complete.

Zones of use were picked out in much the same way as seen in burolandschaft office planning, using planting, changes in level, drapes, and extremely light-

Karregat Centre, Eindhoven, Holland. General view after 7 years use. (Architects: Buro Van Klingeren. Photo: Gerald Perrin)

Karregat Centre. External childrens play area. (Photo: Gerald Perrin)

Karregat Centre. Central concourse area used for roller skating, pop disco sessions, film nights and meetings with a capacity of 2000 (Photo: Gerald Perrin)

Karregat Centre. View of the original pub and cafe area with the library on the right and medical centre to the left, taken shortly after opening. Each unit has now been partitioned off, and the bar/cafe area replanned. (Photo: Gerald Perrin)

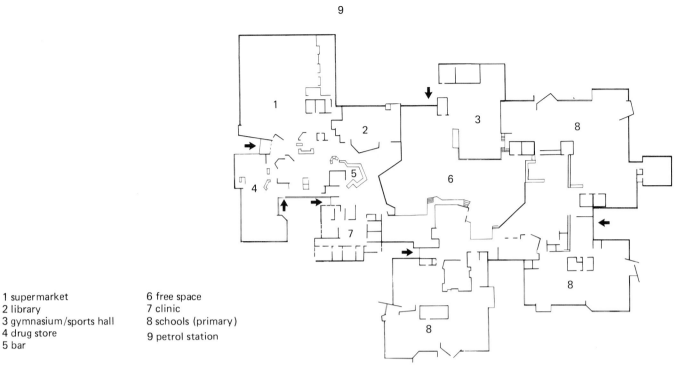

1 supermarket   6 free space
2 library   7 clinic
3 gymnasium/sports hall   8 schools (primary)
4 drug store   9 petrol station
5 bar

Karregat Centre. Plan of complex as originally built in 1972

weight partitions. Services were slung below the roof in a series of loops, again coloured to indicate different activities: and six different points of access as shown on the plan, were originally provided to emphasise the openness, or 'de-clustering' concept of the project.

It was hoped that by removing these formal barriers mutually profitable relationships would develop, particularly between the schools and the community, and between senior citizens and young people. For a time this did in fact happen. Parent participation flourished, greater interest than normal was taken in school work, the children were able to gain much from closer social contact with the grown up world, especially in the field of recreation, and sponsors were delighted at the success of the experiment. All this was however short-lived. After six years the sight and sounds of passers by proved a serious distraction to both children and teachers.

Some of the relationships between user groups resulted in open conflict (for example between the open pub and the adjacent library). Pressures developed, the period of educational innovaton came to an end, and the initial enthusiasm died away and the absence of any form of organised management did little to help matters.

The obvious need at this stage to set a new course was precipitated by the educational authorities who insisted in 1978 on the installation of formal divisions between the schools and central concourse, and alterations to the acoustics, air-conditioning and hygiene services to these areas. This process was repeated in other parts of the building to the point where little of the original interior remained intact. Public access points were reduced to one (other than to the shops), and after years of consultation with the local authority, local residents succeeded in placing the management of community affairs in the hands of a district services committee with considerably more freedom of movement at decision-making level than hitherto. A full time manager was appointed with part-time staff assistance, and an annual maintenance budget of 100 000 guilders was allocated for this purpose.

Today one sees very little of the initial concept apart from the exterior which remains intact. This is still attractive and is set off by mature landscaping of the same high standard seen in many parts of western Europe. Inside, however, elements have become self-contained and traditional in appearance, but still retaining views through windows into classrooms, and the sports hall/gymnasium. The bar/cafe has been completely renovated, and the installation of 1000 litre storage canisters in the bar store have removed the brewer's delivery van from the premises together with the barrels that did so much damage to paving when being unloaded. This is a plus factor just noted by suppliers in the UK. The youth centre has been refurbished, and the sports associations are flourishing, along with the hobbies section which include chess, draughts and photographic clubs. To date over six million guilders have been spent on refurbishment, a figure likely to double when the medical centre moves out in 1983 and other facilities take its place.

The community makes good use however of the central open space which can accommodate up to 2000 spectators (although 1500 are preferred as being more manageable). The various differences in level help give identity to film nights, jazz sessions, and meetings. These attract people from a wide catchment area outside Eindhoven.

Looking back with hindsight, many conclusions can be drawn from experience to date. Some people have felt that the juxtaposition of some original elements was bound to lead to open conflict. Schoolteachers are rarely happy when watched at work by parents. The lack of any formal management did not match up to the intellectualism of the design and the original public consultation was, in the eyes of others, a huge waste of time and public funds.

At the end of the day the users decided they did not like the experiment, the planners received the feedback they were looking for, and the designers got a mixture of praise from other architect/planners, and criticism from the clients. Society has a useful tool with which to make future decisions, although some would argue at a price which is not acceptable.

It is interesting to speculate, however, that had the project received the same degree of highly organised management expertise as at The Cresset Centre, whether the original concept would have faded quite so quickly. In a rapidly changing society the loose-fit planning of the Karregat makes infinitely more sense than the more solid cellular structure used at The Cresset, much of which will probably still be there in the same form in the year 2050 unless removed with some difficulty. A marriage between the two sound principles of each project would appear to be the obvious conclusion, as time will tell when the present rearrangement at the Karregat has had its own reassessment in a few year's time.

The Cresset, Peterborough
This complex of shops, social and recreational services, occupies a 1 ha site serving a neighbourhood unit on the north west side of the city centre. Sponsorship was jointly provided by the county council,

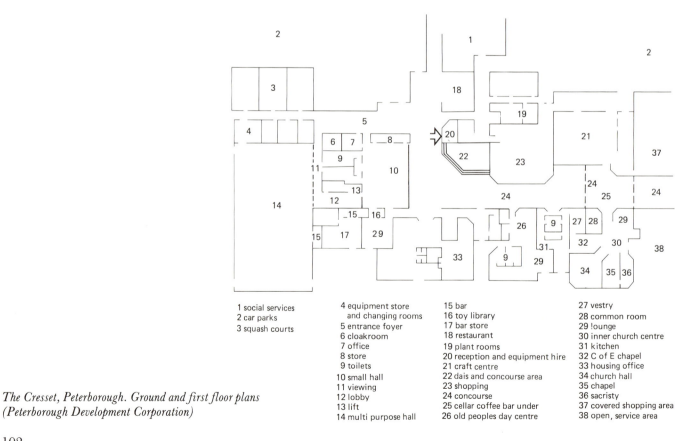

The Cresset, Peterborough. Ground and first floor plans (Peterborough Development Corporation)

1 social services	4 equipment store	15 bar	27 vestry
2 car parks	and changing rooms	16 toy library	28 common room
3 squash courts	5 entrance foyer	17 bar store	29 lounge
	6 cloakroom	18 restaurant	30 inner church centre
	7 office	19 plant rooms	31 kitchen
	8 store	20 reception and equipment hire	32 C of E chapel
	9 toilets	21 craft centre	33 housing office
	10 small hall	22 dais and concourse area	34 church hall
	11 viewing	23 shopping	35 chapel
	12 lobby	24 concourse	36 sacristy
	13 lift	25 cellar coffee bar under	37 covered shopping area
	14 multi purpose hall	26 old peoples day centre	38 open, service area

city council and development corporation, and voluntary societies. On completion, in 1978, the total cost was three million pounds. Control is vested in a company with limited liability status, which by itself is unique in the UK, quite apart from the fact that since coming into operation the centre has been self-financing. It has therefore attracted attention from many countries and from many would-be sponsors within the UK.

The main objective was to provide a much needed centre for community provision in the fields of sport, education, and recreation, with strong emphasis placed upon integration of the aged, handicapped, and counselling agencies. By sharing and meeting one another within this framework it is believed that much better understanding will result between groups of differing backgrounds and capabilities.

Another aim was to fund the costs of running a full community programme out of revenue, especially from the shops, restaurant and bars provided for this purpose. This again at the present time is almost unique in the UK where only a few projects make an actual profit (even when discounting municipal loan sanction charges).

The hub of the project is the main concourse which acts as the central meeting place for major elements on either side, and for all visitors to the Centre. It also serves as a setting for exhibitions of art and local

history, bring and buy sales – usually for charity – and many other informal but carefully managed 'happenings'.

A raised platform at the intersection of the concourse with the recreation centre is frequently used as a stage, exhibition area, and as a setting for recreational chess and draughts tournaments. It is also a popular meeting place for much the same reasons as the sunken amphitheatre illustrated in the Therapeutic Recreation Centre on page 25. Much the same feature can also be seen in the community school project at Sable sur Sarthe illustrated on page 107.

The Cresset, Peterborough. Concourse area, used for jumble sales, meetings, and informal 'happenings'. (Photo: Martin Howard. Courtesy of The Architects' Journal)

The Cresset, Peterborough. Reception is situated just off concourse area adjacent the main refreshment lounge, and is much in the public eye. Security and control in such open surroundings requires special attention. (Photo: Martin Howard. Courtesy of The Architects' Journal)

The Cresset, Peterborough. View of multi-purpose hall used for sport and business hirings. (Photo: The Cresset Centre)

Just off the main concourse is the main reception area for the recreation centre where bookings can be made, equipment hired, and staff contacted by radio call system anywhere in the building. The open plan arrangement confounds the belief held by many managers that access to facilities should be via turnstiles and a tight system of control at all entrances. This system also encourages the public to use the bars and restaurant provided of their own free will, in much the same way as they would in any shopping centre. In the restaurant a waitress service is provided each evening when the demand for a more sophisticated approach is thought desirable. This is yet another departure from standard UK practice in sports centres, where refreshment services are usually of 'motorway' standard, or obtained from vending machines.

The main hall has been conceived as a multi-purpose area which, in addition to providing sports facilities, can be used for wedding receptions, banquets, discos, and meetings. This type of use is accepted as a compromise situation, although considerable attempt has been made to provide the soft furnishings and lighting arrangements called for by the latter.

Considerable care has been taken throughout the centre to ensure access for the handicapped to all major elements. Activities officers are responsible for arranging physical recreation and educational programmes for this specific group of users. Similarly the elderly are encouraged to attend film and slide shows, story reading sessions, and recorded concerts. At the other end of the age scale the young have a coffee bar where they can meet youth workers in their own world of jukeboxes, and wall 'doodles'; a far cry from the more structured arrangement of more conventional youth clubs.

Finishes, as one would expect, have been designed to stand considerable heavy use, with buff coloured facing brick, brick paviours and hardwood much in evidence. Lighting is appropriate for the areas it has to serve, with certain occasional built-in problems such as the use of spot-lighting in the multi-purpose hall where the probability of damage from sports users must be high.

The Centre makes for interesting comparison with the other comprehensive community projects described in this chapter. Compared with the Karregat Centre which has been conceived along similar lines, it has a high degree of caring and professional management. It therefore appears busier, more integrated and more successful in achieving its original objectives. On the other hand the architectural style is dull compared with the Dutch example, and 'fixed' immutably by its use of permanent materials, and finishes. It

therefore lacks flexibility and it will be difficult to rearrange the major elements easily, as at Karregat, if this becomes necessary in the future.

As an example of effective management integration between all age groups in the community it would appear infinitely more successful than any other case study in this section. With a Karregat-style approach to design and planning this example could provide would-be sponsors with most of the clues they need for future buildings of a similar nature.

Wester Hailes Education Centre, Edinburgh
This complex serves a new housing area of 20 000 people on the outskirts of the city, including schooling for 1400 pupils. A single management structure provides for both the school and leisure centre, although both elements have been physically separated as seen on the site plan.

Adults have been given the opportunity of taking part in what is known as a 'second chance' policy, to study for certificates of education together with schoolchildren. The latter are encouraged back in the evenings and when they leave school to take part in the general programme of recreation. Youth clubs and other community groups are offered their own facilities, and the creative arts have been provided with a theatre and hall for music, drama, art, and film society use. Additional courses are provided for business studies, car repairs, typing and cooking.

The campus consists of five blocks, arranged to form internal concourses, quadrangles and car parks. These are linked visually by the use of rendered common brickwork and stained timber frames and fascias. The main feature of the leisure centre is a free form, deck level pool with three interlinked zones for competition swimming, diving and children. It is one of the few examples in the UK to carry this concept into the field of joint school provision.

The pool arrangement comes the closest of any recent aquatic projects in the UK to achieving formal conventional swimming objectives within a loosely-knit leisure framework. This is considerably cheaper than the general European system of providing separate pools for each activity group. The plan follows the same principle as at the Royal Commonwealth Pool by the same architects, where ancillary rooms surround the pool hall and minimise the problem of specular reflection on surface water caused by natural lighting.

The relationship of height to width in this area is excellent, and the strongly modelled ceiling provides one of the best acoustic standards of any swimming pool in the UK. This is normally difficult to achieve where natural lighting is placed over the pool area and

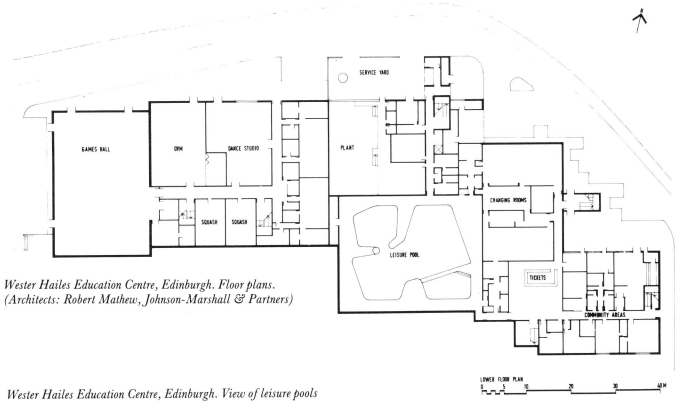

Wester Hailes Education Centre, Edinburgh. Floor plans.
(Architects: Robert Mathew, Johnson-Marshall & Partners)

Wester Hailes Education Centre, Edinburgh. View of leisure pools
with childrens splash pool in foreground. Competition events are
possible in the main irregular-shaped 25 m pool. (Photo: Architects)

105

diffused with plastic liners; another good reason for the planning solution seen here. Internal planting, and a number of 'fun' features such as the stepping stones between the two main pools, also serve to break down noise levels considerably. An attempt has been made to provide some form of competitive swimming in the principal pool by the provision of racing lanes down its length, although the irregular shape at either end must lead to some difficulty in judging results.

Other facilities provided include a large sports/games hall, gymnasium, dance and drama studio, two squash courts and outdoor all-weather and grass pitches. Community involvement also includes a small hall seating 230 people with a small stage platform at one end, two lounges, one intended as a disco space, the other as a lounge bar, and two general purpose rooms.

Completed in 1978, this was one of the first purpose-built community schools in Scotland to allow all departments simultaneous use by the general public. The cost of £5.9 m was provided by the Lothian District Council, and administration is undertaken by the local Education Department working from an adjacent administration wing. The Centre is of particular interest for its higher than normal standards of finish and design flair, especially in the aquatic area, which is on a par with any in the UK at the present time.

Stantonbury Campus, Milton Keynes

Milton Keynes is the largest of the English new towns with a projected population target in excess of 250 000 when completed about the turn of the century. The original recreation master plan called for a series of district scale sports centres throughout the town, of which the first was Bletchley Leisure Centre (see page 000) and the second is this Campus situated in the north-eastern periphery.

The contrast between each recreation centre is considerable. The Bletchley Centre marked the beginning of a trend away from 'pure' sports centres to a more relaxed approach to playing games in a highly sophisticated environment. The Milton Keynes Campus is a highly organised educational resource centre serving three *in situ* secondary schools, and a post-school college, in which 'pure' sport has been provided as an educational tool serving part of the learning process, with no concession made to 'leisure' or the illusory surroundings normally found in such settings.

The focal point of the campus is the Resource Centre which has been designed in 'H' form, with one wing serving dry and 'wet' sports, and the other as as information retrieval centre containing language laboratories, video cameras, tapes, typewriters and a library. The high level link between the two is used by the schools to gain access to the sports facilities during the day, and as an informal refreshment area serving the sports facilities at one end and a small theatre at the other. Doors at either end control access by both schools and the public.

Pool provision is in the form of a strictly conventional scum-channel type 25 × 12.5 m wide main pool with a teaching bay to one side of the shallow end, and an informal viewing gallery at first floor level down one long side. This leads into a meeting area serving as general purpose refreshment room and games space with a servery at one end and higher level galleries above. On the other side of this room is a one-court sports hall with high level galleries on two sides to augment seating at hall floor level for large scale spectator events such as boxing or weight lifting tournaments.

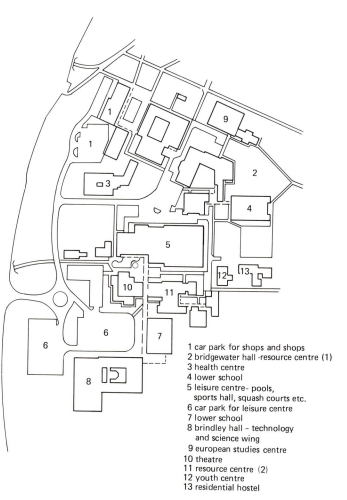

1 car park for shops and shops
2 bridgewater hall -resource centre (1)
3 health centre
4 lower school
5 leisure centre- pools,
  sports hall, squash courts etc.
6 car park for leisure centre
7 lower school
8 brindley hall – technology
  and science wing
9 european studies centre
10 theatre
11 resource centre (2)
12 youth centre
13 residential hostel

Stantonbury Campus, Milton Keynes. Site plan of secondary school resource centre, with indoor sports centre on left. (Milton Keynes Development Corporation)

Ancillary accommodation includes a leisure-conditioning suite (known in the USA as a 'slimnasium'), and the usual changing rooms and administration offices. The status of the latter is one of complete autonomy within the framework of the resource centre. This is one stage removed from the normal community school relationship, and eminently more satisfactory.

Green curtaining has been provided to both ends of the sports hall where clerestory windows have been provided – a feature which was dropped in the middle 1960s due to problems of glare – and the position of the badminton courts down the length of the hall is also unusual in view of this feature. Boarding has been used with a vertical joint as a dado around the lower half of the hall, in which doorways have been finished with an 'invisible' frame lined flush with the inside wall face. The ceiling is lined with a series of inverted timber troughs designed to provide players with good cut-off light angles below.

The building is finished externally with steeply pitched roofs finished with tiles, over red brick walls and brick tiles paving. Good landscaping has helped give a strong feeling of college cloisters and quadrangles to the centre.

The project has been in use since the mid-1970s which is sufficiently long for its reputation to become established as a successful pioneer venture in the context previously described. This has attracted considerable attention from Third World countries, particularly the Middle East and Nigeria. With the introduction of more up to date sports facilities the concept would be a very attractive middle of the road level of provision, and must considerably influence future provision at this scale.

Sable sur Sarthe, France

There is a considerable number of experiments involving community schools throughout the continent of Europe. This example has been selected as being typical of the problems and solutions encountered between preparation of the brief and practical operation some years later.

The town lies 260 km south west of Paris in the heart of a prosperous agricultural region. The fabric of the town however, had been allowed to deteriorate over many years, and in 1975 a series of public consultation meetings were held to invite suggestions for revitalising and improving this situation. These were followed by a survey aimed at assessing the best means of achieving what were considered to be the most immediate objectives. The outcome was the preparation of a brief for a community school, as the best means of bringing together many facets of town life in the one centre.

A meadow near the town's shopping centre was selected as the most suitable site, bounded by a public park and river, and containing an existing swimming pool. A slope of 8–16° was used to plan the building on various levels using a series of mezzanines to achieve physical separation between public and school use during the day. The result of this was to confine uses to specific floors and also to encourage the 'discovery' of the building stage by stage.

Education Centre, Sable sur Sarthe, France. Perspective of centre showing 'stacking' arrangement used to segregate different types of user.

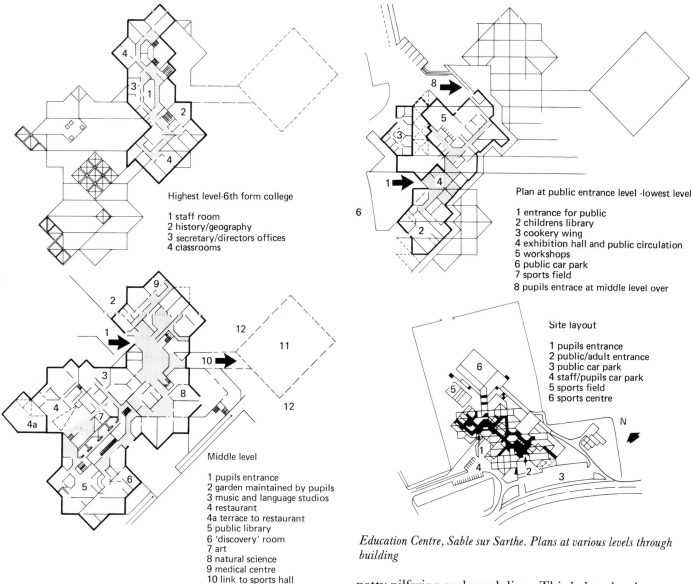

Highest level-6th form college

1 staff room
2 history/geography
3 secretary/directors offices
4 classrooms

Middle level

1 pupils entrance
2 garden maintained by pupils
3 music and language studios
4 restaurant
4a terrace to restaurant
5 public library
6 'discovery' room
7 art
8 natural science
9 medical centre
10 link to sports hall
11 sports hall
12 recreation areas

Plan at public entrance level -lowest level

1 entrance for public
2 childrens library
3 cookery wing
4 exhibition hall and public circulation
5 workshops
6 public car park
7 sports field
8 pupils entrace at middle level over

Site layout

1 pupils entrance
2 public/adult entrance
3 public car park
4 staff/pupils car park
5 sports field
6 sports centre

Education Centre, Sable sur Sarthe. Plans at various levels through building

Elements have been arranged in compatible groupings which achieve a considerable saving in floor area. Teaching units, workshops, laboratories, arts and science rooms, libraries, sports areas, circulation meeting spaces, and administration offices each have their own zone of use. As can be seen from the plans these elements are linked vertically, culminating at upper floor level in a 900 pupil college with a srongly defined house system each with a house tutor. Public access is therefore at lower floor levels, and school at the upper level, with a common meeting ground in the sports facilities. Pupils also have access to the park where they are responsible for a small zoo and botanical garden.

When the building came into use in 1978 a number of operational problems soon came to light, including petty pilfering and vandalism. This led to the closure of all educational areas to the public, and the school being barred from access to the sports facilities. Much of this trouble was put down to the handover of major elements being phased as they were completed. There was also the factor of inadequate supervision and management control due to shortage of staff.

Since the complete handover and the appointment of a full staffing complement most of these problems have evaporated. The building has become fully operational along the lines originally intended with every indication of a successful future. The separation of public from school use, except at contact points in the form of public meeting areas and sports zones is particularly successful, as is the design concept of the building and its enclosing spaces. This does however, illustrate the need for a management input from the outset and this should be written into every future brief of a similar nature.

Chapter 8

Urban rest and leisure parks

Urban play parks are assuming an increasingly important role within the framework of present-day society, especially as open space continues to be eroded by other land uses. The inner cities have been particularly affected in this respect, and the introduction of synthetic materials described in chapter 9, has done little to ameliorate the situation despite increasing the intensity of use of small pockets of available space.

Growing interest has therefore been taken of other means of providing play space, and especially of rehabilitating existing urban parks provided originally in Victorian times along similar lines to West German and Scandinavian examples which appeared in the 1960s and have since proved one of the more successful experiments of this decade. Their name 'rest and leisure parks' derived from the researches of the West German sports philosopher Carl Diem, whose observations of public use of older parks led to their rehabilitation along user patterns he had identified as being mainly associated with 'learning, rest, observation, and play'.

The later case study of the Gruga Park in Essen is typical of many 'Bundesgartenschau Parks' designed between 1960 and 1975, while the Cologne example illustrates another design approach using an overhead cable chairlift as a means of providing visitors with panoramic views of all facilities at a glance.

The much smaller example also illustrated at the Planten und Blomen Park, Hamburg is of a much more recent project which uses a miniature train to take users from one section of the park to another. Water 'cannons' and artificial mounds are provided to stimulate a good deal of intuitive play and design interest, in addition to the lakes, trampettes, and crazy golf courses sited around a natural hill in the centre of the park, used as an observation area and refreshment spot. A feature of all these examples is the excellence of the landscaping on which little expense appears to have been spared, and the short time it has taken for

trees and shrubs to mature, aided by a policy which believes in planting 'big'.

Similar parks although on less ambitious scales may be seen in Holland and Scandinavia, where water has again been used to good effect both for its appearance and use for recreative forms of play, for example sailing model boats. The Amstel Park in Amsterdam has several areas reserved for children's play and pony rides, and the excellent little detail of a slide, located at a major change in site levels.

Bundesgarten Park, Cologne, Germany. Overhead chairlift carries visitors to every part of the park. (Photo: Gerald Perrin)

Bundesgarten Park. Artificial play mounds for children. (Photo: Gerald Perrin)

Bundesgarten Park. Bandstand with Otto Frei tent covers. (Photo: Gerald Perrin)

Planten und Blomen Park, Hamburg, Germany. View of central area linked to other activity areas by miniature railway. The park is one of 4 in the South West of the city near the Aussen Alster Lake. (Photo: N. Polytechnic DMS course)

Canon Hill Park, Birmingham. Trampolining held in one of the open air theatres. (Photo: Jackson and Edmonds)

Canon Hill Park, Birmingham. Plan of complex also known as the Midlands Arts centre for Young People. This is part of Canon Hill Park, opposite the county cricket ground and is being developed by the Canon Hill Trust as an ambitious ten-year project encompassing the complete recreation spectrum. Sport is one of several leisure uses planned into the project. (Architects: Jackson & Edmonds). (By courtesy of the Midland Arts Trust)

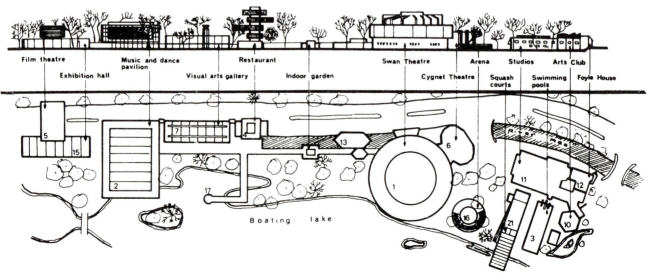

Development in the UK

Few direct comparisons can be seen at the present time in the UK, although many similar features have been included in new town park development, and in the examples later in this chapter. Several alternatives have however begun to appear within the past five years, notably the restructuring of several existing sports centres, as at Eastleigh in Hampshire, into leisure parks where riverside walks, lakes, play mounds, and crazy golf courses are to replace *in situ* sports pitches to be relocated in other areas of the town. In the case of Eastleigh , these will be linked to amenity areas associated with the existing 18-hole golf course. Together with the large indoor sports centre, this centre will form one of the largest recreation complexes on the South Coast, with 'something for everyone'.

One of the features is a planted nursery which will provide much of the material for this long term proposal. This will enable shrubs and trees to be installed in semi-mature form, as in West Germany, to minimise vandalism and make an immediate impact on site.

The examples at Ballymena and Irvine have yet to be fully implemented, but when complete will be among the best in the UK, with many interesting design features associated with local conditions and weather characteristics. The funding of these projects is such, however, that many years often elapse between a start being made and completion, with the result that new objectives appear, and initial enthusiasm wanes. The possibility of private sources of finance being used for these purposes, as part of a planning gain exercise, is being actively pursued despite the political overtones this sometimes generates.

An example of this is the Lee Valley Regional Park where fifteen years elapsed between designation, and the provision of the first major objectives described in the case study, largely as a result of economic constraints imposed by successive governments since 1965. To the north east of this park lies Harlow New Town, where parkland has been gradually developed along a hillside overlooking the Stort Valley, with zones of interest located within natural landscape features. For example, the river itself has been designed as a walkway linking an outdoor canoe and pursuit centre, boating lake, cycle velodrome, and motorbike training centre. A natural hollow has been turned into an area accommodating several thousand people watching pop concerts and firework displays. An old watercress bed has been reformed as a series of ornamental pools, while an old mansion is used as a refreshment centre, attached to a children's zoo and roller skating rink.

An example which comes closest however to 'learning and watching' may be seen at the Midlands Arts Centre for young people at Canon Hill Park, Birmingham, where part of mature parkland has been built on to provide several indoor and outdoor theatres, a theatre workshop, and a boating lake. To these will be added a film theatre and museum to complete the range of 'experiences' offered to users, who already include a fair proportion of adults.

Some international projects

There are many other examples now in various stages of completion in France, USA, and Japan, from all of which common factors emerge. The range of users is obviously very much larger than for the active end of the leisure spectrum alone and the age range is correspondingly wider. The setting for the sports facilities provided is considerably more sympathetic than in many alternative urban areas. Car parking is easier and much more flexible than in conventional sports centres. The opportunity to expand, or to adapt to new and changing user needs is considerably greater. Inter-relationship between sport and the arts within the framework of intelligent landscaping involves a much wider cross-section of society, with long term beneficial factors to all, especially the family unit which is much more likely to participate in this type of environment than any other available to date.

Apart from these conceptual points, practical features to be considered include the desirability for a short term 'impact' pattern of provision, with facilities for longer term infill or adaptation; making the most of existing natural resources; and framing the earliest forms of provision around known existing needs, as in the case of the Lee Valley example.

The obvious success of these projects suggests the possible direction that future large scale sports facilities could take. After all, the Munich Olympic arena is part of a parkland setting. In this way one will come infinitely closer to the ancient Greek concept of sport as an art form, and much closer to the 'illusory quality of life' believed by many to be fundamental to our present existence.

Case studies

Gruga Park, Essen, West Germany
The 81 ha site stands beside the autobahn linking Essen to other parts of the Ruhr Valley. This scheme

Gruga Park, Essen, Germany. Swimming complex with wave pool on left. The whole area often attracts between 25 000 and 30 000 people on fine summer days. One of several restaurants in the park is to the right. (Photo: Gerald Perrin)

Gruga Park. 'Gondola' fun pool. (Photo: Gerald Perrin)

Gruga Park. Outdoor table tennis played on concrete tables. (Photo: Gerald Perrin)

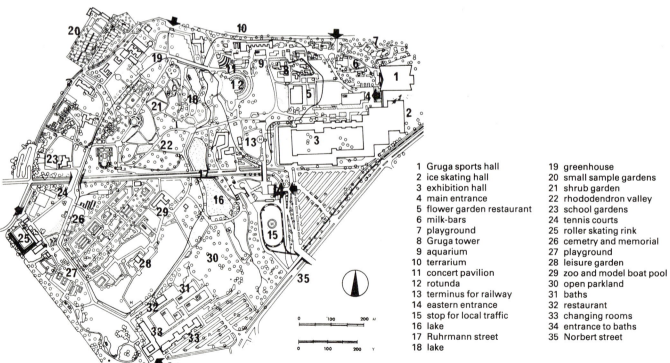

1 Gruga sports hall	19 greenhouse
2 ice skating hall	20 small sample gardens
3 exhibition hall	21 shrub garden
4 main entrance	22 rhododendron valley
5 flower garden restaurant	23 school gardens
6 milk-bars	24 tennis courts
7 playground	25 roller skating rink
8 Gruga tower	26 cemetry and memorial
9 aquarium	27 playground
10 terrarium	28 leisure garden
11 concert pavilion	29 zoo and model boat pool
12 rotunda	30 open parkland
13 terminus for railway	31 baths
14 eastern entrance	32 restaurant
15 stop for local traffic	33 changing rooms
16 lake	34 entrance to baths
17 Ruhrmann street	35 Norbert street
18 lake	

Gruga Park. Site plan

was begun in 1929 as a series of botanical gardens, all of which were destroyed during the 1939–45 war. They were reconstructed by 1952, including the tropical houses and large indoor sports hall – the Grugahalle. By 1962 the outdoor swimming pool complex consisting of two Olympic-sized pools, one wave pool and one Olympic-depth diving pool, and exhibition hall had been added. The Grugahalle was rebuilt to accommodate large scale spectator events including indoor cycle-racing.

In 1965 the park was selected as the site for the Bundesgartenschau, and was enlarged to include land used after 1945 as allotments. The full range of facilities shown on the site plan were completed for the summer opening exhibition, and well over 2½ million visitors a year have been recorded through the entrance kiosks every year since.

The principles used in the design were based upon the zone concepts suggested by Carl Diem described in the introduction to this chapter. Areas were set aside for: learning; observation (botanical gardens, lakes, terrarium, hothouse gardens, and rhododendron valley); rest and leisure (parkland, memorial ground and concert pavilion); and play (roller skating rink, pony riding ground, tennis courts, trampette area, swimming, indoor sports, ice skating hall and adventure playgrounds/pools). Refreshment facilities are scattered throughout the park at strategic positions, and all major elements are linked by miniature railway. An observation tower overlooks the whole site.

Added interest can be found in the area zoned as a small zoo and model ship lake. Wild fowl and flamingoes have been encouraged to breed on various lakes sited at key vista positions. The peripheral planting and hard edge detailing around these waterside picnic areas is of the highest order, and attract many visitors and traditional wedding walkabout parties.

Mature trees and shrubs were planted as a deliberate policy designed to give the park immediate impact, and allow areas such as the Japanese and alpine gardens to develop more slowly within their own micro-climatic conditions. Both hard and soft landscaping are an object lesson in design techniques intended to exploit such features as vistas, enclosures, scale relationships, textures and colour.

Great care has been taken to ensure adequate ground preparation, maintenance (which is highly labour intensive), and general supervision, although vandalism does not appear to be the problem it is in many other countries. The very high quality of the facilities provided in fact seems to command a form of respect from all but the small handful of children who may feel inclined to misbehave – although superintendants quickly appear at the scene of any disturbance.

On warm weekends well over 25 000 to 30 000 people gather around the swimming pools to swim and sunbathe or eat and drink in the restaurant provided for this purpose overlooking the pools. Every half hour a klaxon gives notice that the wave pool is about to start operating and hordes of youngsters rush to the artificial beach on which waves of variable height and direction land.

Admission to the park is by ticket offices at six entry points, one of which is to the pool complex only. Once inside there is no further obligation to pay to use general public areas of the leisure gardens and parkland. Additional charges are however made for any of the optional extras such as pony rides, boating on the gondola pool, or pitch and putt course. Many have found it a very enjoyable way to spend a day with the family for a reasonable outlay financially. The park is a favourite stopping off place for tourists from Holland, Britain and Scandinavia en route south on their holidays.

It is worth comparing this example with the following case study of the Lee Valley Regional Park, if only to note the contrast in scale, speed of development, financial input, and accessibility. Probably the biggest single difference lies in what has been called the 'impatient factor'. People do not appear willing to wait twenty-five years to see planting mature, or facilities provided piecemeal. They prefer to have everything installed in one swift building and planting period, so that when the various elements start to decay or fall out of fashion they can be replaced or rebuilt, as was the Grugahalle on the same site (a saving in itself) and to new requirements.

Confirmation of this policy can be seen all too clearly in the many UK examples which started with so much enthusiasm in the mid-1960s only to peter out ten years later as this drive diminished. The earliest facilities no longer met changing demands, and financing became very much more expensive due to inflation. The Gruga Park still serves as a model urban park worthy of attention for its design skill, philosophy of use, and 'instant provision'. Its impact has been sufficient to provide much food for thought in the long term planning of large scale sports facilities throughout Western Europe.

Lee Valley Regional Park, North London

One of the few regional park proposals of the 1960s to approach fruition in the UK is this example in the Lee Valley running between north London and south east Hertfordshire 37 km to the north.

In the early 1960s the area consisted of disused sewer works, old gravel pits, rusting machinery, abandoned glasshouses (the ground is rich alluvial deposits), power stations and pylons which still dominate the skyline. The potential of the area as a playground for Londoners was recognised by many who knew it well. These included Sylvia Crowe the distinguished landscape architect, and Michael Dower in his article the 'Fourth Wave' published in 1965.

In 1967 an Act of Parliament set up the Lee Valley Regional Park Authority consisting of members from local authorities bordering the valley. Several years were spent in acquiring land, setting up nurseries, researching user patterns, and generally laying down the foundations of development infra-structure now appearing as firm projects attracting by the end of the 1970s over two million visitors a year.

The spine of the proposals was the River Lea (to give its original spelling) and its centuries old 'banks' which rarely exceed 5 km in width. Along these banks, many traditional contact points had been made with north-south traffic routes including the A10 main road to Cambridge, the main line railway to Kings Lynn and Norfolk generally, and the junction with the river Stort at the northernmost point of the valley. High ground and reservoirs act as a physical contraint to the east, and housing development to the west and south. For years, north Londoners had turned a blind eye to the dereliction around them, and had come for weekend picnics, fishing expeditions, boat rides, cycle meets and walks. In more recent years they have been joined by the 'new-towners' from Stevenage to the north west and Harlow to the north east.

Lee Valley Regional Park, Broxbourne Lido. External view to one of several large scale indoor projects located at strategic points throughout the park. This is the first stage of an indoor sports centre sited at the junction of a main railway line and inland waterway system. (Photo: Gerald Perrin)

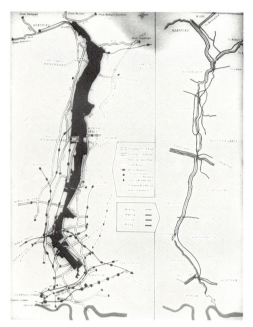

Lee Valley Regional Park, N.E. London. Site plan (Lee Valley Regional Park Authority)

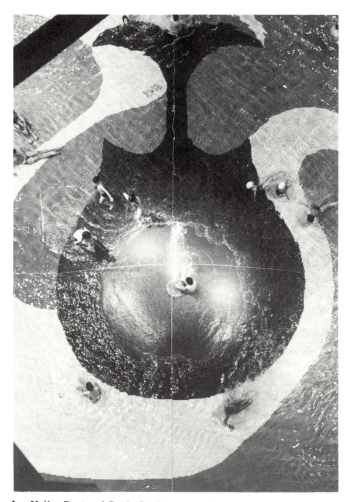

Lee Valley Regional Park. Birdseye view of indoor pool complex, Broxbourne Lido, with the 'whale' clearly seen at the shallow end of the wave pool. (Photo: LVRPA. By courtesy of the Design Council)

It is not surprising therefore to find these contact points as focal points for early development work, as a glance at the park layout clearly indicates. Picketts Lock was the first major project to be opened in 1973, to be followed by the Lea Bridge Riding Centre, King George Sailing Centre, marinas at Springfield and Stanstead Abbots, the Eastway Centre (squash, cycling and outdoor sports pitches), Banbury Sailing Centre, and the Broxbourne Lido (leisure pool). Picnic areas, riverside walks, a countryside park and a model farm (Hayes Hill) were also developed over the same time scale, while a massive planting programme transformed huge areas of the countryside very much for the better.

The valley is still a working lung of London. Each day commuters travel past these facilities en route to the City of London. Gravel workings are still producing sand and gravel for major development programmes in the south east of England. The sewage outfall from the two New Towns is treated in a sewage farm at the north end of the valley, and power is generated for the region nearby. Perhaps therefore the most important point to make is that the Park works, perhaps because of these new facilities and because people have been used to coming there for many years.

The facilities offered are workmanlike and designed for mass user participation at the contact points referred to. Picketts Lock has one of the largest indoor halls in the country intended for multiple use including roller discos, exhibitions, boxing tournaments and mass meetings. In addition there is a two-court sports hall, squash courts, a small free-form pool (intended that way in order not to compete with the Broxbourne Lido), ancillary games rooms, and an 18-hole pitch and putt course adjacent to six all-weather pitches (three floodlit) for soccer, hockey, netball and tennis.

Lee Valley Regional Park. Lea Bridge Riding Centre. General view of indoor equestrian centre. (Photo: LVRPA)

Broxbourne Lido stands besides the river Lea at a traditional centre for fishing, sailing, rowing, and boating on narrow boats catering for a thriving holiday trade. The main line station is less than 500 m away. The huge glass enclosed outline of the building forms a landmark for some distance which, like the Bletchley pyramid (see page 70), tends to attract visitors as much out of curiosity as anything else.

Inside several pools combine to give a 'fun' image by means of their free shapes, wave making machinery, 'waterfall', spouting 'whale' and high level enclosing glazing (bronze tinted) allowing views out to the landscaping around. Little concession has been made to competition requirements, and with a maximum water depth of 1.2 m little opportunity is provided for serious swimming or diving of any kind – the ultimate perhaps in 'bobbing' pools. A high level walkway leads to a refreshment area overlooking the pools, and will eventually lead to a dry sports project on the other side of the river. Sunbathing areas have been laid out on the south and west sides of the building for long stay users. Structural steelwork over the pool is exposed and painted light green as a feature of the overall environmental quality of the building.

The Lea Bridge Riding Centre is the first of three intended to provide basic indoor and outdoor training facilities for beginners and recreational use, or occasional horse shows. When the other two centres are completed they will be linked by bridlepath making it possible to ride the full length of the Park, 37 kilometres (23 miles), on horseback. The character inside the Centre is traditionally workmanlike, and expressed by the exposed structural framework, facing brickwork and brick paviors to circulation areas.

A PA system has been provided for class instruction. Outdoors are paddocks for grazing the twenty-

Lee Valley Regional Park. Fashion show at side of main pool, Broxbourne Lido. (Photo: LVRPA)

five horses and ponies, and a menage to introduce riders to outdoor work within a controlled area until they are ready to ride to the nearby Walthamstow and Leyton marshes.

Water-based interests have been provided with marinas, sailing hards, repair shops, toilets and refreshment rooms at key points along the river, and rehabilitated gravel workings. All these make it possible to explore the Thames estuary and upper reaches of the Thames at one end of the park, and the attractive open countryside at the other.

New changing pavilions have been provided for the many sports fields at the southern end of the Park. Hackney Marshes has over one hundred soccer pitches used at the same time each Sunday morning during the playing season. In the same location, the Eastway Centre is being developed as a major indoor sports centre, which includes twelve squash courts, a two-court sports hall, and outdoor playing areas. Another feature of this Centre is a cycle road racing circuit and clubhouses as the focal point for the many enthusiasts traditionally found in this part of London.

The decision to build the national rowing centre near Nottingham has affected the proposal for a 2000 m rowing course in the centre of the valley, although a strong local rowing tradition exists which will find expression in the many sections of the river suitable for this purpose until new facilities are finally provided. Future plans for a tower and hotels indicate the possibility of some commercial involvement which is much needed to inject the massive capital required to complete the original master plan. The decision not to proceed with the proposed main link road, or an alternative monorail system could influence future strategy considerably.

When completed (although development will then continue on an *ad hoc* basis as new needs appear) the project will compare favourably with similar parks in continental Europe, for example the Ruhr Valley Regional Park in West Germany, and may serve to encourage the development of similar areas of dereliction, elsewhere in the UK.

The main lessons to have been learned from this particular example are that there must be a strong local user tradition for the activities proposed, with sufficient flexibility in the original master plan to allow for changing needs, and ideally, sufficient capital should be made available at the outset to ensure that all primary objectives are completed within as short a time as possible. The latter in particular demands a strong political commitment from all concerned and it is perhaps this factor more than any other which provides the main point of departure between UK projects at the present time and those elsewhere.

Irvine Beach Park and Magnum Leisure Centre, Scotland

It is unusual to find a New Town developing tourism as one of its industries, but the location of Irvine as a seaside town overlooking the Firth of Clyde and Isle of Arran make it ideally suited for this purpose. This has not been an easy process thanks to years of industrial dereliction and waste deposited in considerable bulk within walking distance of miles of unspoilt beaches. Despite their background these have long been used for day outings and picnics by Glaswegians.

The master plan designated 61 ha (120 acres) of this land as a leisure park and sports centre, and reclamation was begun in 1975 by the town's Development Corporation. The work began with the removal of the more invidious areas of waste deposits, and ended with topsoiling and reshaping the reclaimed land into the present parkland. Sand dunes were replanted with hard-wearing grass, and mounded to provide interest. Viewing space for spectators watching play on one of the sports pitches was also provided.

Zones of privacy were provided for those preferring peace and quiet and a park and ride transportation

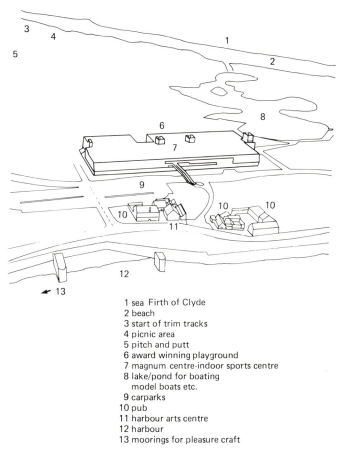

1 sea Firth of Clyde
2 beach
3 start of trim tracks
4 picnic area
5 pitch and putt
6 award winning playground
7 magnum centre-indoor sports centre
8 lake/pond for boating model boats etc.
9 carparks
10 pub
11 harbour arts centre
12 harbour
13 moorings for pleasure craft

Irvine Beach and Leisure Park and Magnum Centre, Scotland. Layout of project with Magnum Indoor Centre in foreground. (Irvine Development Corporation)

system was introduced to avoid cars entering this area. (Special provision was made for the elderly and handicapped to reach the beach in their own cars – one of the few concessions to motorised forms of transport). Stage one was opened in 1978 consisting of a 12 ha (30 acre) lake suitable for canoeing, rowing, and sailing model boats, an artificial ski slope, tennis courts, a trim track (for fitness training), bowls greens, roller skating rinks, crazy golf course, rifle range and several sports pitches. Later additions will include facilities for yachting, wind-surfing and swimming.

The focal point and heart of the park however, is the Magnum Leisure Centre opened in 1976. As its name implies, this is one of the largest indoor recreation complexes in the UK, with a two-court sports hall, indoor bowls hall, ice-skating and curling rink, cinema/theatre, two swimming pools – one of which is a free-form leisure pool – squash courts and ample facilities for social interchange and refreshments.

Dual use is encouraged in the sports hall and cinema/theatre with the frequent programming of conferences, exhibitions and seminars, in typical sea-side tradition. The Centre was sponsored by the local authority (in this case Cunninghame District Council) who is also responsible for administering the Beach Park as a whole.

The use which has been made of these facilities has exceeded all expectations, and at times more than 10 000 people are on the premises at any one time. The unpredictable nature of the weather in this area however, as in the case of the Dutch polder towns development, more than justifies indoor leisure facilities on the scale seen here. It would seem more than appropriate if future provision were to be biased towards other forms of indoor facilities, including those for the arts – using the parkland as a pleasant linking agency similar to that seen in Holland and West Germany, or the Tivoli Gardens in Copenhagen on which large parts of the concept are modelled.

The spin-off effect of this development has already made a significant difference to tourism in the area, and to the appearance of the old town and harbour of Irvine, large parts of which had been given a facelift in best Civic Trust fashion. Whether the older inhabitants welcome such changes, or the influx of visitors, especially to the Magnum's skating facilities, is another matter, although in terms of income this must be to the advantage of all local ratepayers. Getting the cost of running the Centre down from the near £1m per annum mark however will remain a problem until

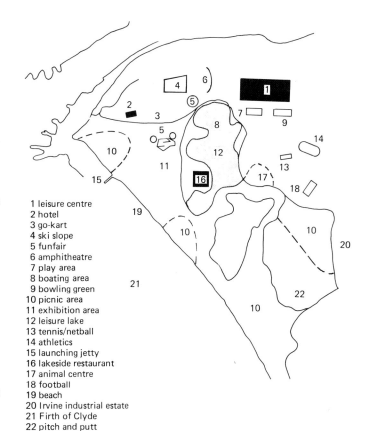

1 leisure centre
2 hotel
3 go-kart
4 ski slope
5 funfair
6 amphitheatre
7 play area
8 boating area
9 bowling green
10 picnic area
11 exhibition area
12 leisure lake
13 tennis/netball
14 athletics
15 launching jetty
16 lakeside restaurant
17 animal centre
18 football
19 beach
20 Irvine industrial estate
21 Firth of Clyde
22 pitch and putt

Irvine Beach and Leisure Park and Magnum Centre. Site plan

Irvine Beach and Leisure Park and Magnum Centre. View of ice rink with curling 'bullseyes' in foreground. (Photo: Director of Lesiure, Cunninghame District Council)

117

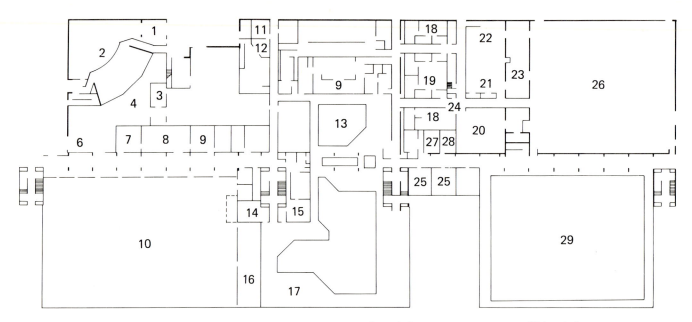

either loan repayments have been made or staffing is reduced by the installation of more automatic devices along West German lines.

Ballymena Town Park, Northern Ireland
Although implementation of these proposals is still some way off, the concept behind this 105 ha project is very similar to that at Irvine Beach Park in Scotland.

The site designated for the development is situated between the town centre and the adjacent M2 motorway, through which the River Braid will feed two large lakes which will be stocked with game fish. Bird sanctuaries are to be encouraged on artificial islands in the lakes, which school parties can observe, together with plant life of the area, as part of conducted tours organised between local schools and the park management. Sculpture will be sited in appropriate parts of the site. Other areas will be laid out as bog and ornamental gardens, livestock paddocks for the annual Balleymena Town Show, daffodil trial areas, and a riverside walk beside the lakes.

The town sports centre will form a focal point in the plan and will include a two-way facing grandstand for spectator events on both sides of the main arena. A cycle track, kart track, and ancillary sports pitches complete the 'stadium' element of the park. A nature trail will link this to other sections and neighbouring residential areas.

When completed, the project will attract visitors from much of mid-Antrim, and like Irvine, will derive a substantial income from tourism. Much will depend however on the availability of finance to complete the park in as short a time as possible if it is to gain maximum benefit from these proposals.

1 workshop	16 heated area
2 stage	17 main swimming pool
3 switch room	18 female sports changing
4 theatre seating over	19 male sports changing
5 plant room	20 practice room 1
6 store	21 practice room 2
7 male changing	22 practice room 3
8 cloakroom and skate hire	23 store with target range over
9 female changing	24 foyer entrance hall over
10 curling/skating rink	25 toilets
11 staff	26 sports hall
12 office	27 female bowls changing
13 teaching pool	28 male bowls changing
14 main pool store	29 bowls hall
15 sauna lounge	

Irvine Beach and Leisure Park. Lower level plan of Magnum Centre

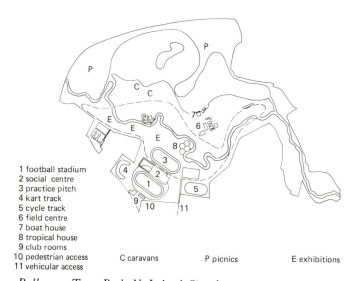

1 football stadium
2 social centre
3 practice pitch
4 kart track
5 cycle track
6 field centre
7 boat house
8 tropical house
9 club rooms
10 pedestrian access
11 vehicular access

C caravans   P picnics   E exhibitions

Ballymena Town Park, N. Ireland. Site plan

118

Chapter 9
Stadia

The opportunity to design and build stadia on the scale described in this chapter only rarely occurs. When the opportunity does arise the project is usually hedged around with intense political activity at local and national level which more than anything does much to shape the final planning and appearance of the final concept.

The influence of the Olympic movement

The modern Olympic movement is typical of this process, and yet has provided the vehicle for many of the most impressive examples of sports architecture seen this century, although at a cost many would argue had been unacceptable to the host countries concerned. Tokio (1964), Mexico City (1968), Munich (1972), Montreal (1976) and Moscow (1980) have all contributed to this process, raising standards of building just as much as those of the athletes performing in them.

If a choice had to be made between these projects, Munich would probably emerge as the concept which came closest to the Olympic ideal of harmony between sport and the arts. This had the flowing form of the roofscape by Otto Frei, reflecting the landscape forms below, and since 1972 has been used for 'happenings' and arts-orientated events on a growing scale.

Olympic facilities however represent only a fraction of the stadia built around the world since the 1964 Tokio Games. The World Cup soccer series, Commonwealth Games, Mediterranean and Asian Games, have all contributed to this movement, as have the growing number of sponsored tennis and baseball events. Each has added something unique to stadia design, whether it is the floodlighting towers in the South American examples, or the special electronic scoreboard seen in the 1980 Moscow Olympics.

The most significant development, however, to appear in the past decade has been the new role of stadia as centres for everyday community recreation . This is particularly the case of the generation of stadia beginning with the Real Madrid project, and continuing with the Dusseldorf Rheinstadion example (see page 125), which have been concceived specifically along community lines.

The traditional reluctance of professional clubs to share with the community (even where thcsc may be members of the club concerned) has been a large obstacle to similar development in the UK, especially in the world of soccer. This is further compounded by tax laws which provide no incentive to improve or rebuild facilities which in many cases were first used in Edwardian times.

It is refreshing, therefore, to see the way recent development at this scale of provision on the European mainland has taken the initiative in the design and planning of many recent imaginative stadia. These buildings incorporate features which many feel are essential to meet present-day standards of comfort, hygiene, and design sophistication.

The stadium at AFC Eindhoven, for example, is one of the first to be rebuilt in Holland on the site of the old ground, where orange-coloured plastic seating has been provided for 75% of the spectators, with covered accommodation for all. Floodlighting masts are slim and elegant, and ample car parking space is provided even though the ground is located in the centre of the city. All exits are spacious and adequate enough to ensure reasonable crowd safety conditions which are now universally required. The quality of the grass on the soccer field is above average and looks most photogenic on colour TV, for which purpose the fescue was selected.

Dusseldorf stadium, described later, is an example of a new project on a site located just outside the city periphery. In addition to the seating and cover conditions referred to at the Eindhoven ground, there is a wide range of additional sports facilities for round-the-week use by the public, at a nominal charge per head.

The Peace Stadium at Yokahama on the other hand is an example of high technological innovation which includes devices to move large sections of stand seating according to the game being played. It includes retractable baseball pads, artificial grass to the main arena, and floodlighting which can be adjusted to three levels of illumination depending upon whether it is required for match play, training or colour TV broadcasts.

In the Sharjah Stadium in Saudi Arabia similar technology has been installed in anticipation of a rapidly growing market in the sports field. In many respects the clients concerned have obtained the latest ideas relating to stadia planning, with none of the growing pains experienced in many developed countries. Problems of maintenance however remain – as they do in most African states – and it has been interesting to see the appearance in 1980 at the Moscow Olympics of several electronic devices requiring little or no maintenance skills.

Upgrading of existing facilities

It is at the level of the local 'stadium' however that there exists most scope for upgrading existing facilities. Examples are at Harlow (see page 77) and Paris, where synthetic materials have given a new lease of life to facilities long past their best.

The capital investment for these projects is however high, and experience shows there is also a reasonably high labour content involved in maintaining these surfaces in good condition. On the other hand they enable many more players to use them in all weather conditions, and surfaces give the adequate playing characteristics looked for by the present-day athlete. The arrangement of the training ground in the centre of Paris, would appear to meet most of the problems associated with inner city play space, although the material used could be one of many now on the market for such locations.

Such materials are only part of the answer, however, to extending the period of use. Floodlighting is equally important, and it has been noticeable that even at this level of provision standards have improved appreciably over the past decade. At full stadium level the improvement in design and technology has been even more marked, with many recent examples refined to sculpturesque lines when seen in the context of an urban landscape.

Scope for further improvement exists in establishing a synthesis between planning, design and technological objectives, geared to the needs of a public increasingly looking for improvement, innovation, and standards probably more geared to the world of entertainment than sport.

Case studies

Stadium Olympiapark, Munich, Germany
The 280 ha site stands 4 km from the city centre. The decision to choose Munich as the setting for the 1972 Olympic Games involved not only the construction of the sports facilities, but also a new network of communications involving the underground, federal railway, trams, motorway system and parking arrangements.

Olympiapark, Munich, Germany. Aerial view of Frei Otto roof which gives the complex its particular well-known character. The 290 m tower and its revolving restaurant, was one of the few existing features when work commenced in 1966. (Architects: Benisch and Partner. Photo: Olympiapark, Munich)

Olympiapark. View of conical steel pylons which support the stadium roof. (Photo: Olympiapark, Munich)

Olympiapark. Interior of velodrome, which has a seating capacity of 5000 around the afzalia-boarded track. (Photo: Olympiapark, Munich)

The only extant features on the site were the 290 m high television tower, a well-known Munich landmark, and a mound of rubble which had been formed into toboggan and ski runs. Otherwise it was flat, monotonous, and completely barren of landscaping quality. The decision was therefore taken to make the project the subject of an international architectural competition (with a first prize of 100 000 DM). Considerable emphasis was placed in the brief on achieving harmony between the buildings and their surroundings, in much the same manner as the Greeks had done 2500 years earlier.

The extent to which this has been achieved in the winning design by Benisch and Partner can be judged from the illustrations, but can probably be better assessed by the fact that the Otto Frei-inspired 'tent' covering to the stadium and surrounding buildings has since become internationally renowned, and the flowing curves of the spaces between these elements are still a delight to walk around today. Reading through the architects' submission to the international jury, it is clear how they arrived at this particular solution by simply following Greek philosophy involving the use of elements such as Alpheios (river – in this case an existing canal), Kronion (hill – which already existed apart from reshaping), Altis (central area – which was used here to form the core of the design in

the form of an 8 ha lake), Propyla (tower), and Iera Odos (way).

Construction began in 1966 and was completed six years later. The project was paid for with funds provided by the Federal Government, the State of Bavaria, the City of Munich, television and sweepstake lotteries, several sports organisations, and other states. Funds were also raised by the worldwide sale of specially minted coins.

Olympiapark. General view of 2000 m rowing course still used regularly for regattas and rowing events

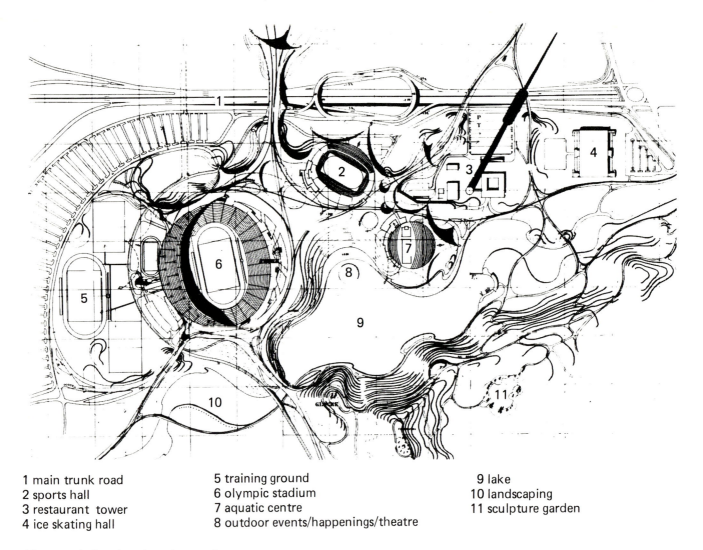

1 main trunk road
2 sports hall
3 restaurant tower
4 ice skating hall

5 training ground
6 olympic stadium
7 aquatic centre
8 outdoor events/happenings/theatre

9 lake
10 landscaping
11 sculpture garden

Olympiapark. Site plan of complete complex

For many people the most remarkable design feature is the 75 000 m² of translucent acrylic glazing forming the 'tented awnings' to the west stand of the stadium, the sports hall and swimming centre. This is carried on a steel cable mesh system curved in two directions to avoid the possibility of 'flutter' and, in turn, on tall double conical steel pylon clusters selected for their known resistance to buckling. The complete assembly was prestressed before erection.

The flowing lines produced by this arrangement have been repeated at ground level by the shape of the forum surrounding the stadium, and the footpath system leading in all cases to the central area and lake. Around the latter, earth mounds have been formed to provide additional terraces, avenues of trees and informal areas for occasional 'happenings', lakeside concerts, folklore displays, readings, and exhibitions.

To paraphrase the architects' report again 'here would be the setting with its facilities for serving Sport and the Muses, which could create an atmosphere during the Olympic Games of contact between the youth of the world in the sphere of sport and culture'.

With the active support of park management, the grounds have today become a rest and leisure centre, occasionally activated by sports events of an international importance. As, for example, during the 1974 World Soccer series when the stadium was the setting for the opening and closing matches of the tournament.

In addition to the roof covering, the design of the stadium has a number of other original features since copied in later, similar sized projects. One of these consisted of sinking two-thirds of the amphitheatre below ground level by an average depth of 4 m in order

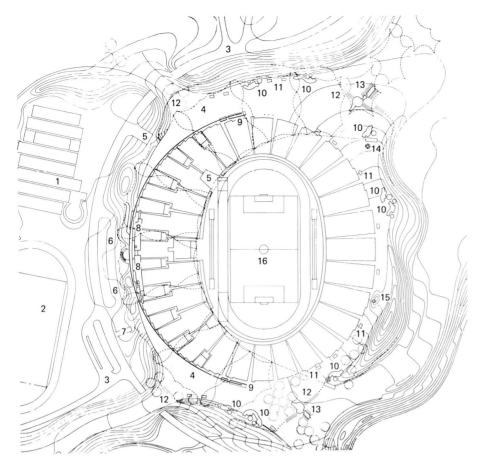

1 warming-up hall
2 warming-up ground
3 delivery road
4 entrance level
5 service approach and
  marathon gate
6 approach for Press and
  honorary guests
7 sportmen s'entrance
8 control platform
9 indicator board
10 kiosk for supplies
11 toilets
12 entrance controls
13 sale of tickets
14 first- aid station
15 olympic flame
16 ground and track

Olympiapark. Plan of stadium

to allow the 75 000 capacity crowds to enter from the highest point of the outside Forum, and to disperse *en masse* within 15 minutes from twenty eight spectator segments around the ground. Only the west stand is above ground level. In shape this approximates to a circle with the longitudinal stands rising to a maximum height opposite the centre line of the soccer pitch, thus providing closer viewing for the maximum number of spectators, emphasising the roof profile, and giving views out to the landscaped areas beyond.

Other secondary features, some of them now well-known, include a heated coil system under the turf playing area to avoid frost action in cold weather; areas behind both goalmouths completely covered with the same synthetic finish as on the running track; a floodlighting system giving 1875 lux, partly mounted on four masts (two on the roof of the west stand), and partly suspended below the roof line; a matrix system for the two electronic scoreboards with 10 lines of 34 characters; and a loudspeaker system clustered at midpoint on the main roof hawser.

Other facilities include seating for 45 000 people (54% under cover), restaurants, and the usual press and television accommodation. In other parts of the grounds are the Olympic sports hall seating 7000 –14 000, which includes an ice rink, cycle track and a 200 m indoor athletic track, all of which can be illuminated for colour television broadcasts (1875 lux); an aquatic centre seating 2000, which was reduced in size (very sensibly) after the Games; a Velodrome seating 5000, with an afzalia boarded track; and an ice stadium seating 7200. The tower has a revolving restaurant seating 200 which overlooks the whole complex.

Since the Games, the Olympic village has been used by the University of Technology as a sports high school and research centre. There have been none of the scenes of dereliction which followed many preceding Games facilities, due largely to the foresight of all concerned.

Today the Park is fulfilling a major role as an amenity and sports centre for the city, with daily excursions for the millions of sightseers recorded each year. At weekends the park is vibrant with the many uses previously described – a justifiable success by any modern standards. Individual facilities still compare

Crystal Palace National Sports Centre, S. London. Close-up view of terraces on older west stand, showing method for supporting cantilevered roof by means of pylon clusters. (Greater London Council, Architects Department. Photo: Gerald Perrin)

Crystal Palace National Sports Centre. Detail section of roof support to newer east stand. (Photo: British Steel)

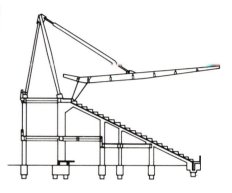

SECTION THROUGH LATEST STAND

favourably with those at the most recently held Games, apart from the almost inevitable progress in automatic security devices, or electronic gadgetry. These advances are minor however compared with the big step forward in design concepts taken by this project, which will almost certainly influence subsequent Games until the turn of the century, and beyond.

Crystal Palace National Sports Centre, South London

The sports centre stands on part of the site formerly occupied by Paxton's famous Crystal Palace National Exhibition Centre, gutted by fire in 1936. Today a television transmitting station serves as an equally well known landmark in this part of south London; an oasis of some 14.50 hectares of mature trees and shrubs surrounded by busy roads and railways.

The original brief called for facilities which would 'meet the needs of amateur training in a centre of national calibre, as exist in many other countries competing in international and Olympic events'. After fifteen years some doubt has been expressed as to whether the facilities opened by the Duke of Edinburgh in June 1964, are still adequate for this purpose. Many of these are no longer comparable to the standards seen at overseas centres of excellence as described in chapter 6. The policy of making facilities available for local community use has however been successful, although there has been a noticeable increase over the past decade in the number of international events, and national training courses held at the centre, when the recreation programme has to be temporarily suspended.

The stadium on the other hand, despite many defects in surfaces, internal planning, and sightlines, has come to be regarded as a good example of small scale stadium design. Engineering principles have been translated into an interesting architectural solution, much copied in other parts of the world, especially in Third World countries.

By comparison with many national stadia overseas, this 38 000 seat example is insignificant, and contains few of the refinements looked for today in stadium planning, and seen for example in the studies described of the Rheinstadion, Dusseldorf, or the Peace Stadium, Yokohama. It does however have a compactness, and human scale sometimes missing in these other examples, and the elegance of the slightly curved covered sections to both stands is much admired.

The older, west, stand has been designed to make the most of a falling site by bringing spectators onto the terraces at the uppermost level. A feature which gives the entrance elevation at this point a single-storey appearance, much enlivened by the pyramid clusters of masts supporting the steel-section cantile-

vered roof, on inclined front cable ties. The latest addition on the east side of the arena has eight of these assemblies along the 122×27.4 m length, arranged behind the back seating. Each pyramid is capped by a box section forming the apex of the A-frame in each case.

Seating is orange-coloured and blends well with surrounding landscaping, while providing a sense of excitement and 'occasion' for those attending international meetings. The floodlighting towers of mid-1960 design consisting of three-legged parallel-sided supports each 50 m high and carrying forty lamps, are distinctly dated, especially if compared with those illustrated on page 132. Track surfaces have also been superseded by improved materials now being used worldwide at this type of facility.

By overseas standards a general programme of upgrading all facilities would have taken place many years earlier, and by West German standards it is probable the existing facilities would have long since been demolished and rebuilt to present-day requirements. It is probable, however, that UK acceptance of making do with things as they are, together with the general shortage of funds traditionally associated with sports provision, will see few changes to status quo unless forced by national prestige, or a real desire to keep pace with other countries.

Rheinstadion, Düsseldorf, W. Germany

This is one of the most comprehensive stadia projects to have been completed in the past decade, even by West German standards. It has been selected for this case study however not for its scale of provision, but because management objectives have been framed around the principle of allowing the project to function as a community sports and recreation centre, whenever it is not required for large scale events. A similar policy has been advocated for some time in the UK with little response apart from a few isolated examples, and then not at the level seen here.

The stadium has replaced an earlier building which opened in 1926 with an international match against Holland, and was the host in 1974 for the World Cup soccer series, and in 1977 for the European Games athletic championships. The total cost of construction when completed in 1972 after a four year contract period, was 52 million DM.

The range of facilities now provided in the 50 ha site is impressive. They include an indoor swimming pool with telescopic roof for use in fine weather, three 'in-line' outdoor heated pools for diving, competitions, and training, two 400 m running tracks, an indoor athletics training hall with a 200 m track, field event practice areas, and sprint straights, 42 outdoor tennis courts, an archery range, 50 000 m^2 of recreation and

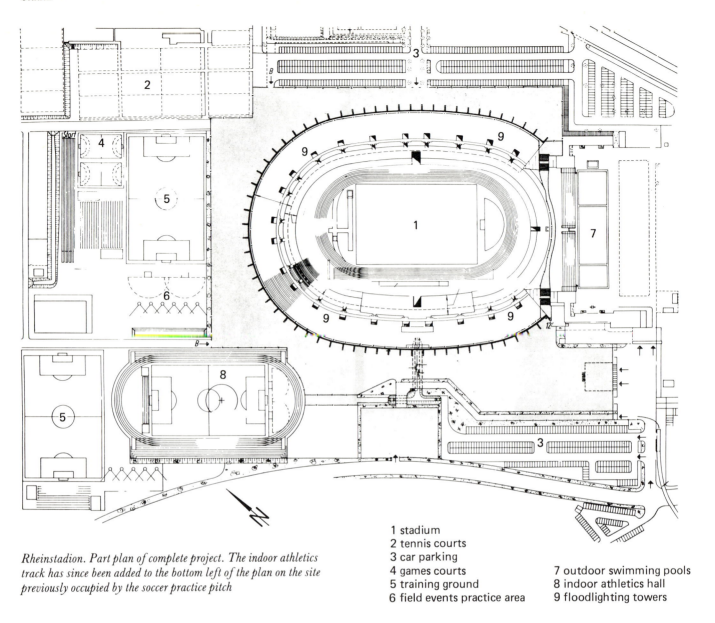

Rheinstadion. Part plan of complete project. The indoor athletics track has since been added to the bottom left of the plan on the site previously occupied by the soccer practice pitch

1 stadium
2 tennis courts
3 car parking
4 games courts
5 training ground
6 field events practice area
7 outdoor swimming pools
8 indoor athletics hall
9 floodlighting towers

Rheinstadion, Düsseldorf, Germany. Aerial view of stadium, swimming pool complex, tennis courts and car parking for 25 000. Since the photograph was taken a second athletics track has been added to the left of the stadium together with an indoor athletics training hall with 200 m indoor track. (Landeshaupstadt, Düsseldorf. Photo: Landeshaupstadt)

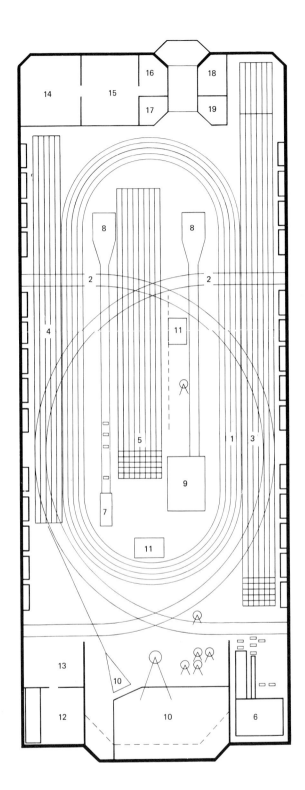

amenity space, much of it around the outdoor pools, parking for 25 000 cars, and a sports hostel for entertaining visiting teams and players.

A sophisticated system of public transport involving the use of trams and buses runs a shuttle service to and from the ground to the city and nearby international airport. Generous circulation space in and around the main grandstand allows good access to all internal spectator areas with none of the near stampede conditions that one has come to associate with most UK soccer grounds during the season.

The total ground capacity is 68 000 of which 32 000 people can be seated, and 36 500 provided with cover. Seats are of tough orange-coloured polypropolane and each has a back rest. Seating tiers have an easy rake with 400 mm risers and 800 mm steps, and give excellent sightlines to all parts of the playing area.

The stands are arranged in a horseshoe shape and consist of 61 precast concrete frames and steel supports, the upper finials of which give the stadium its elegant architectural character, noticeable from some distance. Each finial supports the 32 m long cantilevered roof by means of steel cables as seen in the section.

The frames are in turn supported on piles taken down 7 m into underlying bedrock, with shallow foundations under the inverted 'V' of each frame buttressed by ground beams taken across to each pile cap.

The playing area and track facilities are lit by four 42 m high floodlight clusters on slightly angled masts similar to those now seen frequently throughout Europe and South America (see pages 128 and 132). Additional lighting giving a total of 1500 lux (suitable for colour television requirements), is provided by individual fittings positioned just below the leading edge of the roof.

1 200 m track
2 curve practice track
3 100 m sprint practice track
4 110 m hurdle practice track
5 8-lane sprint
6 long and triple jump with assisted take off
7 pole vault
8 shot put into nets
9 high jump
10 changing rooms and sanitary areas
11 reception and offices

Rheinstadion. Plan of indoor athletics training hall

An electronic scoreboard is provided which is powerful enough to be read in most daylight conditions; although it is not as sophisticated as that at the Lenin Stadium in Moscow for the 1980 Olympic Games.

The back-to-back seating and terrace arrangement between the stadium and outdoor swimming pools has been cleverly disguised by tree and shrub planting. The latter has been used to soften each of the amenity areas around the stadium.

All facilities can be booked and used for as little as 1 DM per person a day, a level of subsidy rarely seen elsewhere. In addition to this a phone-in system is available to newcomers and visitors which puts them in touch with local sports organisations and coaches throughout the city.

This is another example of the great potential a project like this can harness for the public benefit, given the same breadth of imagination, and the finances to put this into practice. It also illustrates many of the design trends associated with present-day stadia (see also the example at Split, Yugoslavia, page 130), which have strongly influenced many subsequent projects in Europe, Japan and South America. All of these add up to a level of sophistication far above that of stadia built between the wars, especially in the UK.

Peace Baseball Stadium, Yokahama, Japan

This project is of interest for a number of design and construction features. The brief required the ground to be available for sports events to international standard, meetings, and exhibitions, with occasional large-scale 'happenings' such as pop concerts or festivals. For all of these a total seating capacity of 30 000 was considered to be adequate.

Given these requirements, the limitations of natural grass was clearly understood at an early stage in the pre-contract discussions, when the decision was taken to cover the whole ground area of 13 000 m² with artificial grass. The time factor involved in arranging different seating arrangements, and many other pieces of apparatus in order to stage different activities, was also taken into account. In view of this provision was made for the installation of mechanical and automatic aids of a highly sophisticated nature designed to reduce staff-intensive operations to a minimum. For example, different seating arrangements can be provided by means of push button controls, which give optimum viewing conditions for basketball, football and field sports generally.

Similarly, lighting illumination levels can be varied to suit the needs of high level competition, training, and minor competitions. These levels vary from 2500 lux at the striker's end of the field, to 1500 lux on the outfields, and are provided by six lighting masts each 43 m high, with 118 floodlights on each. (These are considered to be desirable for good colour television pictures).

Excellent sightlines have been provided by arranging seating angles at 30° to the horizontal. Two segments each carrying 3000 spectators can be moved mechanically into position behind the striker for baseball matches. The pitcher's mound can be lowered on hydraulic supports below ground level when the ground is required for other uses. When in the lowered position the mound is covered by a 7 m diameter aluminium disc which in turn is covered with artificial grass. The whole sequence takes less than half an hour, compared with three days using earth and turf.

Peace Baseball Stadium, Yokahama, Japan. View of main arena seen by striker. The wall below the scoreboard forms a good sight screen, against which to see the ball. (Photo: Philips International)

Peace Baseball Stadium. View of pitchers mound which can be recessed into the ground when not required. (Photo: Philips International)

This is without doubt one of the best organised stadia to be recently completed, and indicates the general direction now being taken towards the inclusion of labour saving devices where multi-purpose use is looked for by the client.

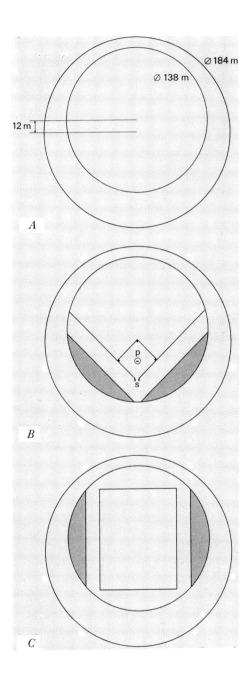

A

B

C

Peace Baseball Stadium. Diagram showing three seating arrangements made possible by automatically controlled movable seating sections.
A. Basic layout for baseball when more people wish to sit at strikers end of ground
B. Second baseball arrangement with the movable segments placed parallel to foul lines
C. Arrangements for general sports use. (Philips International)

Sharjah Stadium, Saudi Arabia

The number of stadia built in the Middle East over the past decade has increased significantly as funds have been directed in this direction to meet the growing need for inter-country tournaments, and for local recreation. Many new ideas have been incorporated including the use of synthetic surfaces, and floodlighting methods, up to international standard.

The Sharjah stadium is typical of this process and is interesting for the range of facilities provided in addition to the main arena, and the way in which the architectural form follows traditional Islamic patterns. As many designers from the West have come to realise, many of these patterns are based upon commonsense principles of encouraging good cross ventilation and providing shade within a cultural formula which has characterised the region for very many years.

Shade has been provided over the stand seating in the form of eight *in situ* hyberbolic paraboloid concrete umbrellas. These were first tested in a wind tunnel on a model which provided the basis for the final design, together with a computer analysis of these tests. Perforated screens at either end of the stand encourage cross ventilation from prevailing winds to pass below precast concrete seating units, while giving the distinctive architectural appearance one has come to expect in this part of the world.

A 400 m synthetic running track encloses a grassed soccer pitch, lit by four floodlighting towers housing sufficient luminaires to provide full colour television broadcasts from the ground. These also light the

Sharjah Stadium, Saudi Arabia. View of grandstand and floodlighting tower (Architects: Robert Mathew, Johnson-Marshal)

adjacent 50 m 8-lane swimming hall, squash courts, gymnasium, 6-lane bowling alley, games rooms, refreshment and social areas. Administration offices complete the project.

Stand seating for 2400 is very small by western standards bearing in mind the overall scale of provision on the site, but is in keeping with present-day needs. Extensions can be added as required on space left for this purpose at either end of the existing stand.

It is interesting to note the way in which a considerable number of ancillary sports facilities have been provided for day-to-day use, a lesson only recently learned even in the West, if economic sense is to be made of such a large capital investment.

Stadium, Split, Yugoslavia

The 1979 Mediterranean Games were hosted by this impressive stadium seating 50 000, constructed in only three months.

The distinctive appearance is provided by an eliptical space frame which reaches a height of 45 m at its peak, formed by a series of hollow metal sections arranged between an outer arch 261 m long, and an inner ring 214 m in length, supported during construction on ten temporary columns. The combination of semi-octahedron and tetrahedron space frames is extremely strong, and has been designed to withstand anticipated gusts of wind up to 180 km per hour (50 miles a second).

Another feature of the design is the way in which seating has been provided for every spectator, very much in keeping with present day trends on the European continent. Floodlighting towers have been omitted as a result of the elliptical arch arrangement over the seating, the outer rim of which is used to mount rows of metal-halide lamps performing the same function as conventional tower-mounted fittings. The appearance after dark is exceptionally striking, and almost sculpuresque when seen from a distance. The overall concept heralds a new approach to stadium design as urban 'sculpture' which is quite unique at the present time.

Split Stadium, Yugoslavia. View of stand showing the eliptical space-frame construction forming the roof. (Architects: Boris Magas. Photo: British Steel)

Synthetic surfaces and track and field event design

The use of synthetic surfaces has become widespread in the past ten years. This has been due partly to lower running costs than those associated with grass or cinder surfaces, and partly to much better wearing qualities.

Most new tracks now being installed have polymer or rubber finishes in place of cinders or shale, and many existing tracks have recently been up-graded along similar lines to the example illustrated at Harlow Sportcentre in the UK. The use of artificial grass which has been so prolific in the USA is also beginning to spread to other parts of the world, especially where the central playing area in stadia may be required for other uses, as in the example at the Peace Stadium, Yokahama, Japan.

Other applications for both materials can be seen in many inner city areas, where play space has always been at a premium; or in public 'kick-about' areas and childrens' playgrounds, where the safety aspects of these surfaces has much to recommend them. An increasing number of bowling greens are also being laid using artificial grass (as in the example at Eastleigh Sports Centre) and it may also be found on a considerable number of pitch-and-putt courses or practice greens around club houses. Several first division football clubs are also in the process of installing or considering synthetic grass as the main playing surface in the UK now that international regulations have approved its use.

The average cost of a 400 m running track (together with all field event areas), or soccer pitch surfaced with artificial grass, was (at 1980 prices) around £¼ m in the UK. It is treble this figure in developing countries, such as Nigeria, where transportation problems add considerably to the cost of raw materials.

A sound, well-constructed base is essential to the wearing quality of these surfaces, as is the need to provide for good rainwater drainage around the perimeter of these playing areas. To achieve the latter it is necessary to instal a slight crown to the centre of the pitch, and to fall running tracks to the inside where water can share a common drainage disposal scheme with the pitch. The latter arrangement is also required by international regulations and is a help to runners on the bends.

It has been found desirable to place the responsibility for both sub-base construction and finishes with the supplier of the latter who normally acts as the main contractor. Many suppliers will give a five-year guarantee with their materials, and some seven years. It is well, therefore, to bear in mind that the two inner lanes of most tracks will wear out more quickly than others, if management subsequently allows these to be regularly used for training purposes. In this case the guarantees may not apply.

Design trends are tending to reduce the amount of natural turf around arenas to the minimum, and for the 'D' behind both goalmouths to be replaced entirely by synthetic surfaces. The trend in many training areas, such as the example shown at Vincennes, Paris, is to completely cover the central area with the same material as the track, where it can be used for warm-up practice, sprinting, and for the field events.

The location of the field events is a matter for local preference. Although the most recent trend has been to place either the long and triple jump, or pole vault run-up in front of the main (west) grandstand, and therefore right in the public eye as a spectator attraction.

It is becoming fashionable to place the water-jump off-centre at the north end of running tracks, as in the Harlow Sportcentre example illustrated which owes much to current French practice. As standards continue to improve in all the field events it is possible that some events such as javelin throwing, may have to be accommodated elsewhere.

The approximate construction period for new tracks and central playing areas is in the order of five to six months, although weather conditions often influence this time factor considerably. It is also worth bearing in mind that temperature can play a large part in determining speed of construction.

Stadium floodlighting

The floodlighting of outdoor sports facilities, especially those in stadia, has become considerably more sophisticated over the past decade, in order to meet the changing requirements of colour television, and the different needs of training, local matches and top international events. Each host nation for the latter has improved standards to those of its predecesor, especially where the events involved have included the Olympic Games or World Cup Soccer Series.

For example, the decision to hold the 1978 World Cup series in Argentina, resulted in the reconstruction of three old grounds and the construction of three new stadia, each with the latest facilities for press, film and television. One result was to improve floodlighting arrangements to standards of excellence hitherto little seen in South America, as may be judged from the accompanying illustrations.

Levels of illumination have gradually risen to between 1500 lux and 2500 lux, with the average at around 1800 lux. Masts are between 42 and 52 m high, with lamps angled slightly to the ground as in the example illustrated at Velez Sarsfield stadium, Buenos Aires. Most are used in combination with subsidiary lamps usually mounted behind seating or at roof level with an assymetrical arrangement designed to provide the higher levels of illumination behind the main television camera. Secondary light

Mendozo Stadium, Argentina. Detail of 52 m high floodlighting tower. (Photo: Philips International)

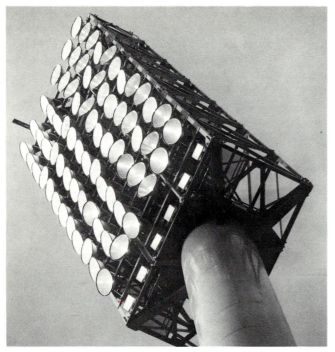

Velez Sarsfield Stadium, Buenos Aires. Detail of 42 m high floodlighting tower. An internal spiral stepladder provides access for maintenance to the combination of metal halide and halogen floodlights. (Photo: Philips International)

Mendoza Stadium. Detail of rectangular light fittings along the roof at a height of 26 m above ground to give the necessary vertical illumination for colour TV broadcasts. (Photo: Philips International)

Riyadh Stadium, Saudi Arabia. View of floodlighting towers which can provide three levels of illumination for training sessions, match play and colour TV broadcasts. 15 halogen light fittings on each tower are used to light the stands. The average height of each tower is 45 m. (Photo: Philips International)

sources are provided immediately opposite to equalise the horizontal illumination.

Metal halide lamps are commonly preferred, in tandem with tungsten halogen for secondary lighting of areas such as terraces or access paths. Four masts are normally used to provide the main light source for all playing areas, as in the example at Mendoza where circular fittings have been used, in combination with 392 rectangular 2 kW metal halide lamps placed on the roof of the main stand.

The stadium at Riyadh with a running track around the soccer pitch, has lighting devised to meet the needs of training (400 lux), local events (800 lux) and televised events requiring between 1000 and 1400 lux illumination. The arrangement is also assymetrical with two masts on the television camera side of the ground carrying thirteen rows of floodlights, and two masts opposite carrying eight rows, each with ten floodlights with single 2000 W high pressure metal halide fittings. The average mounting height is 45 m. Fifteen halogen fittings light the stands with power provided directly from a diesel generator in case of a mains power failure.

The design of towers at this level of provision has generally tended to favour circular steel shafts with internal spiral staircases for maintenance inspections, similar to those seen at Velez Sarsfield, or Düsseldorf. Secondary floodlighting systems are required for ancillary facilities such as outdoor tennis courts, swimming pools or training areas, in order to maximise use after dark. Levels of illumination are generally between 300 and 500 lux, provided on individual posts around 12 to 14 m high, or on catenary cables hung over the playing area. These can often double as light sources for general circulation paths and car parking.

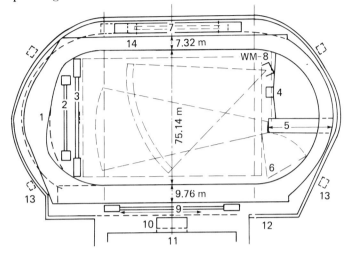

1 water jump	9 long and triple jump
2 pole vault	10 stand
3 long jump	11 pavilion
4 high jump	12 judges stand
5 javelin	13 floodlighting
6 shot putt	14 6 lanes back straight and bends :
7 sprint/warm up	8 lanes on home straight
(marked out for pole vault)	WM water metre positions (4)
8 hammer and discus	

Harlow Sportcentre. Plan of 400 m running track and field event areas, upgraded in 1980 by addition of synthetic surfaces

Vincennes Stadium, Paris. View of ground completely surfaced with synthetic material. (Photo: Resisport Ltd)

Appendix: Olympic regulations governing sports installations

The following diagrams are based upon the report *'Regulations Governing Sports Grounds'* supplied by the Mexican Olympic Committee to whom the author is deeply indebted.

As amendments are made from time to time by governing bodies for sport it is advisable that they be checked by national sports associations/councils before starting work on site. In the UK further details and advice can be obtained from the Technical Unit for Sport, The Sports Council, 70 Brompton Road, London SW1.

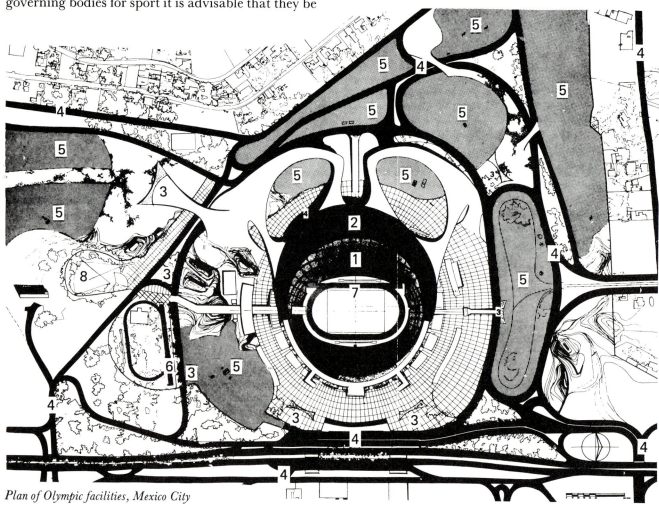

Plan of Olympic facilities, Mexico City

1 former stadium	5 parking
2 extension	6 warming-up track
3 controls	7 running track
4 circulation	8 warming-up, field events

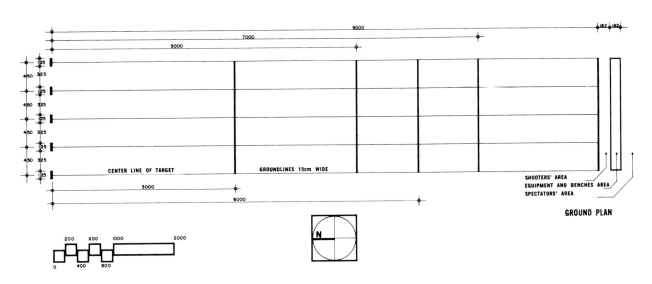

GROUND PLAN

Distances shown to be marked out on ground

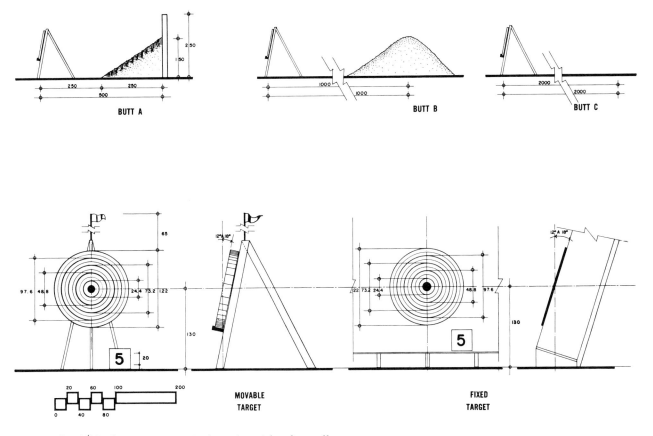

BUTT A

BUTT B

BUTT C

MOVABLE
TARGET

FIXED
TARGET

Archery. South/North orientation required together with safety wall
5 m behind targets, 4 m high

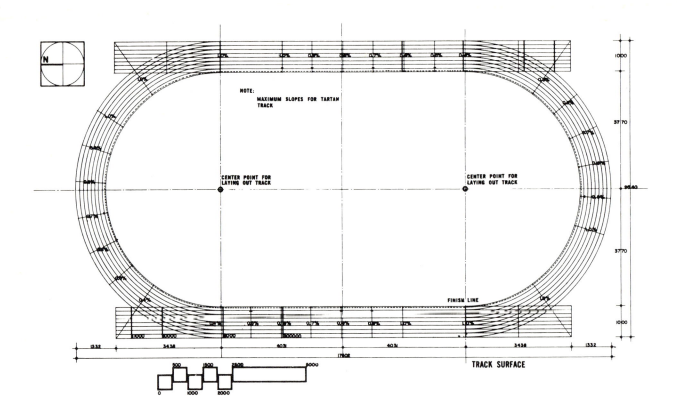

Plan of Olympic (8 lane) track. Each lane is 1.22 m wide.
Maximum slope across track (normally to the inside) 1%

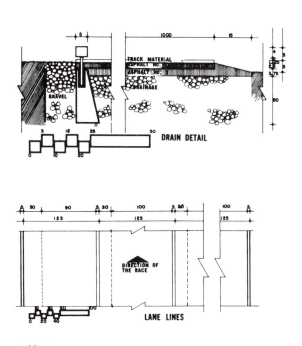

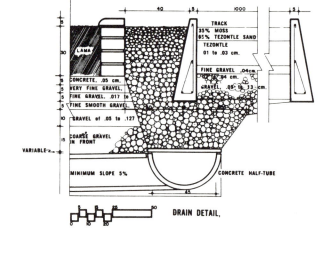

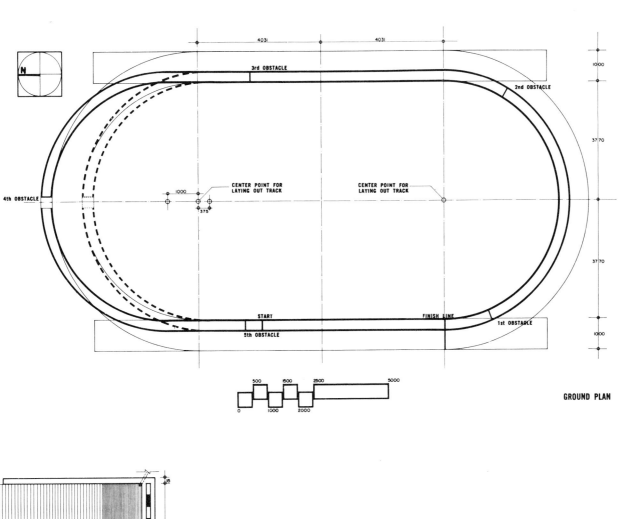

GROUND PLAN

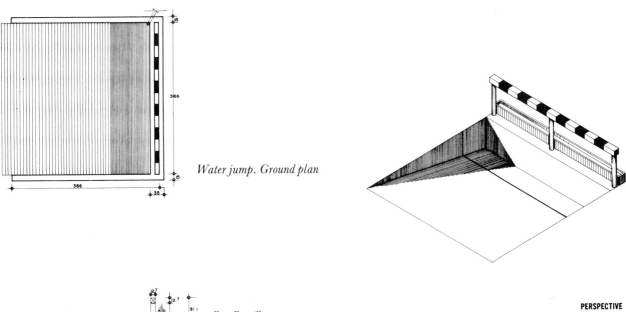

Water jump. Ground plan

PERSPECTIVE

Water jump. Cross section

Steeplechase. Five obstacles including a water jump are placed 78 to 84 m apart. The race is run over 3000 m

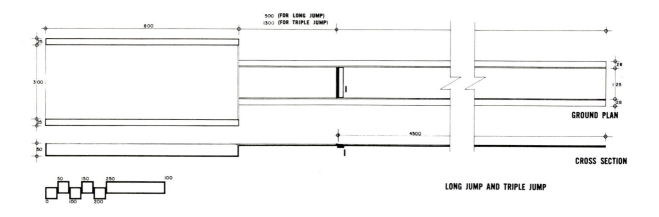

LONG JUMP AND TRIPLE JUMP

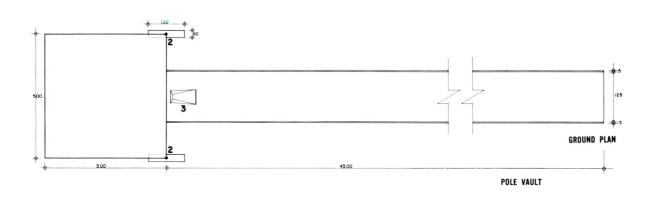

POLE VAULT

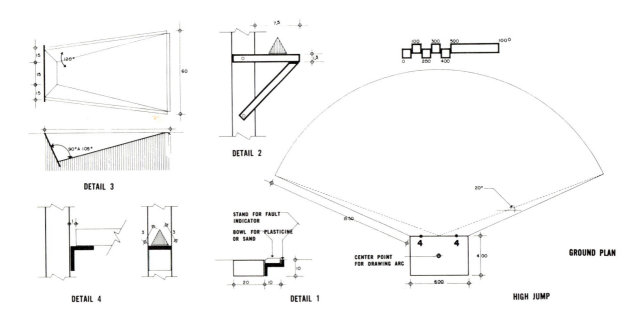

Long jump, pole vault and high jump

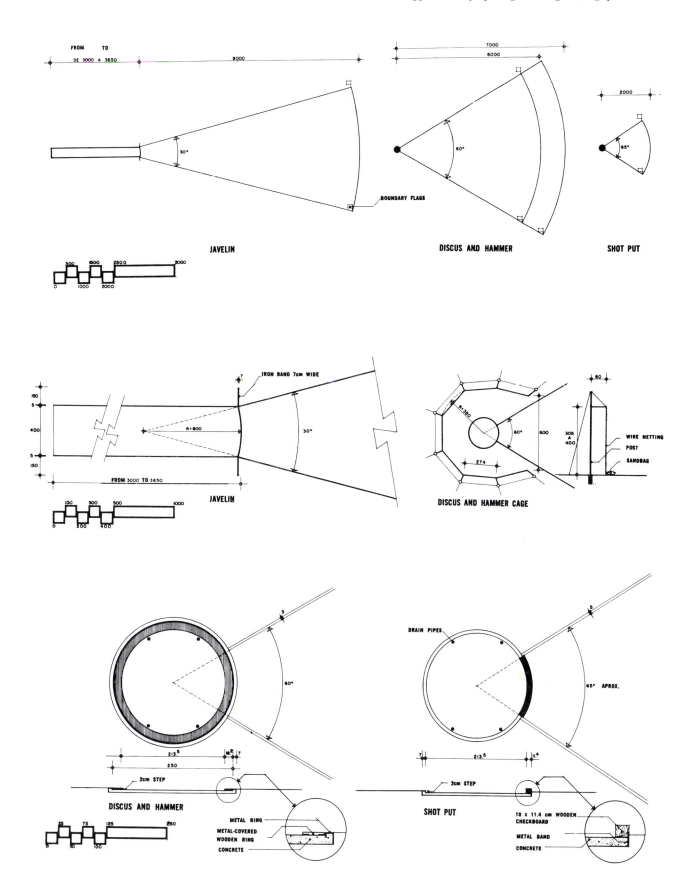

Discus, hammer and javelin

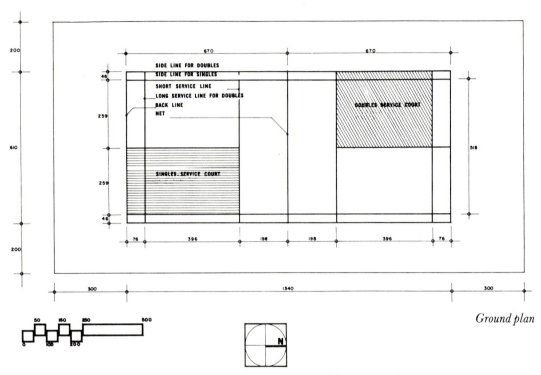

Ground plan

*The centre net line is not marked out on court.
All markings, 38 mm wide*

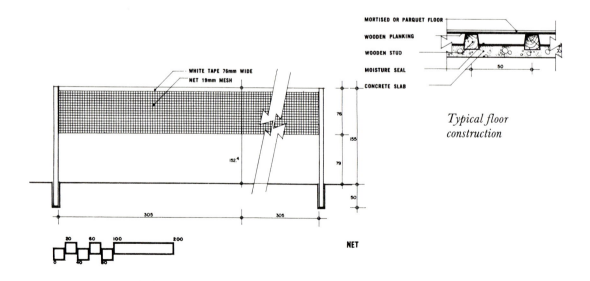

*Typical floor
construction*

Badminton

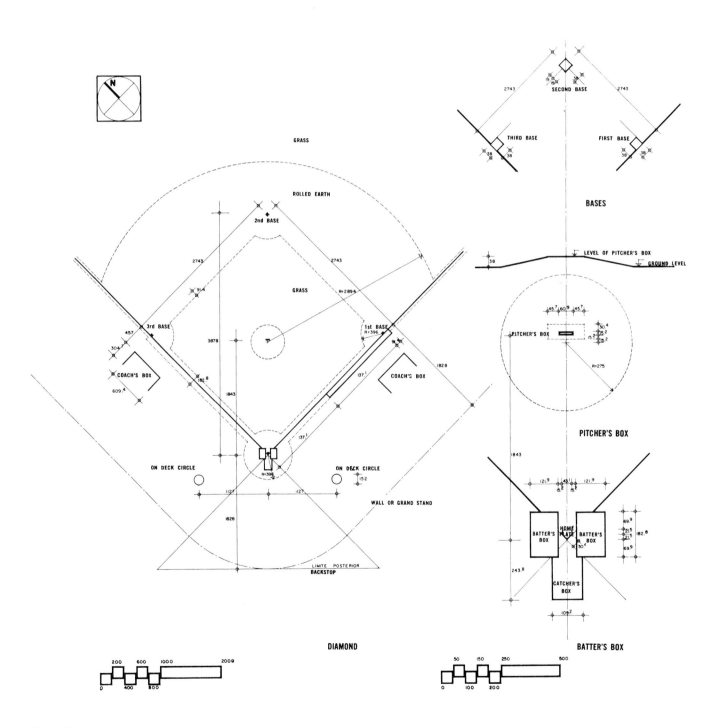

DIAMOND

BASES

PITCHER'S BOX

BATTER'S BOX

Baseball

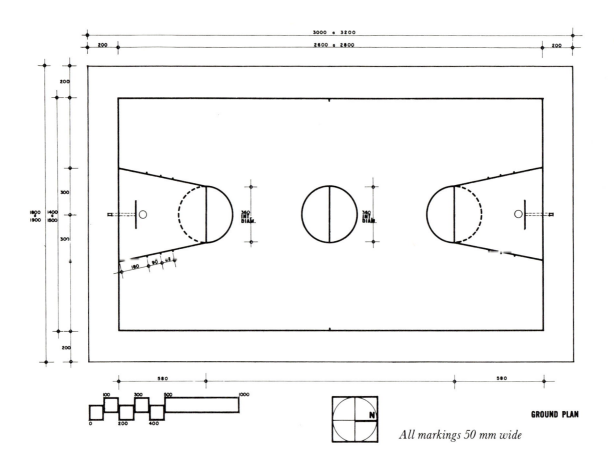

GROUND PLAN

All markings 50 mm wide

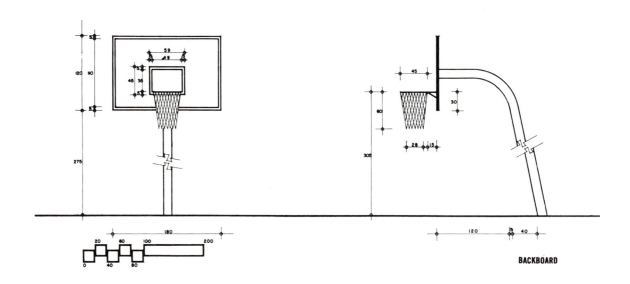

BACKBOARD

Basketball. Backboards are often hung from ceilings or walls where dimensions allow

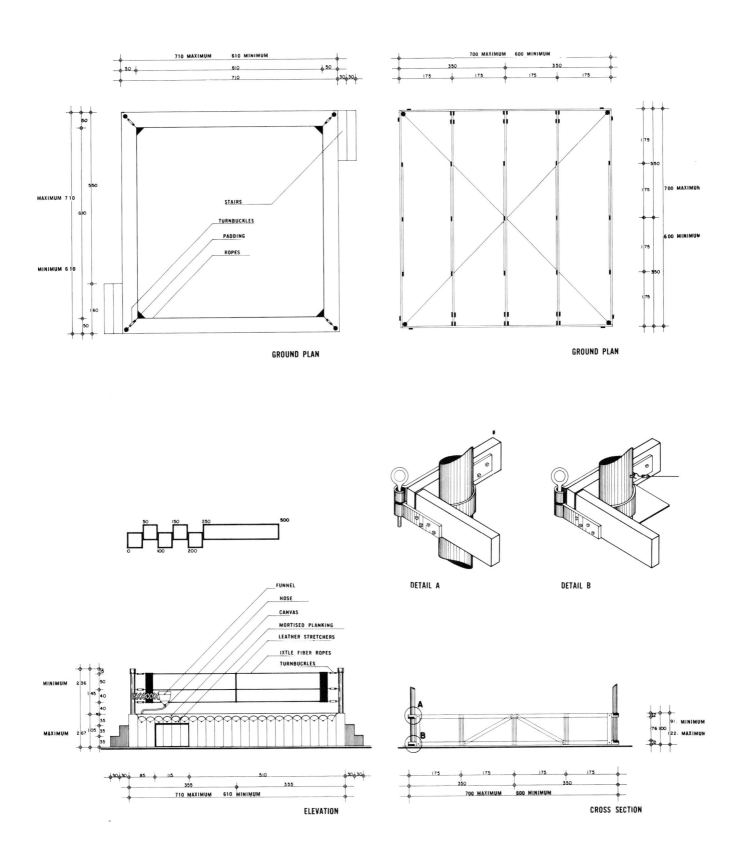

Boxing. 750 lux minimum lighting required above ring

143

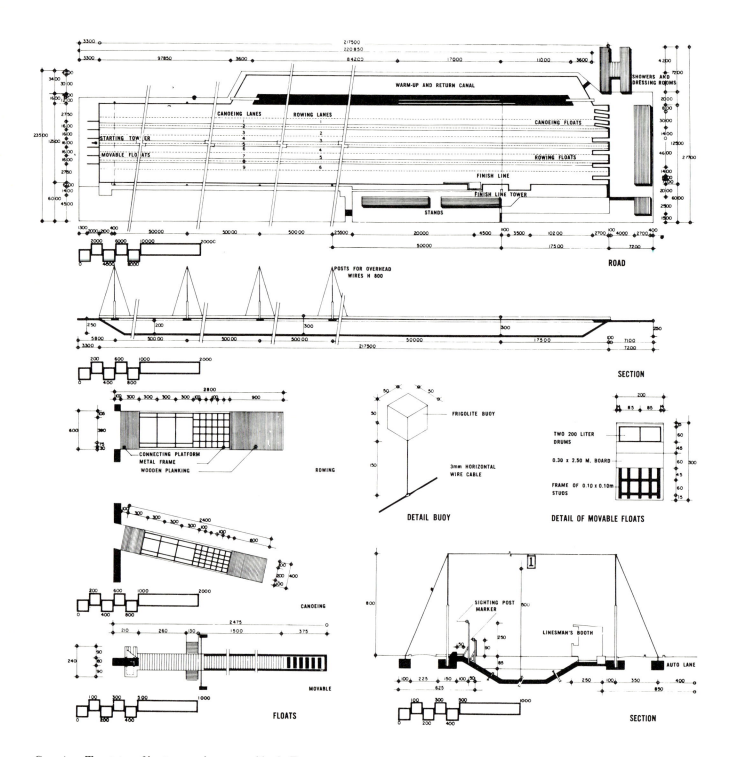

Canoeing. Two types of boat are used: canoe and kyak. Events are held on three different types of water:
1 calm water with straight lines.
2 downstream on rivers with slalom gates.
3 large areas of water.

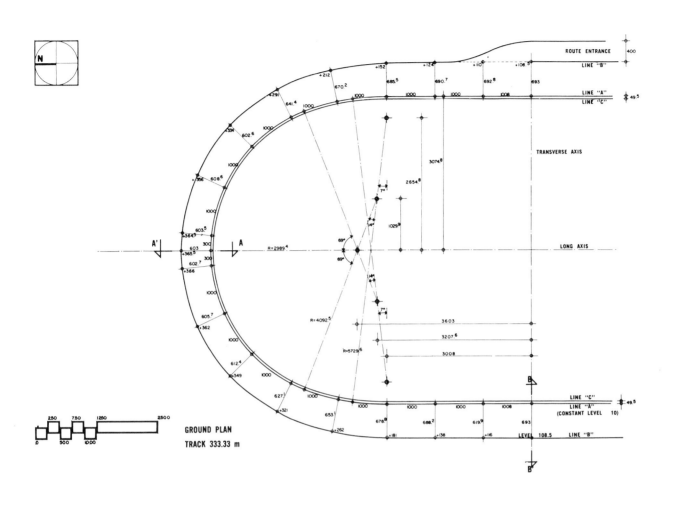

GROUND PLAN

TRACK 333.33 m

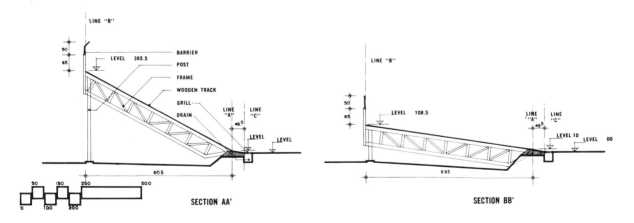

SECTION AA'

SECTION BB'

Cycling. Velochrome arrangement. The main characteristic of the design is the use of transition curves permitting a gradual change in the radius to allow cyclists to go from straights to the minimum pachuis curve by a uniform rotation of the handlebars

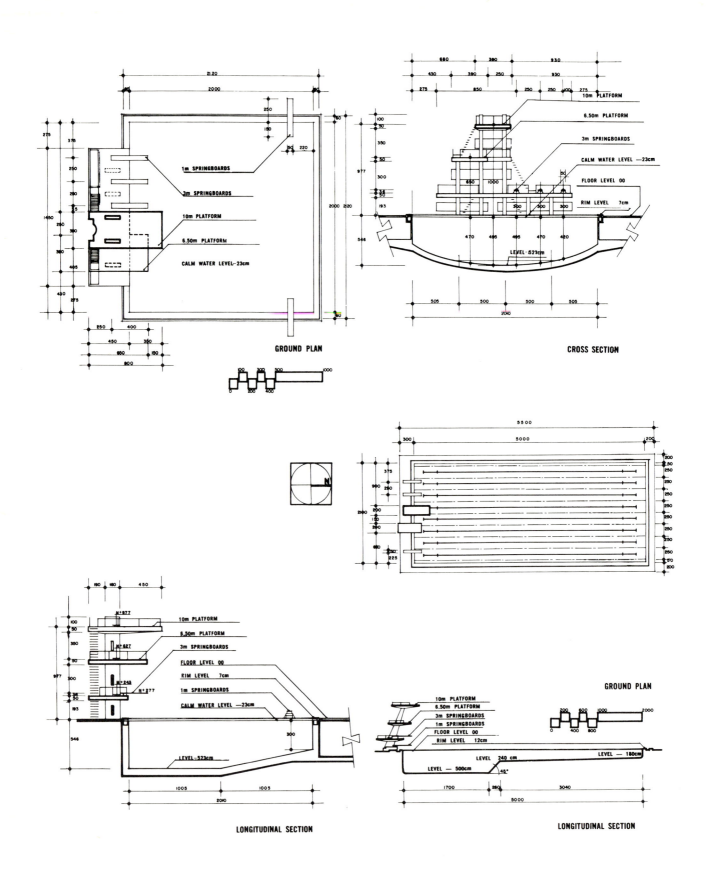

GROUND PLAN

CROSS SECTION

LONGITUDINAL SECTION

GROUND PLAN

LONGITUDINAL SECTION

Diving. All platforms should be stationary, non-skid and 2 m wide

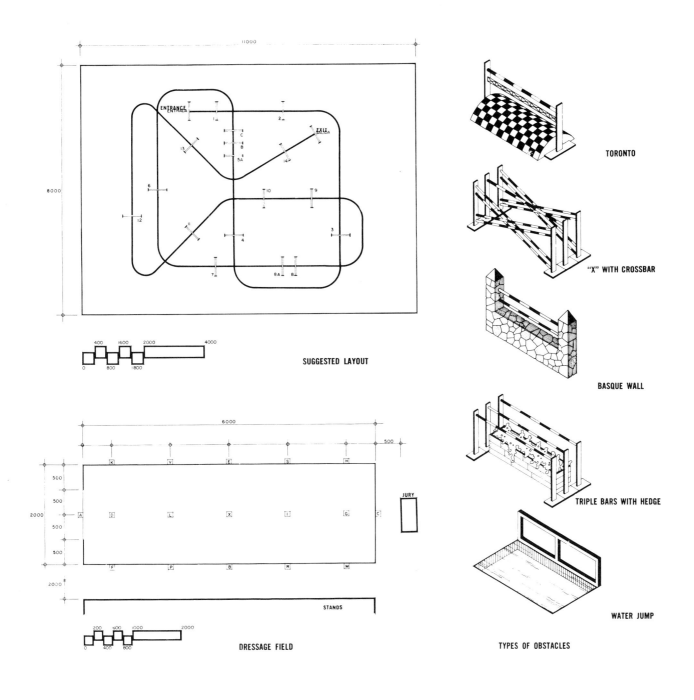

SUGGESTED LAYOUT

DRESSAGE FIELD

TORONTO

"X" WITH CROSSBAR

BASQUE WALL

TRIPLE BARS WITH HEDGE

WATER JUMP

TYPES OF OBSTACLES

*Equestrian. These events are three-day, Olympic Grand Prix
dressage, and Grand Prix jumping*

147

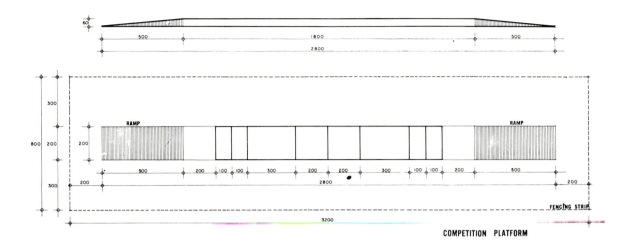

COMPETITION PLATFORM

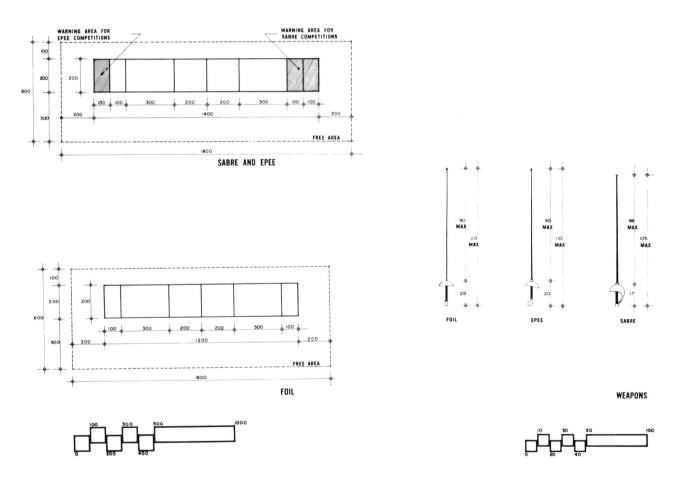

Fencing. There are three divisions of competition: foil for men and women; epee and sabre for men only

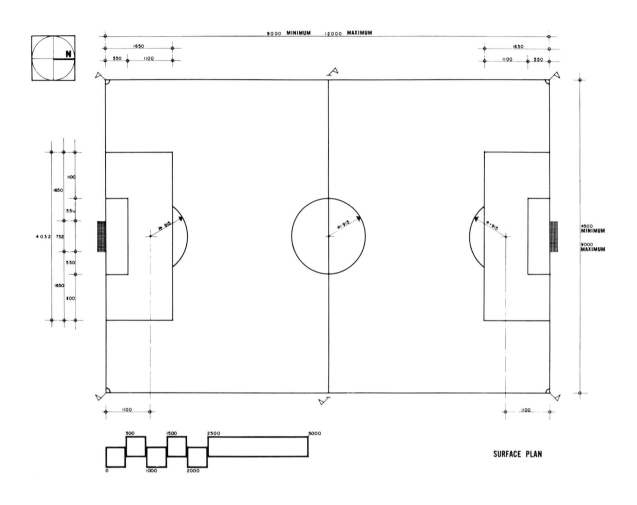

SURFACE PLAN

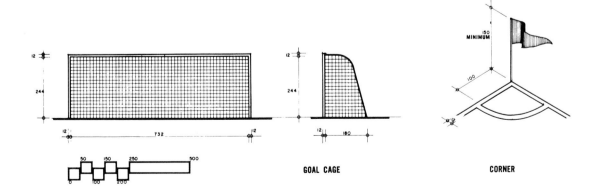

GOAL CAGE

CORNER

Football

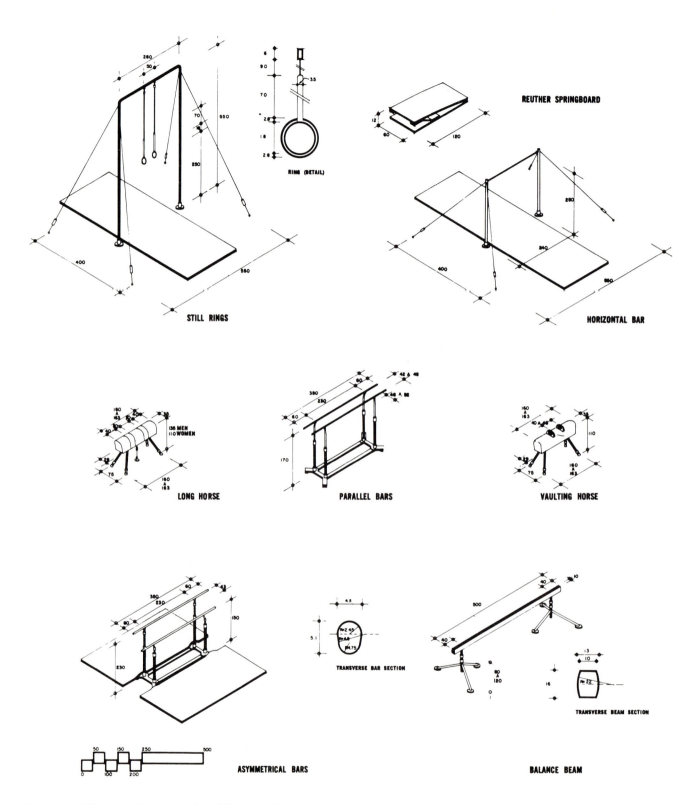

STILL RINGS

RING (DETAIL)

REUTHER SPRINGBOARD

HORIZONTAL BAR

LONG HORSE

PARALLEL BARS

VAULTING HORSE

ASYMMETRICAL BARS

TRANSVERSE BAR SECTION

BALANCE BEAM

TRANSVERSE BEAM SECTION

Gymnastics. The mens' division consists of floor excersises,
pommelled horse, rings, long horse, parallel bars and horizontal bar.
The womens' division is floor exercises, side horse, assymetrical bars
and balance beam

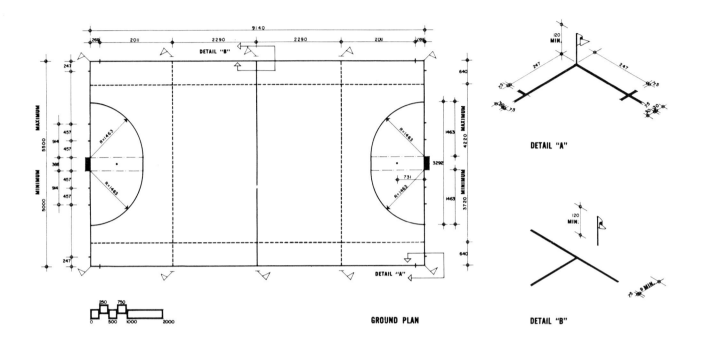

GROUND PLAN

DETAIL "A"

DETAIL "B"

Markings are 75 mm wide

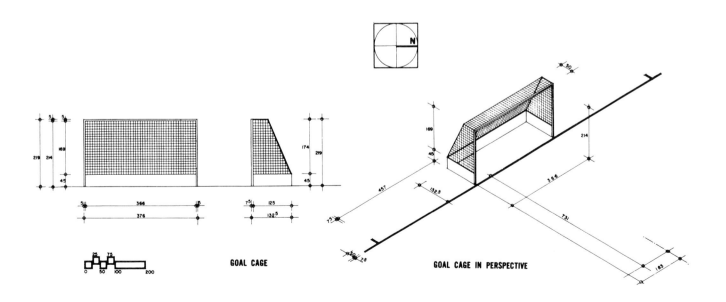

GOAL CAGE

GOAL CAGE IN PERSPECTIVE

Hockey

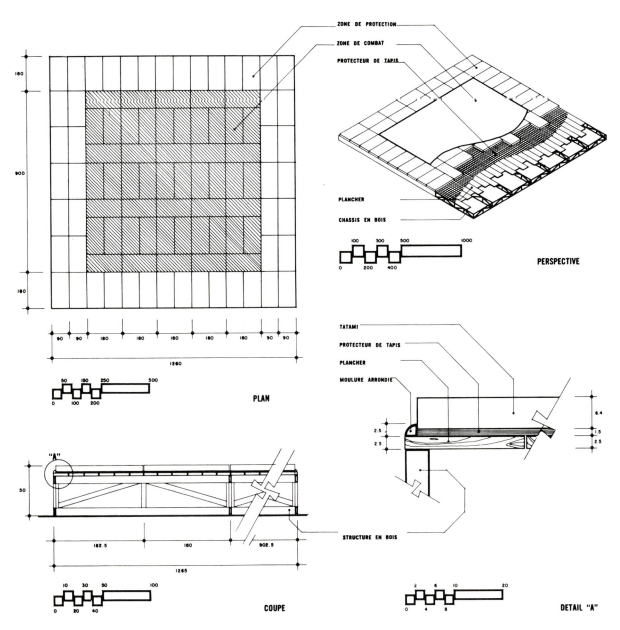

ZONE DE PROTECTION
ZONE DE COMBAT
PROTECTEUR DE TAPIS
PLANCHER
CHASSIS EN BOIS

PERSPECTIVE

PLAN

TATAMI
PROTECTEUR DE TAPIS
PLANCHER
MOULURE ARRONDIE

STRUCTURE EN BOIS

COUPE

DETAIL "A"

Judo. The common construction of the Tatami is of 'lomoto'
(matting) and 'toko' (rice straw). Foam rubber is permitted for youth
and childrens' competitions

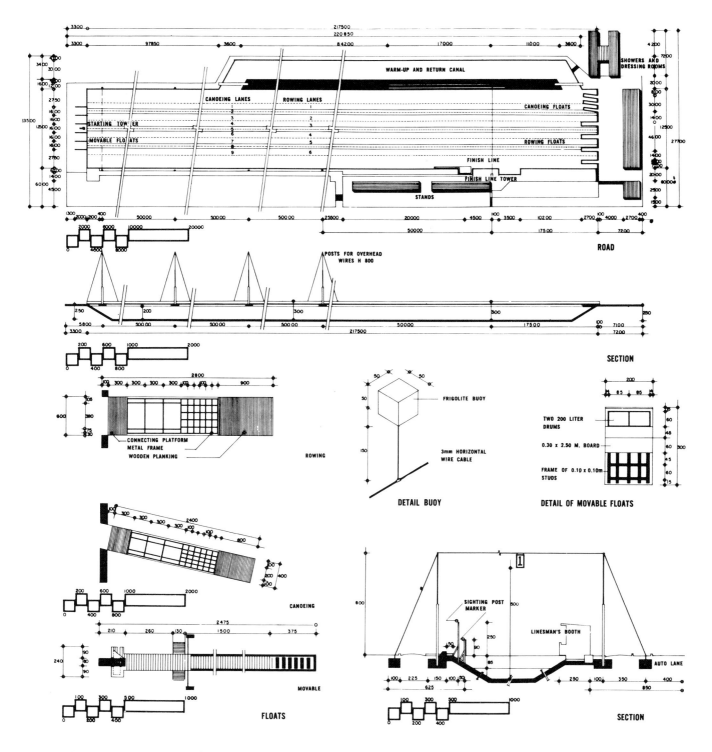

Rowing. The main requirements are for a course 2000 m long, in a straight line, 25 m of open water before the starting line and 100 m of opne water beyond the finishing line for pull-up distance

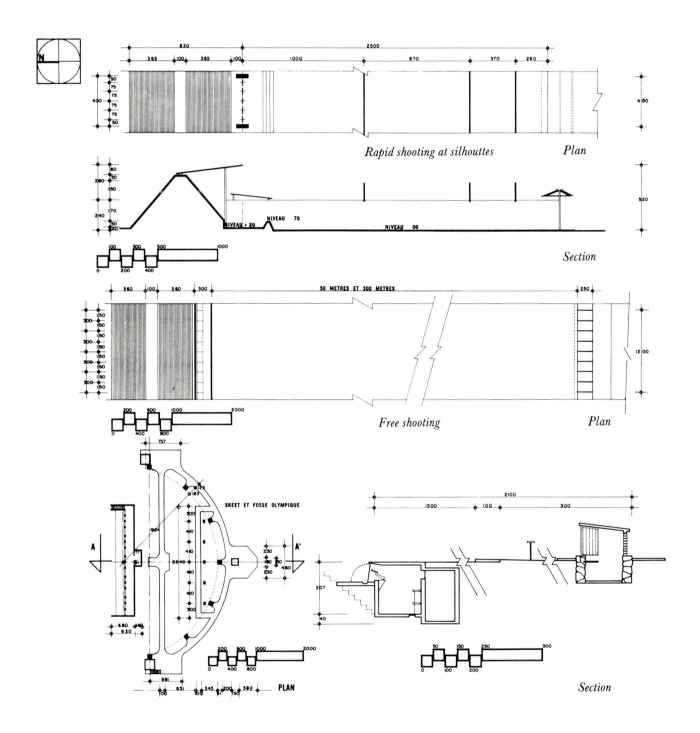

Rapid shooting at silhouttes — Plan

Section

Free shooting — Plan

PLAN

Section

Shooting

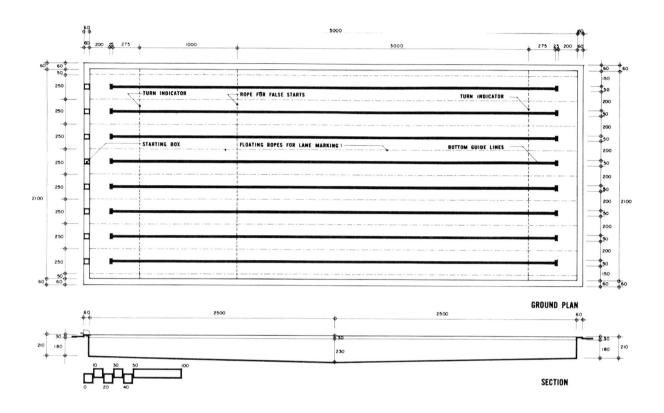

GROUND PLAN

SECTION

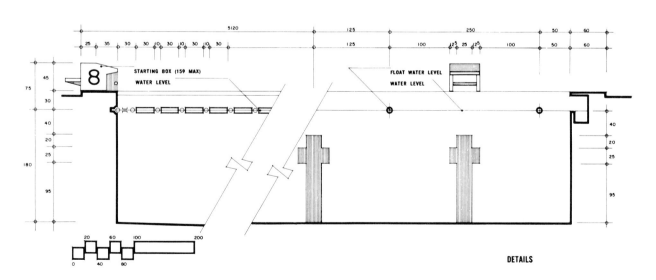

DETAILS

Swimming

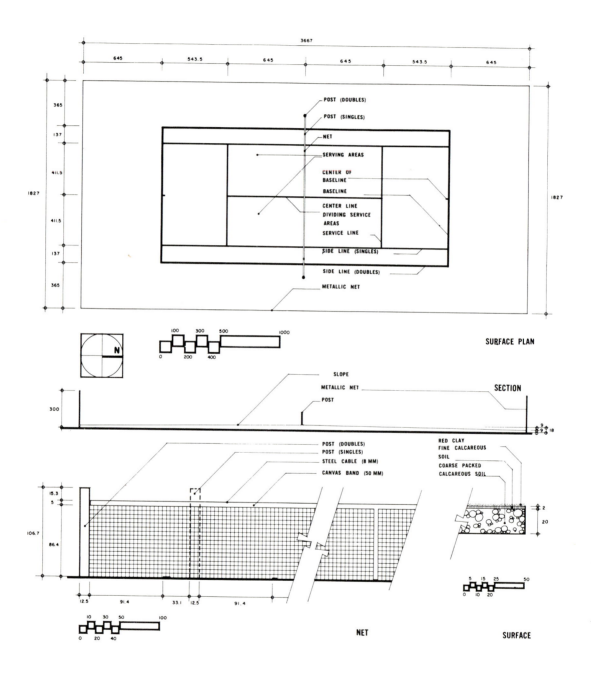

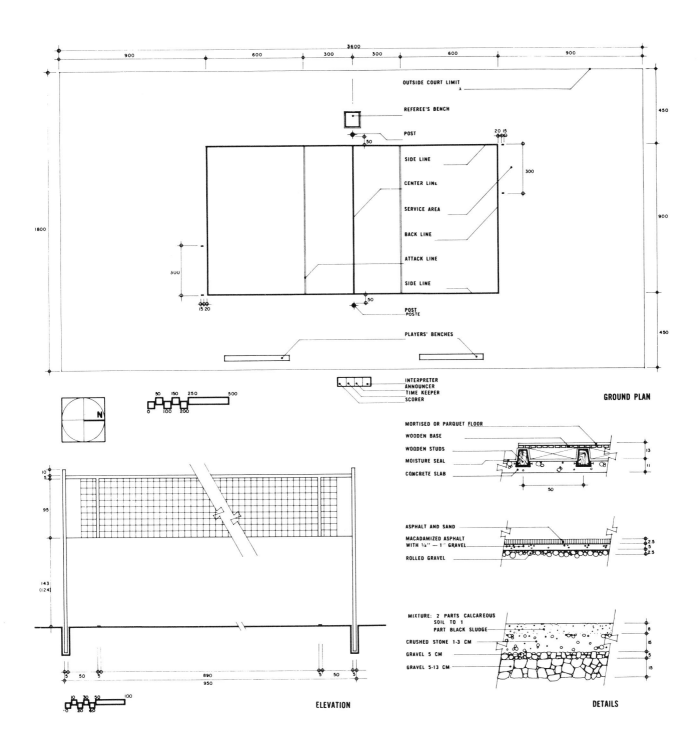

OUTSIDE COURT LIMIT

REFEREE'S BENCH

POST

SIDE LINE

CENTER LINE

SERVICE AREA

BACK LINE

ATTACK LINE

SIDE LINE

POST
POSTE

PLAYERS' BENCHES

INTERPRETER
ANNOUNCER
TIME KEEPER
SCORER

GROUND PLAN

MORTISED OR PARQUET FLOOR
WOODEN BASE
WOODEN STUDS
MOISTURE SEAL
CONCRETE SLAB

ASPHALT AND SAND
MACADAMIZED ASPHALT
WITH ¼" — 1" GRAVEL
ROLLED GRAVEL

MIXTURE: 2 PARTS CALCAREOUS
          SOIL TO 1
          PART BLACK SLUDGE
CRUSHED STONE 1-3 CM
GRAVEL 5 CM
GRAVEL 5-13 CM

ELEVATION

DETAILS

Volleyball

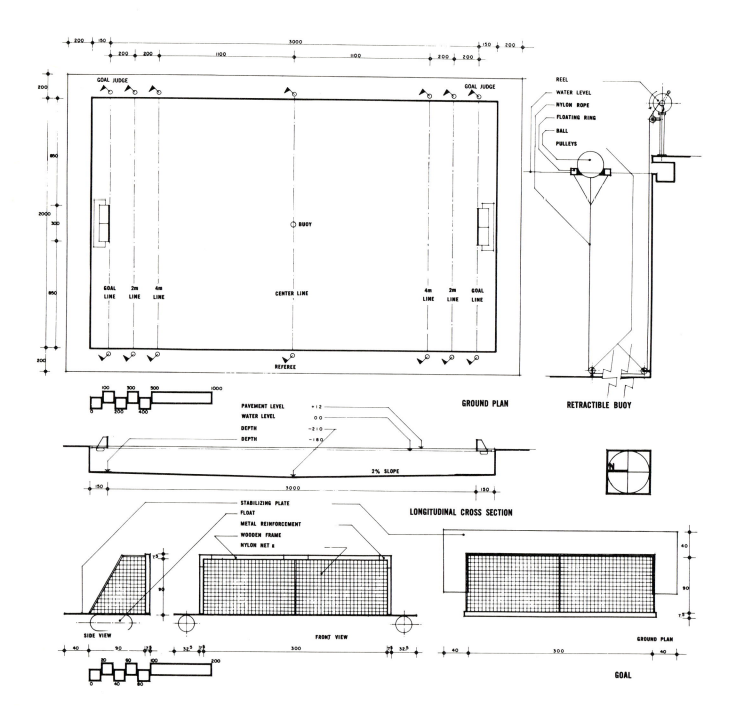

GROUND PLAN

RETRACTIBLE BUOY

REEL
WATER LEVEL
NYLON ROPE
FLOATING RING
BALL
PULLEYS

GOAL JUDGE

GOAL JUDGE

BUOY

GOAL LINE 2m LINE 4m LINE

CENTER LINE

4m LINE 2m LINE GOAL LINE

REFEREE

PAVEMENT LEVEL   +12
WATER LEVEL   00
DEPTH   −210
DEPTH   −180

2% SLOPE

LONGITUDINAL CROSS SECTION

STABILIZING PLATE
FLOAT
METAL REINFORCEMENT
WOODEN FRAME
NYLON NET 8

SIDE VIEW

FRONT VIEW

GROUND PLAN

GOAL

Water polo

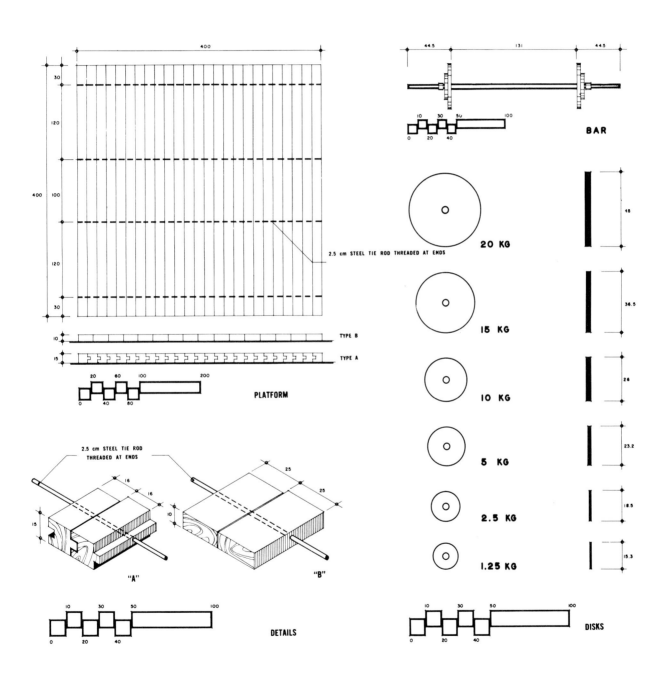

PLATFORM

BAR

DISKS

DETAILS

2.5 cm STEEL TIE ROD THREADED AT ENDS

20 KG

15 KG

10 KG

5 KG

2.5 KG

1.25 KG

"A"

"B"

TYPE B

TYPE A

Weightlifting

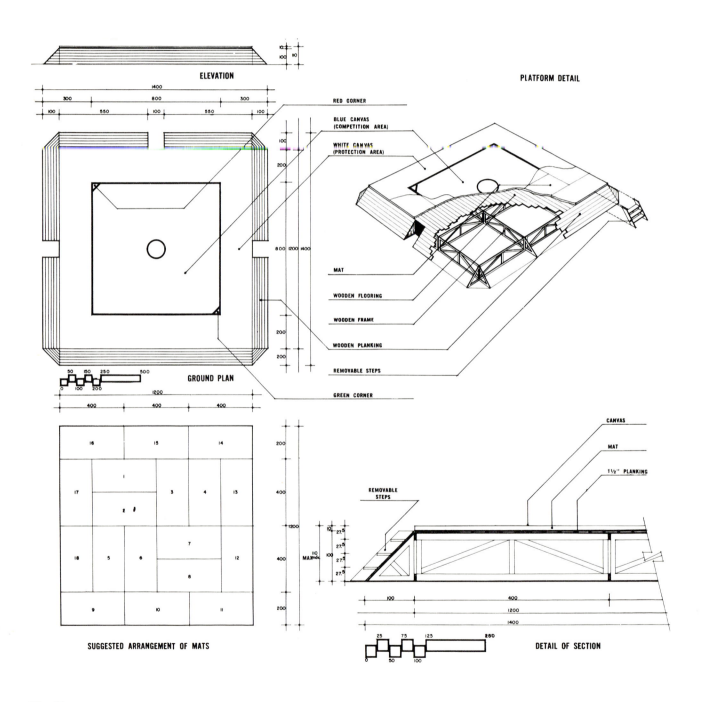

ELEVATION

PLATFORM DETAIL

RED CORNER

BLUE CANVAS
(COMPETITION AREA)

WHITE CANVAS
(PROTECTION AREA)

MAT

WOODEN FLOORING

WOODEN FRAME

WOODEN PLANKING

REMOVABLE STEPS

GREEN CORNER

GROUND PLAN

CANVAS

MAT

1½" PLANKING

REMOVABLE
STEPS

SUGGESTED ARRANGEMENT OF MATS

DETAIL OF SECTION

Wrestling

Index

161